Ronald Skirth was born in 1897. When he left home to fight in the First World War he was nineteen years old. He served on the Western and Italian fronts, returning home in 1919 after the war had ended. He married his teenage sweetheart Ella in 1924 and their daughter Jean was born five years later. Skirth worked as a teacher until his retirement in 1958 and in 1971 set to work on what was intended to be a brief account of his early romance with Ella, their separation by war and their reunion two years later. In the intervening fifty-three years he had never spoken of his war experiences and, as he wrote, they soon began to get the better of him. He filled hundreds of pages with his handwritten account, plus the postcards, letters and documents which he had kept for more than half a century. The resulting memoir, on which this book is based, was donated to the Imperial War Museum by his daughter Jean after his death in 1977.

Duncan Barrett is a writer and editor. He grew up in London and studied English at Jesus College, Cambridge. He is the co-author of *Star Trek: The Human Frontier* with his mother Michèle, whose research into shell-shocked survivors of the First World War introduced him to Ronald Skirth's story. He recently edited Vitali Vitaliev's *Passport to Enclavia* and was Assistant Editor of *Bobby Baker: Redeeming Features of Daily Life*. He also works as an actor and theatre director.

THE
RELUCTANT
TOMMY

Ronald Skirth

Edited by Duncan Barrett

PAN BOOKS

First published 2010 by Macmillan

First published in paperback 2011 by Pan Books
an imprint of Pan Macmillan, a division of Macmillan Publishers Limited
Pan Macmillan, 20 New Wharf Road, London N1 9RR
Basingstoke and Oxford
Associated companies throughout the world
www.panmacmillan.com

ISBN 978-0-330-51374-6

1 3 5 7 9 8 6 4 2

A CIP catalogue record for this book is available
from the British Library.

Printed in the UK by CPI Mackays, Chatham ME5 8TD

Visit **www.panmacmillan.com** to read more about all our books
and to buy them. You will also find features, author interviews and
news of any author events, and you can sign up for e-newsletters
so that you're always first to hear about our new releases.

Contents

Foreword

After the war was over, Churchill called it 'the bravest little street in England'. Chapel Street was a cul-de-sac in Altrincham, Cheshire, but that one street alone sent 161 men to the Great War to fight for king and country. Although that statistic is awesome, there were communities all over the country who could boast almost as much. A huge proportion of those who went never came back.

On the wall of the tiny Saxon church in the hamlet where I have a home in west Berkshire there hangs a wooden plaque. On it are inscribed the names of nearly twenty men who left the rich agricultural land upon which they worked to fight in some foreign field. There are far fewer family names. The Wiggins family sent four; two other families sent three – fathers, brothers and sons.

Ronald Skirth was one of those myriad men from across Britain who went. Somehow he came back. Somehow he managed to locate and arm the conscientious objector within himself, ultimately saving not only his life but his sanity too. Skirth is one of the very very few 'Tommies' who not only experienced and survived the First World War but also managed to write vividly about it. The memoirs of the officers and politicians of the time are legion; the offerings of the underclasses are sparse. Ronald Skirth's remarkable book contributes one of the rarest of perspectives. It is of a man who came to hate the killing and who came to find mechanisms for frustrating it, even mis-directing his guns to give the enemy a chance of escape.

As a child in the 1950s the proximity of the Second World War might have served to obliterate my awareness of the First had it not been for the portrait above our dining-room mantel.

My grandfather, Lieutenant General Sir Thomas D'Oyly Snow KCMG, KCB, peered down at proceedings adorned in full fig and rows of ribbons and medals. He was discussed in reveren-tial terms, occasionally even boastfully. General Thom com-manded the Fourth Division under Sir John French and was regarded within the family as a hero first class. He had led the retreat from Mons in 1915. This was seen, and is still seen by some, as snatching some kind of victory from a very palpable defeat. The Somme was never mentioned, though he was there too.

The British army of the First World War has been described as 'lions led by donkeys'. If Ronald Skirth was a 'lion', Thom Snow was ultimately a 'donkey'. Thom spent the battle of the Somme eight kilometres back in the comfort of a rural chateau writing to his wife Charlotte about the beauty of the French countryside. On the day he wrote, 4,000 of his men perished in a morning.

Thankfully Ronald Skirth was not among them, and the 'reluctant Tommy' survives even after his own natural death, to provide an essential historical perspective.

Jon Snow, London 2010

Introduction

*'On 3 October 1916 I was a slender callow youth
of eighteen who looked about sixteen and a half.'*

When Ronald Skirth sat down in January 1971 and began the
journal on which this book is based he had no intention of writing a war memoir. What he intended to write was a 'Love Story'
– an account of the teenage romance between himself and his
wife Ella: 'our meeting and what followed it, then our parting
and final reunion'.

The couple had met in 1916, when Ronald was eighteen and Ella just fifteen and a half. By the time he was called up for military training ten weeks later, they had fallen head over heels in love. Parted for nearly two years (he was repeatedly denied home leave), they continued to write regularly, and remained faithful to each other until the war's end. A few years later they were married and, as Skirth himself puts it, 'lived happily ever after'.

This was the story that he sat down to write. But before long his war memories began to take over – memories which he had done his best to forget in the intervening fifty-three years – and the wartime interlude in his 'Love Story' swelled to fill hundreds of pages.

To think that at the outset I envisaged one exercise book bare-ly filled! But then I didn't intend to include the war episodes which have taken up so much space. As a result, my 'Love Story', which was to tell of how a teenage romance grew into an adult relationship, developed into its present dispropor-tionate size, mainly because I hadn't allowed for the fact that once you start reminiscing you enter a kind of world-without-end; one memory brings back another and that brings back a third and so on, ad infinitum, it seems.

An inexplicable compulsion would not allow me to exclude accounts of the episodes about which I have written. They are in my book because they forced themselves into it.

The result was an astonishing account of one man's experiences of the First World War, a scrapbook of letters, postcards, diary entries, maps and photographs detailing a remarkable personal journey – geographical, philosophical and spiritual.

Skirth clearly felt ambivalent about what he ended up with.

His intention had not been to write a 'detailed, complete auto-biography', yet he had to concede that

> in spite of . . . my original intention, these pages <u>are</u> auto-biographical and this 'work' (– is that being pompous?) is a kind of autobiographical Scrap Book. I suppose in a way it has become a Portrait of Me – and that portrait would be insincere and lack honesty if it didn't tell you how I reacted, what I thought, said and did during the three most eventful, – and possibly most important – years of my life.

At the same time, Skirth's ambition to produce a love story was fulfilled. He christened the folders in which he wrote 'Ronella', and the stories those folders contain are a kind of a paean to the girl from whom he was separated for so long, and to the love they both kept alive against all the odds. Nearing the end of the memoir he asserts defiantly, 'what I <u>have</u> written I claim to be a Love Story in spite of the fact that more of my pages are concerned with the war-separation of the two lovers than of their times together, – in spite also of the fact that in dozens of the pages the heroine makes not one single appearance'.

As the scope of the memoir changed, so the scale of it expanded dramatically. Skirth's daughter Jean remembers Ella's frustration as her husband's pet project dragged on for months and months – 'Oh yes, he's at it again,' she would tell her over the phone – and her relief when he finally finished it.

Ella was understandably shocked at what she read: far from the charming romance she had been promised, she was confronted with some pretty horrific war stories – stories which Skirth himself had never told her in their nearly fifty years of marriage. It must have been a difficult time for both of them – writing the journals made Skirth remember more, and many of those memories were traumatic – but it did help to clarify some things: 'Her one complaint is that I didn't tell her of these happenings years ago; they would, she says, have helped her to understand certain actions and states of mind which at times puzzled her . . . [T]hey are now, as the saying has it, "out of my system" and I think I am the better for having told of them.'

The quantity of material that Skirth produced is quite remarkable, not least for a man by this point in his mid-seventies. Once started, it seems he just could not bring himself to stop. At several points he indicates that he is nearing the end of the project – 'I have just one more story to tell' – and then something changes his mind, and he goes on to relate another.

Even after he had reached the end of the story proper, Skirth kept returning to his journals – adding to, editing and amending what he had written, even after suffering two strokes. As a result, the finished product is something of a palimpsest. Some sections exist in multiple versions, while elsewhere odd pages are blacked out or missing, presumably consigned to the 'W. P. B.' – the waste-paper basket.

Skirth originally wrote for two reasons: first as a 'pleasant pastime', a project not unlike the holiday scrapbooks and photo albums he was forever compiling, and intended, like those albums, for the eyes of his nearest and dearest; and second to provide some 'manual exercise' for 'finger joints threatened with immobility from arthritis'.

He was well aware of what a remarkable tale he was telling – on a number of occasions he describes his war experiences as 'extraordinary' – and it must have struck him that it might be of interest to readers outside his family circle. His aerial photographs of the Passchendaele battlefield may, he says, be 'the only ones in existence' and of considerable interest to 'military historian[s]'. Later he claims that the official history of a part of the Italian campaign is based on a fabricated report of a battle which never even happened: 'only two people knew that <u>no</u> attack of any kind whatsoever was made'.

As far as is known, the only people Skirth showed his journals to were Ella – who read them day by day as he was writing them – and Jean, to whom he gave them before his death five years later. However, he often shared his holiday scrapbooks with friends, and it is possible that the war stories were passed around to a trusted few. Towards the end of the final journal he hopes that Ella won't be embarrassed if the card she wrote that morning is 'seen by any eyes but mine'.

At times Skirth seems to be writing for someone not known to him personally: 'if you have ever smoked an Italian cigarette you will understand why they raved over ours.' . . . 'If you have <u>seen</u> Garda, and Como, Lugarno and Maggiore you will know what I mean. I hope that one day you will.'

When he defends his pacifist beliefs, he imagines his reader as an interlocutor in a kind of ethical debate: '"Oh yes," you'll say, "we understand and sympathize." But what you overlook is the fact that there comes a time when a nation <u>has</u> to fight; when there is no alternative. How much are your principles, sincere as they may be, worth then?' This may be more of a rhetorical device than anything else, but it suggests that Skirth must have at least wondered who might one day read his words. Later he poses the question more directly: 'I thought, <u>one</u> day, I'll write <u>our</u> story down . . . but if ever I did, would anybody want to read it?'

Although Jean Skirth was given her father's journals before he died in 1977, it wasn't until two decades later that she read them in full. Over the years she would dip into them now and again,

coming back to those sections which appealed to her, but finding much of the material too upsetting. Then in 1999, twenty-
two years after her father's death, a combination of her own
health concerns and the approaching millennium made her feel
that she should finally 'do something' with what he had left her.
After discussing various options with friends and relatives, she
came to a decision: she would donate the majority of the memoir to the Imperial War Museum, with whose staff she knew her
father had been in contact, while retaining the more personal
sections in a separate volume. For the first time she read
through his five ring binders from beginning to end, dividing up
the sheets as she went along.

Jean was never quite sure whether this was what her father
would have wanted. The memoir was very personal to him and
he had been upset when she had showed it to a friend without
asking his permission. But she felt that his was a story that
ought not to be forgotten and that it should be placed where
interested parties could read it. She was very relieved to hear,
from the IWM, that others found the memoir as fascinating as
she had – it made her feel that she had done the right thing.

I first became familiar with Ronald Skirth's story as a result
of my mother's research for her book *Casualty Figures* (2008).
She wrote about him as one of a number of men who survived
the First World War after suffering from shell shock. Despite the
company of other fascinating life stories, it was his narrative
that stood out, in part because of his remarkable conversion
to conscientious objection, which brought Ian Hislop – then
researching a Channel 4 documentary, *Not Forgotten: The Men
Who Wouldn't Fight* – to the IWM archive to read his story. I
remember a paper my mother gave to promote her book: in
the question-and-answer session that followed, what everyone

wanted to know more about was Skirth. Clearly this was a story that resonated widely – a remarkable story of love, conscience and integrity, as inspiring as it was shocking. I felt that it deserved as wide an audience as possible, and to be read in its protagonist's own words.

I contacted Jean Skirth and obtained her permission to edit the memoir for publication. Fortunately, Skirth's handwriting is for the most part very clear, though the volume of material is considerable. The Imperial War Museum archivists were extremely helpful, allowing me to photograph the journals so I could do the bulk of the transcribing work elsewhere.

Jean gave me access to the fifth, private, volume of the memoir, from which the opening and closing parts of the story here are taken, as well as the section on Skirth's home leave. Without these sections I felt the memoir would be missing its heart: the love story against which the rest of the narrative takes place. She also kindly showed me some of her father's old photo albums, from which the pictures of him and Ella reproduced here are taken.

Finally, thirty-eight years after the memoir was completed and nearly a century after the events which it describes, Ronald Skirth's story is available in his own words as a published book.

The bulk of what you read here is as it exists in the original five journals. I have had to abridge them considerably, cutting down Skirth's 185,000 words to a more manageable length. Many of Skirth's asides and observations quoted in this Introduction do not re-appear in the main text, where I have tended to let the story speak for itself, removing much of the author's commentary. My approach has been to preserve as much of the story as possible while cutting back on digressions, asides and apologies.

I have modernized a few spellings and made small changes for the sake of clarity and flow. I have also imposed a more straightforward chronology. In the journals, even after extensive reordering by both Ronald and Jean Skirth, there is a lot of jumping to and fro. As he admitted, 'I have . . . wandered from high roads on to low roads, by-roads and cul-de-sacs. I've gone forwards, backwards and sideways in my journey of recollections, picking up bits and pieces all the way. This "book" contains what was left after the waste-paper basket had been emptied over and over again.' The Imperial War Museum archivist puts it rather more baldly: '9023 99/53/1. Private Papers of J. R. Skirth. Very interesting but anecdotal and disjointed ms memoir (4 volumes, 688pp in total).' Skirth's gift for anecdotes is one of the great strengths of his work, but the narrative you hold in your hands is I hope a little less disjointed than the original.

Writing more than half a century after the event, Skirth knew that 100-per-cent accuracy would be impossible. 'I write these accounts fifty-five years afterwards. That's a huge span of time to elapse and a hazy memory may play tricks with truth. It would be an impossibility to recreate with complete and absolute accuracy the thoughts, feelings, opinions and reasoning of months more than a half-century past.' Quoted dialogue, he freely admits, cannot be taken as verbatim: 'I cannot reproduce the conversation . . . word for word. It is too long ago . . . I'll set it down as I think it must have been.'

Perhaps most problematically, the crucial letter in which Skirth wrote to Ella of his conscientious objection to killing never reached her; as he predicted, it '[went no] further than the Officers' Mess'. He was forced to reconstruct it from memory. 'It is quite impossible for anyone to say after fifty-odd years

"This is exactly what I wrote on that day." The best I can do is to declare that what follows is as near the actual truth as I can make it. The gist . . . remain[s] indelibly engraved in my memory.'

Where I have spotted inconsistencies and errors I have silently corrected them. For example, in the same reconstructed letter Skirth writes, 'People who think like me (– and unfortunately I've only met <u>one</u> who does –) are called Conscientious Objectors.' This one sympathetic person is presumably Raymond Raggett, who Skirth didn't in fact meet properly until *after* he wrote to Ella, so I have removed the reference in the letter. Later he writes, 'Ray knew that conscription was going to be introduced before the end of [1916].' One of them must have been mistaken since the Military Service Act had been passed in January of that year. Again, I have changed the offending sentence.

Skirth undertook a lot of research at the time of writing, both scouring his own collection of war memorabilia and consulting with authorities such as the Imperial War Museum and the Italian Tourist Board.

In regard to the historical accuracy of the actual happenings I have chosen there is no doubt in my mind whatever. Wherever I have needed verification of dates or locations I have consulted appropriate books in our Public Libraries. My own little diary-journal has been invaluable in bringing back to me, – where I needed it, – the personal details which make the stories individually mine and no one else's. I refrained from re-reading semi-fictional or documentary records by professional authors, e.g. Remarque's *All Quiet on the Western Front*, in order not to be influenced in any way by 'outside' sources. I <u>did</u> re-read some of Sassoon's and Owen's War

Poems, because they were contemporaries and to a certain extent, kindred minds of mine. (But they, alas, only saw their war through the eyes of the Officer Caste.) Robert Graves, yes and Hemingway, yes because they fought on the same fronts as I did.

However, despite this extensive research Skirth often chooses to fictionalize or at least work up his material for dramatic advantage. He clearly felt that this was his story and he had the right to make whatever changes he saw fit. When he includes an extract from the official report on the Battle of Asiago Plateau, he is reconstructing it from memory, not research. And even when he reproduces his own diary entries, it is not always clear how genuine the imported text is. He claims that his little black book is the primary source for much of the memoir – 'Without [it] I couldn't have recalled half of what I have written' – but this source is unfortunately now lost. (Jean believes that after he worked up his stories into their present form Skirth got rid of it, along with the other memorabilia which didn't make it into the scrapbook.)

Skirth claims to quote directly from this original diary, although he confesses to polishing its prose: 'The account was scribbled hurriedly . . . I have allowed myself the liberty of expanding its style into something approaching standard English.' But what exactly did the black diary contain? There are apparent inconsistencies. Near the end of the memoir Skirth writes that between his 'knock-out' at Passchendaele and his climbing of 'Mount Hippo' a year later he didn't write in the journal, yet he reproduces passages apparently taken from it which fall between those two events. Unless these were in fact written in another (unmentioned) book, they should perhaps be taken with a pinch of salt, as a narrative device rather than authentic primary sources from the war years.

Some of the facts in his story Skirth changes deliberately, though perhaps out of a sense of propriety more than anything else. Throughout, he claims to have been a member of '239 Siege Battery', but a postcard from his Italian friend Giulio gives the game away: it is addressed to 'Bombardier Ronald Skirth 12033 R.G.A. 293 Siege Battery, Italian Expeditionary Force'. The Officer Commanding 293 was not the 'R.A. Snow' of Skirth's account, but a near namesake, Major H.S.R. Snowdon.

Skirth offers neither apology nor explanation for these changes, which is surprising since elsewhere he is at pains to justify his more creative reconstructions of events. So exactly how truthful is Skirth's story? It is hard to be certain, though the basic facts – where he served and with whom – do all check out. At times his memoir seems less an autobiography than a novel, but he strongly denies that, beyond the occasional burst of poetic licence, it is in any way fictional. 'Had this been a work of fiction,' he writes, certain particulars would have been arranged differently, but 'I must be sincere and truthful . . . I am not writing a novel, a play, nor a film-script, but of the small part of a Great War in which I participated. What I did, what I saw and how it affected me.'

As it happens, Ronald Skirth 'saw' the war from a relatively unusual perspective. As a non-commissioned officer he straddled the boundary (often uncomfortably) between the officer caste and the rank and file, a boundary which was even more pronounced in the artillery than it was in the infantry. 'By virtue of my job, I had to live in a sort of No Man's Land. I belonged neither to the officer clique nor to the rank-and-file. My work segregated me from the latter and made me associate with the former.' His critique of the officer caste is very clear: '[T]hey had the "cushier" life. They rarely suffered the miseries and hardships of the rank and file. They <u>saw</u> our war, but didn't <u>live</u> it.'

This is putting it mildly. Throughout 'My War' (as Skirth terms it, with perhaps a deliberate double meaning) his most obvious enemies are not the Germans and Austrians across no-man's-land, but his own superiors. His commanding officer is described as 'the person I grew to hate more than any of my country's enemies'. Gradually, all his respect for the 'officer-gentlemen hierarchy' is stripped away – and with it fall the other great institutions: the Church of England, the government and the royal family (not to mention the munitions makers and the propagandist press).

Skirth's developing moral qualms about the war placed him in an even more ambivalent situation. His conscience forbade him from taking lives, and yet stuck out in the field he was in no position to declare himself a conscientious objector. (Even Siegfried Sassoon, the most famous of the COs, would wait until he was back in London before doing so – and Sassoon was a decorated aristocrat, while Skirth was a relative nobody with a history of being bullied by those in authority.) He became, in his own words, a 'sheep in wolf's clothing', outwardly a dutiful combatant, while inwardly a pacifist.

Skirth's acts of military sabotage – deliberately targeting guns to miss human targets – generate controversy even today. Ian Hislop, in his *Not Forgotten* documentary on conscientious objectors, found Skirth's approach disquieting: 'It's quite an extraordinary admission, and it's not a comfortable one to read. Yes, he's preserving the life of the enemy, but is he in some way endangering the life of his own troops?' Skirth is adamant that no men were harmed as a result of his actions. He states quite explicitly that during this time the only casualties sustained by his battery were self-inflicted – the result of disastrous incompetence which he did his very best to prevent.

Nonetheless, feelings run high. When I've told Skirth's story to people, it has been met with a mixture of fascination, celebration and hostile criticism. One dinner party very nearly descended into chaos as a result of the ensuing debate while an early book talk was hijacked by a man who couldn't understand why no one else was as outraged as he was. I have been astonished at the anger Skirth's actions prove capable of inspiring nearly a century after the event. One librarian told me about an enraged customer who marched in and slapped the book down on his desk, declaring that its author should have been shot. (Intrigued, he took a copy home himself, and came to precisely the opposite conclusion.)

Since *The Reluctant Tommy* was first published almost a year ago, its harshest critics have claimed that Skirth is either a liar or a fantasist – that, whether through old age and the delayed effects of shell shock, or out of a malicious desire to discredit men he personally disliked, he wrote not a 'sincere and truthful' account, as he claims, but a highly biased narrative that distorts the events he describes.

Perhaps unsurprisingly, they have uncovered a number of discrepancies between the memoir and other historical records, which they believe undermine Skirth's credibility. Some of these are specific factual quibbles: Skirth's claim that the men were not allowed to wear shorts in Italy is contradicted by photos of some of them doing so; the boat he shipped out on was indeed hit by a submarine, but before, not after, his own channel crossing; the official history of the Italian campaign does not 'specifically praise' 293 Siege Battery, but makes a general remark about siege batteries in the area; the precise medals he describes being awarded to his colleagues do not always tally with those mentioned in official records, and occasionally he 'promotes' another man too early, or too late. Such minor factual errors I am inclined to ascribe to faulty memory after more than fifty years – in any case, they do not affect the narrative of the memoir overall. Perhaps Skirth's belief that he was personally singled out for punishment in not being granted leave, when it seems that this was relatively common practice, can be put down to a combination of 'memory play[ing] tricks' and a misunderstanding on his part at the time, given that he already felt so victimized by those in authority.

Other differences between Skirth's account and official records must perhaps be put down to artistic licence. Jock Shiels, 'the best friend I ever had', was indeed a real person, and did die in action on the Western Front – although not on the date specified in the memoir. While some of Skirth's comrades have names that closely associate them with real people, others do not, and it is hard to be certain of the extent to which each character matches up to an original person. Real figures may have been amalgamated, or transposed from one situation to another, and after such a distance of time it is not impossible that individuals may have been unintentionally confused. With this in mind, and given the distress caused to some descendants of Skirth's colleagues by characters whose names closely resemble those of their relatives, I have in some cases added an extra layer of anonymity by now changing their names more completely.

Perhaps the most significant area of disagreement between Skirth's memoir and historical sources is in his description of a fatal gun accident which he claims the army covered up. It is hardly a revelation that this account is at odds with the official story since it is, in effect, a conspiracy claim. Those who refuse to countenance the possibility that it might be true, generally fall back on rather weak generalized assertions – the very idea of such a conspiracy is 'fanciful'; that such an accident could have occurred is 'inconceivable'. There are powerful myths at stake here – whether historical, political or, for some readers, familial – if we choose to believe what Skirth is telling us.

Again, there appear to be factual errors in Skirth's account of the incident, in particular concerning the exact numbers of dead and wounded, although one man from Skirth's battery did certainly die on the night in question. Perhaps it will never be possible to know beyond doubt exactly what happened nearly a century ago. My own view is that the tenor of Ronald Skirth's memoir is one of honesty and truth-telling, and I would not dismiss what he says too lightly, even if he does deviate from specific facts in order to craft an engaging story. Gore Vidal writes that 'a memoir is how one remembers one's own life, while an autobiography is history, requiring research, dates, facts double-checked'. Skirth's narrative certainly falls into the former category – it is not a history book, and if taken as such it is rightly viewed as 'unreliable', to the extent that the Imperial War Museum are currently reviewing its status within their archive. But taken as an intensely personal account of one man's experiences at the most pivotal moment of his life, I believe that it more than stands up to any criticism levelled against it. I encourage you to read the memoir for yourself, and make up your own mind about who to believe.

And so to the ethics of Skirth's pacifist conversion, and the actions he claims to have taken as a result, deliberately mis-targeting his guns to give the enemy a chance to escape. Some readers find it astonishing, even reprehensible, that a soldier could do such a thing, although in fact Skirth's behaviour is not without precedent and the 'Live and Let Live System' that developed during the First World War has been documented elsewhere. To me, Skirth's actions seem an understandable, desperate attempt to preserve his sanity and moral compass, both of which had taken a severe battering. Those who condemn him would do well to place themselves in his shoes: a sensitive, amateur soldier only nineteen years old whose ideals had been shattered and whose friends had all been blown to pieces – not, to his mind, the victims of an enemy attack so much as of the men who ordered them to place their lives in unnecessary danger. Prevented by those same superiors from leaving the front line (his leave, which should normally have been granted after six months at the most, was deferred for a further fifteen), Ronald Skirth took the necessary actions for his own mental and spiritual survival, and was courageous enough to risk imprisonment, even death, by informing his superiors of how he felt in the most tactful way he could devise: by allowing them to read his confession in a censored personal letter.

The strength of Skirth's convictions (as revealed in the Postscript to this volume) are likely to surprise many readers, but they are a testament to the extreme nature of his experiences. Perhaps equally surprising, given his 'disillusion[ment]' as a young man, are his optimism about the future and his confidence in those long-haired, strangely apparelled 'youngsters' of the early 1970s who he knew would grow into our leaders: 'From the young people of to-day will emerge the leaders of to-morrow. They will make mistakes, as everyone does. But they won't be guilty of the colossal blunders of their predecessors . . . [who] plunged us into war because they hadn't the vision to do anything else.'

If Skirth were alive today, perhaps his optimism would be tempered a little. As I sit writing, the BBC News website carries the headline UK MAY HAVE 40-YEAR AFGHAN ROLE.

Duncan Barrett, September 2009 and February 2011

Acknowledgements

I am grateful to my mother Michèle for uncovering Skirth's journals in the depths of the Imperial War Museum's archives, and for her expert advice on how to deal with them; also to Rod Suddaby and his staff at the IWM for their generous assistance in bringing the story into print. Thanks are due to Georgina Morley, my editor at Pan Macmillan, for her immediate confidence in Skirth's story, to Jon Elek at A.P. Watt for his tireless work representing it, to Ruth Petrie for her suggestions on how to move it forward and to Tania Adams for her sensitive editorial input. Kate Hewson and Philippa McEwan have brought their considerable skills to bear on the book, and have been a pleasure to work with.

To Nuala Calvi I owe a huge debt for her support, encouragement and shrewd advice. I think she knows something of what Ella must have felt as her husband spent months on end squirrelling away at his journals. For her patience throughout the process I am very grateful.

Finally, thanks to Jean Skirth, Ronald's daughter, who was determined that his story should not be forgotten and who gave every possible assistance in getting it published, more than thirty years after his memoir first came into her possession. If her father were alive to see his book in print, there's no doubt to whom it would be dedicated: to Ella, who lit up his life and made those most difficult and traumatic of years just about bearable.

Ella, aged seventeen.

I keep six honest serving men
(They taught me all I knew);
Their names are What and Why and When
And How and Where and Who.

Rudyard Kipling

CHAPTER ONE

Our Love Story

If it was a children's fairy tale, I think it would go like this.

Once upon a time there was a schoolboy and a schoolgirl who fell in love. He was eighteen and she was only fifteen and a half.

A few months after they met, he enlisted as a soldier and went off to foreign lands to fight for his country. And the old folk said, 'That's the end of <u>that</u> little romance. She's too young to know her own mind; she'll soon forget <u>him</u>.'

But the boy and the girl knew they wouldn't ever forget each other.

After they had been parted for a year, the girl's friends began to say, 'Why don't you find another boy to go out with and enjoy yourself?' But she didn't want another boy because she believed her sweetheart when he wrote to say that though they were apart he loved her more than ever. So, although she sometimes felt sad, she said nothing and continued to smile to herself.

When a year and a half had passed the friends said, 'That boy is having a good time with all those foreign girls. He won't want you now. Why don't you forget him?' They thought she was lonely and felt sorry for her. But she was not as unhappy as they thought because she trusted her sweetheart and believed him when his letters told her he still loved her. So she still said nothing and went on smiling.

Then, after many exciting adventures, the boy came home from the wars and stopped being a soldier. And the boy and the girl found that they loved each other more than ever.

And very soon he left her again to go to the Big City for two years' studying. When holidays came the lovers were able to be together and were very happy indeed. But even after he had finished his studies they couldn't be together for long because the boy was not rich and had to go away to seek his fortune.

By this time most of the girl's friends had got married. They thought the girl envied them and teased her by saying, 'He'll never marry you. If he loved you he wouldn't keep you waiting so long.'

But she knew in her heart that one day he would, so she took no notice of their teasing, said nothing and went on smiling to herself.

Suddenly, one day eight long years after they had first fallen in love, the boy who was now a grown man came back from the Big City and said, 'I've found a nice little home for us to live in. Will you marry me?' And the girl said, 'Yes, I'd love to!'

And all the people who had teased and who had thought

the romance would never come to anything were glad that they had been proved wrong. They all came to see the wedding and whispered to one another, 'Aren't they a lovely couple?'

And, of course, the boy and the girl lived happily ever after.

It isn't often that real life works out like a fairy tale, but this one summarizes our own love story exactly.

But there was much more to it than that, – as you can see from the length of this book. To begin with, I would like to write about times and events before Ella and I met. Then I'll tell of our meeting and what followed it, then our parting and final reunion. It is all so conventional, conforming to the pattern of all love stories: Boy meets Girl, Boy leaves Girl, Boy returns and marries Girl. So conventional when it is put down like that, but anything but 'ordinary' in actual fact! I don't think I would have troubled to write this story of an ordinary boy and an ordinary girl, if extraordinary things hadn't happened to one of them.

So here is our story, a collection of recollections, a scrapbook, a hotch-potch, a medley. It doesn't follow any pattern at all, except that it has a middle that is sad, a beginning that was happy, and an end which we hope won't come for a long time yet.

Childhood Days

I have always regarded Sussex as my own county although my family didn't come to live there until I was eight. It was the county in which I grew up, the county that adopted me. Ella was pure-bred Sussex, born within sound of the sea like her father before her.

When I was twelve I was fortunate enough to win a scholarship to a grammar school. (This was quite a noteworthy achievement as only forty free places were available to the whole country.) The new school was co-educational, so half of my classmates were female. At that age I wasn't particularly fond of girls' company. I considered I had more than a fair share of it at home. (I had two sisters, one two years younger and the other seven years younger, and quite often I had to act as nursemaid to the little one.) With two sisters and their friends at home and a hundred girls of assorted shapes and sizes at school I shouldn't have been a shy type. But I was.

Anyway in those days trains excited me far more than girls. My new school was at Rye and to get there from Bexhill required a rail journey on two different companies' lines, seventeen miles in each direction. To a train-mad youngster like me the unlimited free rail travel my season tickets entitled me to was a magnificent bonus.

The girl who is going to play an important part in this story, Ella Christian, was nine then. She lived about half a mile away. She didn't interest me much, though I knew her brother, who was three years older than I, because we had both attended St Barnabas 'C of E' School; that is before I went to grammar school. Their house bordered the school playground and the football with which my friends and I played always ended up, sooner or later, among the cabbages in their garden. I knew her father because he sang bass at the church where I was leading choirboy and his blacksmith's forge had been on my way to school. I could never pass by without pausing to watch the brawny smith and his mate strike sparks from the red-hot horseshoes.

Mother had become housekeeper to a handsome, pale-faced young doctor who had set up his first practice in our rapidly growing town. Dr. Stokes was a bachelor and a splendid pianist. His piano was in his surgery-cum-sitting room, ours in the room behind it, our drawing room. I was allowed to practise only when the doctor was out.

My sisters and I were forbidden entry to the surgery. But whenever the sound from that room indicated that the doctor was playing I would tiptoe unobserved and put my ear to the keyhole to listen. I was sure I would never be able to play like that.

One afternoon, to satisfy my curiosity, I disobeyed orders. I had been thrilled by the doctor's playing earlier and wanted to know what such exciting music could be. It was still on the piano: a book of the Piano Sonatas of Mozart.

Then, for some unaccountable reason, I took from its shelf one of the doctor's heavy medical books, put it on the floor and opened it. I was eleven or twelve at the time, and would read anything and everything I could lay my hands on. Chance arranged that this afternoon I should discover those 'facts of life' associated with conception and childbirth. I devoured the print and studied every illustration.

Flushed with excitement and guilt, I was just closing the book when disaster overtook me. I heard the door open and in walked the doctor. I was caught red-handed and red-faced. I couldn't speak. I dared not look at his face. As I scuttled past all I saw were the gloves he was coolly removing. Now I should be for it! But the days went by and nothing was said. 'What a sport!' I thought. 'He hasn't split on me.' And as if that wasn't enough to merit hero worship, a few weeks later this happened.

It was the time in the evening when I did my piano practice. I was a willing pupil and practised assiduously. My only concern was that the doctor might overhear my boyish efforts and think them rather feeble.

This particular evening, by the light of two candles, I had just finished working on the Bach Gavotte I was going to perform at a forthcoming exam. I felt like playing something simple and relaxing. I took down a book of assorted pieces and opened it at Schumann's 'Traumerei' ('Dreaming'). My teacher hadn't taught me this one, but I rendered my own version.

I had just finished the last chord when I had that feeling of being watched. I turned my head. The door was ajar and in the gloom I distinguished the dim figure of Dr. Stokes. He said, 'That was excellent, Ronald, excellent!' then vanished.

I blew out the candles, closed the piano and went up to my bedroom. I couldn't bear to let Mother see me cry. But the tears in my eyes were tears of joy.

Up till then I had somehow felt that piano playing was girlish: that a boy ought to prefer playing football. But, if the doctor thought piano playing was worth-while then I needn't worry. If it was O.K. with him, it was O.K. with me.

By the time I was fifteen and Ella was twelve we had come in contact with each other fairly frequently through our church's social activities, at vicarage garden parties, amateur concerts and in the Sunday School where we both became very young, – and very inexpert – teachers to groups of slightly younger children.

Perhaps I should tell you what sort of lad I was in my mid-teens. Well, I was about average in height and below it in girth: far too 'skinny' for my own liking. I had hair whose colour was in course of changing from very fair to nondescript brown. I could never keep it in place without sousing it with water. (Hair oil was much too expensive.) On the field of sport I didn't compare too favourably with Ella's brother Ernest, who was a stone heavier, a boxer and captain of a football team of his age group.

However, I could boast (– though I didn't –) of one sphere of athletic activity in which I was his superior: swimming. It is rather strange that although his family were all Sussex born not one of them liked the sea.

My only other athletic ability was in cross-country running. I was a fair performer in the gym, could do a bit of rowing and played twice, not very successfully, for the School's Second Soccer Team.

The defects in my character were a rather timid, slightly effeminate manner, two clumsy feet and an intense love of such un-masculine things as 'nature', old buildings, poetry, music and art. I was also very happy in my own company.

Our families were acquainted before Ella and I became friends. Father, whose breakdown in health had been the reason for our moving to the seaside, had recovered sufficiently to begin light open-air work. He became an Insurance Agent, a contrast to the position he had held in the silks department of Debenham and Freebody's in London, where my parents met. Each Monday, my father would call on Ella's mother on business matters.

During my years at Rye Grammar School I spent little time in my home town except at weekends and during holidays. All my close friends were in far-away Rye – and seventeen miles was far away in those days!

Ella had taken notice of me, she confesses. I was almost always, she says, alone and carrying a red-covered book. She thought me rather unsociable. I don't think I had taken much notice of her, – then.

Leaving School

Wiser people than I have put forward theories as to whether environment or heredity exert the greater influence on a child's character formation. I can cite one case where there is no doubt whatever, – my own. Neither my father or mother had any artistic interests, neither were musical. But I was most fortunate in growing up under the influence (if that is the right word) of two of the most beautiful towns in Britain. Rye was one of them, Winchester the other.

For three happy years while my father was convalescing we had lived in the tiny Hampshire village of Ropley. Every second Wednesday my father would drive into Winchester on business matters. If there were no school, Mother and I would accompany him. What a glorious sensation it was bowling along the lanes in the trap behind Polly the mare, especially if, on one of the few straight stretches of road, I were allowed to take the reins for a brief spell!

Some days, Mother would take me sight-seeing. I must have been more of a liability than an asset – interminably asking questions and wanting to go further and further afield. Of course it was the cathedral which attracted me most. I was allowed to enter and wander about alone while Mother took a well-earned rest on one of the seats in the Close.

Its immensity overwhelmed me. I wondered how men were ever able to build a carved stone roof so high and wide. If the choir should be singing, or the organ should be playing, the beauty of it all would so overpower me that my eyes would fill with tears. (I could never understand why, unlike other boys, I used to cry when I was happy.) I would make sure they were all wiped away before I rejoined Mother.

Although the little town of Rye boasted no great cathedral, its impact on me was as great. I loved its steep, cobbled streets, its half-timbered and weatherboarded buildings, and of course its splendid church on the hilltop which locals claimed to be the finest in Sussex. You never walked its streets in good weather without passing half a dozen artists at work. As a schoolboy I had wanted to become an architect, but there were no training facilities available so that ambition had to be abandoned. I settled on teaching instead.

I remember my last day at Rye Grammar School very clearly. It was the day after the school had officially broken up for the Easter holidays. I was there were to collect my few remaining belongings and to say goodbye to any friends I had previously missed. The only member of the teaching staff I wished to see was Mr. Matson, who had been my House Master throughout the six years of my attendance. He made me a pleasant little parting speech: 'Good Luck, Skirth! I remember you once told me that your ambition was to become an architect. Not many of us are able to follow exactly the career we would choose. Well! there wouldn't be many architects if chaps like us weren't around to teach them the three R's first. Teaching may be the worst-paid job you could take up but it's the most worth-while.'

After a parting handshake I recall the thought that came into my mind. 'Good old Mattie! If I become half as good at the job as you are, I'll be content.'

Just before I left the building I chanced to stray into the hall, and there I saw something which provided me with perhaps the most pleasurable surprise in the whole of my days at school. A sign-writer had just finished adding two names in gilt lettering to the Honours Board which hung there. The second name was mine. (One of my form-mates and I had succeeded in gaining 'First Class' Matric Results in all subjects.) I was thrilled to the core that I had been able to leave Rye Grammar School with a pleasant souvenir to remember me by.

Now I had one more duty to perform which, should it prove successful, would make my day.

Journeys between home and school had to be broken at Hastings, as there were no through trains. For this reason I had to carry two separate season tickets, which made me feel terribly important. But to-day I had a special reason for making use of the break in my journey. Instead of waiting on Hastings' No. 1 Platform for my second train I left the station and walked down the approach road to the foot of the hill, where the local Recruiting Office was situated. Bexhill knew me too well and had already turned me down twice. I didn't intend to risk a third refusal. This time I was going to enlist in the Army even if it meant making a false declaration of age.

The Hastings Recruiting Officer wasn't quite as thorough as his Bexhill counterpart, with the result that fifteen minutes after I had entered his office as a civilian I walked out as a soldier. I didn't _feel_ any different and I didn't _look_ any different but I had signed the necessary papers, sworn the necessary oath, taken the King's Shilling and become a deferral member of H. M. Royal Garrison Artillery. My call-up would come, I was told, at the end of my apprentice-teacher training. Walking back up the slope to the station I proudly wore the khaki brassard (armband) with the crown upon it which as a volunteer for the armed forces I was entitled to display until I reported for full-time duty.

When I arrived home and told my parents, their reaction pleased me immensely. It seemed that my father had been told of my two previous attempts at enlistment. (I had thought them to be secret!) They were proud of me and glad I was convinced it was my duty to offer my services to my King and Country. I am sure, though, that Mother's hopes were the reverse of mine when she considered which should come first: my call to the colours, or the ending of the war.

I had brought from school some documents of great importance to my future. One was an application form for St. John's College, the teacher-training extension of the University of London. I also had a very satisfactory letter of recommendation from my Headmaster. 'To-morrow,' I said to myself, 'I'll go and see the Reverend Mortlock and scrounge a testimonial out of him.' He had known me since I was eight and had some influence with the authorities in London.

All my hopes were fulfilled. The vicar did his bit and in due course I was informed that I had been accepted as a Resident Student from the end of the following September. In view of 'special circumstances', no fees would be chargeable for my residence or tuition, apart from a nominal £25, which I would have to provide out of my own resources. I was more than delighted at the news, chiefly because it meant that my parents would not be required to bear a financial burden beyond their means.

The school to which I was appointed was the one I had attended before I left to go to Rye. I was under the guidance of the same splendid Headmaster who had helped me to win my scholarship six years before. The appointment proved to be one of the greatest strokes of good fortune that ever came my way.

How the Love Story Began

I fell in love with Ella at seven o'clock on the evening of 26 July 1916. It was a beautiful day, – sunny and warm. That morning, an unmarried, romantically minded, lady member of the school staff had asked me a rather personal question: 'Haven't you got a young lady yet?' (The term 'girl-friend' hadn't come into use then.) I had replied, 'No, thank goodness,' but my answer hadn't prevented her from inviting me to what we called a 'Musical Evening' in those days.

Now I disliked parties intensely, but the suddenness of the invitation, the fact that the dear lady had been very helpful to me and my inability to think of a valid excuse for declining all combined to require me to accept as gracefully as I could. 'Good!' she said. 'There is going to be someone there whom I would like you to meet.'

The 'someone' was a slim, blue-eyed, fair-haired damsel dressed in a summery frock of blue and white. Never before, I thought, had I seen a girl look so pretty.

As I have told you, Ella and I were not strangers. All the same we were formally introduced.

I had thought her a quiet, serious, reserved type of girl. It wasn't long before I discovered her to be almost the opposite, not often serious, quiet sometimes, but reserved hardly ever!

In the months before this meeting I had seen her about the town with her friend Muriel, who I knew pretty well. She and I used to travel on the same train to and from school (she only to Hastings, five miles away). I occasionally walked home with her as I didn't have to go out of my way to do so; I tolerated her but wasn't very keen. There was an air of fussiness about her I didn't much care for. To use an expression of the time, she 'fancied herself' too much. I supposed it was because she went to a private school. Her father owned a prosperous dairy business.

I'd never spoken to the girls when I saw them out together. I had come to the conclusion that I could live quite happily without female company. It was thrust on me both at school and in my home. I had experienced the sorrows of unrequited love, three or four brief but, to me, intense 'love affairs' with class-mates. (In each case the girl concerned was either completely ignorant of my adoration or completely indifferent to it.)

What I didn't know then was that Ella had been taking an interest in me before we became acquainted. She thought I would be quite 'nice to know' if I wasn't so serious, aloof and wrapped up in my own thoughts.

Now to get back to the party. For the very first time the two of us were together at close quarters, with no Muriel present to dis-tract attention. One look at Ella and all the 'passions' of my recent past were as though they had never happened. I was captivated.

Tea-time over, the 'company' present joined together in a sing-song, with me performing at the piano. The songs we sang were the popular ones of the moment and occupied our time up till around 6.30.

Soon our hostess produced an album of piano duets and asked Ella and me if we would choose one to play together. Ella turned over the pages, stopped at her choice and showed it to me, say-ing, 'If you'll play the Primo I'll do the Secondo,' which is only jargon for, 'You play the top part and I'll do the accompaniment.' (This meant that any mistakes I made would be very noticeable, whereas any she might make would most probably be covered up. Not that she had any such thought in her mind of course!)

I'm sorry to say neither of us can recall the composer of the little piece we played, a 'Piano Duet in D for Four Hands'. I happened to be rather good at sight-reading music and our per-formance was adjudged to be an outstanding success. It was a wonder, since I was streaming with perspiration because of the proximity of Ella's body to mine. You had to sit close together to perform a duet and that was the closest I'd ever been to a girl. (I don't count my sisters as girls in this connection.) I had never felt quite as shy and awkward before.

By the time we'd finished it must have been five minutes to seven. We were given a brief rest while one of the men rendered 'Asleep in the Deep'. This was a 'must' at that time for everybody who could sing bass. Then our hostess invited Ella to sing. She said she would if I would play for her. Of course I agreed.

The song was one of the 'drawing room' ballads so popular in that pre-radio era. It was entitled 'Love, Here Is My Heart'.

Before that evening I had never heard it. It didn't matter. When her clear, warm, sweet voice entered after the brief piano introduction I was sure it was the loveliest sound I had ever heard. The banality of the words seemed transformed into pure poetry and I was completely enchanted. By the time we reached the final notes I was deeply, – irrevocably, in love.

We left the piano and sat side by side while the others made their contribution. When Ella whispered, 'Thanks very much: you played very nicely,' I could find no words to express my happiness.

I remember every detail of those musical moments. I can't remember a thing about the rest of the day. No doubt I took her home, – it would be twenty minutes' walk.

Ella has interrupted my account to remind me that I did. Because, she said, it was getting dark and she didn't like walking through blacked-out streets. (Yes, we had a 'black-out' in World War One.)

I have already told you of the qualities which attracted me so strongly towards her. But there was one, which I was unable to put into words earlier, which I believe was the reason for her special appeal. It was something which I had never observed in a girl of her age before.

I suppose every fifteen-year-old maiden is allotted some degree of charm and feminine beauty; if she is unlucky she may have little of either; if she is fortunate (as Ella was) she will have both to a generous extent. If she is exceptionally lucky she will also possess some of this extra 'something' which I find so difficult to describe. You <u>saw</u> it. It showed in the way she moved, the way she sat, the way she held herself. 'Dignity' is too solemn a word for it. It had no relationship to self-pride, vanity or conceit. I believe that only a girl who was unaware of the fact that she was both beautiful <u>and</u> charming could possess it . . . this special, individual quality which . . . I think I have the word at last! . . . we call poise. Yes. That <u>is</u> the word. <u>Poise</u>.

Of course, it was a combination of all her other qualities with this self-command which I found irresistible. So much so that when, as we walked towards her home in the fading daylight when the party was over, and a kind of sixth sense told me that she liked me too, my joy was almost ecstatic.

Those are the reasons why, when memories of that far-away summer's day come back to me, I declare that it was a <u>lovely</u> day. Had it teemed with rain morning, noon and night I would still swear it to have been the loveliest day of the whole year. The twenty-sixth of July 1916 was a date for me to remember. If there is <u>one</u> day in a lifetime more important than any other, the one in <u>my</u> lifetime was the one of which I have just written, – the day on which the Love Story began.

In the weeks that followed we met frequently. I discovered her to be a very different person from the quiet reserved girl at the party. She was vivacious and gay and in many ways my opposite. She never appeared to let anything worry her and went through life smiling gaily. (Except on the infrequent occasions when she sat for a photograph. Then she was always caught in a pose uncharacteristic of her happy personality.)

I was, I suppose, the dreamer, the idealist, the emotional one of the pair: up in the air to-day, down in the dumps to-morrow. Ella was the practical one, gifted with as much intelligence as I had and much more common sense. While my head was crammed with a lot of highbrow bookish nonsense, hers had room for dealing with the practical problems of life. I walked along with my head in the clouds; she had both feet fixed firmly on the ground.

I used to accuse her (falsely) of being incapable of deep feeling, – especially in the early stages of our little love affair. At eighteen I was deeply in love; at fifteen and a half Ella wasn't. But, let me hasten to add, she did like me very much and the better she got to know me the stronger her affection grew.

In many respects we were ideal companions. Our mutual love for, and ability to take part in, music-making came first. We both loved the country, travel, the same sort of entertainment and usually laughed at the same kind of jokes. In her company I was less serious-minded. In my company she was less frivolous.

At the time we met, Ella was 'contributing to the war effort', as they called it, by acting as a milkmaid. Perhaps that's misleading. I believe I mentioned Ella's friend Muriel, whose father was a dairyman. Owing to men being called up for service he was short of staff. His 'snooty' teenage daughter took over one of the milk-rounds and talked Ella into being her companion.

As it turned out, it was jolly hard work. I often passed the two fifteen-year-olds carrying the milk pails to their customers' door-ways as I cycled to the beach for my pre-breakfast swims. They began their round at 6.30 sharp.

Some afternoons Ella acted as Nanny to a little four-year-old whose father was away at the war. She and Frankie would spend fine afternoons in the park, and whenever I was free I would be there too. Frankie, like me, adored Ella and soon admitted me to his small circle of special friends. It was my expertise in making his sailing boat behave that qualified me for that privilege. It seems the yacht would always capsize on the afternoons when I wasn't at the boat pond. Ella says that when she was getting him ready for his afternoon outing he would invariably ask, 'Will the MAN be there to-day?' I had no name: I was the MAN while his daddy was away. Ella's reply used to be 'Perhaps', with 'I hope so' added sotto voce.

It was a strange coincidence, – but we both intended entering the teaching profession. Until she was old enough to take her entrance examination she was staying on in the Infants Department of her old school as a Monitress. This was a very underpaid and overworked position.

The July day that we met had been my last as Apprentice-Teacher before the five-week-long summer holidays began. I had been accepted for training in London and was due to start at the end of September. One can't enjoy many pleasures without at least a little money, and the tiny allowance which was all my parents could afford wouldn't stretch to giving a girl-friend a good time. (We didn't 'go Dutch' in those far-off days.) So I looked around for a job, and found one that just suited my circumstances.

I worked as a junior (– very junior –) clerk in the offices of our local 'rag', – the *Bexhill on Sea Chronicle*. I had to be not only accounts and filing clerk but lino-type operator's assistant and distributor of our newspaper to the wholesale newsagent's shop! (I used my own cycle for this.) I enjoyed it all, learning each job as it came my way. Five and a half decades later I can tell you the exact number of copies we printed every Friday, – one thousand, seven hundred and fifty, – each priced at one half-penny! Not exactly Fleet Street tycoonery, but to me, then, it was Big Business, for it meant I now had a pound a week for myself (and my girl) and Mondays and Thursdays free for 'courting'.

The more deeply I became involved with Ella the more concerned I grew about another matter, the war. Ella didn't know, but technically I was already in the Army. Under the Derby Scheme, students still at school were allowed to finish their courses. Mine had just been completed. Hence my concern: if the College didn't get me, the Army would, or vice versa. Either way Ella and I would have to part. So far I hadn't plucked up the courage to tell her.

The summer of 1916 was idyllic. Perhaps all summers are when you're in love, – especially when it's first love. It must have rained sometimes but in our memories the sun shone every day, the sky was always blue and the sea always silver. We walked along the Promenade, or wandered through the corn fields, or over the gorse-covered Downs, happy to be in each other's company. On the warmer days we swam, – or rather I did while Ella sat patiently on the beach. When finances allowed we played tennis in the park and more often than not I had to eat humble pie.

We were fortunate that her parents both approved of our friendship. They didn't leave us together, though, so they weren't taking any chances.

Ella's father, who years before had frowned on my capers in church when I was choirboy in front of his stall, wore a poker-faced expression which belied his pawky sense of humour. As for her mother, she was the opposite of the typical mother-in-law-to-be, being sweet, kind, understanding and very good-looking as well. They both liked me and we spent many happy evening hours at Whist and Rummy.

I told you how music brought Ella and me together and that it was Ella's singing voice with which I fell in love. At her home one evening I discovered that she was quite as accomplished a pianist. (Up till then she had played very little except as my partner in duets: she preferred singing she said.) On top of her piano lay a beautiful presentation edition of the Piano Sonatas of Mozart. The album intrigued me because it was the same volume I had seen on Dr. Stokes's piano some years before. I opened it, and attached to the inside of the cover was 'Presented to Ella Christian for Pianoforte . . . Trinity College of Music'. She admitted to having won it as the First Prize for piano-playing in her age group the year before. Then she produced a handsome book of *Lives of the Great Composers*, another prize she had won.

She was 'two-up' on me in that respect! But all I could do was love her more. I certainly couldn't feel jealous.

We weren't restricted to our own performances for musical entertainment. True, we had no TV or radio broadcasting, no L.P.s, etc. But at Bexhill we did have a small resident orchestra, which received a subsidy from the rates. After all, at an up-and-coming seaside resort, holiday makers were entitled to hear 'good music'.

A few years before, a crescent-shaped concert hall had been constructed by hollowing out the low cliff which overhung our promenade. Then a semi-circular pier-head-like structure was built over the beach, and in the centre of the circle thus formed an open-air bandstand was built.

In suitable weather Bor and Paikin's orchestra dispensed music from the bandstand, surrounded by two-penny deck-chairs, while non-payers could walk around the Promenade deck or stand and listen. Bor and Paikin were two most accomplished musicians who, having escaped from some political upheavals in Eastern Europe, had settled with their families in our town. They had the most amazing skill in 'arranging' compositions written for full orchestra to suit their own small combination, so we had excerpts from opera, symphonies, serenades, etc.

Numerous vocalists and instrumentalists made early appearances at Bexhill's Colonnade, – many to achieve high reputations later. Ella and I attended as many of their concerts as we were able, and if the guest singer of the day sang a song Ella particularly liked I would buy a copy and we would practise it together. We owe an enormous debt to Messrs Bor and Paikin, – they widened our musical horizons tremendously and gave us many hours of unadulterated pleasure.

On my 'pay-night' (Saturday) I usually treated Ella and myself to an outing. On the third Saturday (or maybe the fourth) we had been either to the Colonnade concert or the pictures, – we can't remember when our first cinema was opened – and as usual I accompanied her home. At her garden gate I was most daring. I put both arms round her, pulled her close and kissed her boldly on the mouth. She didn't resist in the slightest. I was so elated I ran the whole mile home.

Some time later she coolly informed me that she had wondered when I was going to make a start!

My Confession

The summer holidays were over. We were on our way home from the last of the August evening concerts. Ella's parents insisted on her being in by 10 o'clock so we had twenty minutes to ourselves.

It was very, very dark on the sea front. It was black-out time on account of the Zeppelin and aeroplane raids on London. (They, by the way, were important causes of the prosperity our town was enjoying then. Many people had come from London to our area, which was regarded as safe.) The black-out was good for young lovers like us because the Promenade shelters were ideal for courting. No one would recognize you.

It was one of those rather sultry evenings when sound carries a long way. We could hear the distant muffled rumbling of guns in Flanders, a hundred miles away from us.

We snuggled up together in the first unoccupied shelter. I couldn't feel as affectionate as usual because of the worry in my mind. I had resolved to tell her my secret that evening.

I did so, as gently as I could, concluding light-heartedly with 'They'll have to be in a pretty bad way to want me to fight for them. I don't think I'll be much good as a soldier.'

Ella was silent.

'Everyone expects us to do our bit,' I continued. 'All these women with white feathers about! But I didn't join because of that,' I added hastily.

It was too dark for me to see Ella's face. Then she said, 'But Horace isn't going.' (Horace was her sister's young man.) 'Not until they fetch him!'

I asked her whether she wanted me to be like that, and she whispered, 'No.'

'Well, I'm already in,' I went on. 'Don't worry. I'll only be at Cooden.' (Under the Derby Scheme, a recruit could choose his regiment; as the Royal Garrison Artillery had a training camp at nearby Cooden, I had opted for them.) 'We'll be able to meet whenever I'm free. Anyway, they won't want me yet.'

We strolled home slowly, Ella holding tightly to my arm. In me there was a mixture of joy and sorrow. I was sorry, very sorry, at the prospect of our parting, yet glad to find that Ella was sad on my account. That was the night she realized she loved me.

The blow fell the last week in September. I was to report for service with the Army on 3 October. I had to inform my college of the call-up so my entry could be deferred indefinitely.

It was nine weeks to the day from our first meeting when my

'papers' arrived. The war news was depressing. Things weren't going at all well.

When I gave the news to Ella she took it calmly.

'What did I say? They'd have to be in a bad way to want me. Oh well, I suppose I'll have to go and help them out of their mess,' I joked. I was trying to put a brave face on, but Ella didn't think it funny.

Our boy and girl courtship had lasted sixty-nine days. Would it survive a separation? Nobody but we thought it would, and we had no means of telling until the test came.

Ella saw me off at the station. I had begged my family not to come. My feelings were very mixed. I think I was pleased at the thought that I was fulfilling an obligation to my King and Country and at knowing that my parents were proud of me volunteering for service. I was sad at the parting, – at reaching the end of the ten happiest weeks of my life. Sad, and humble too, when I saw the tear roll slowly down her cheek. I believed it was the first time anyone had wept for me.

Learning to Be a Soldier

As it turned out, that train wasn't taking me to Cooden. I was 'reporting' to Catterick, 300 miles away.

On 3 October 1916 I was a slender callow youth of eighteen who looked about sixteen and a half. Direct from the shelter of home and school I was flung into the deep-end of a world which I hardly knew existed. The Army certainly had a job on their hands if they were to transform me into an adult fighting man in the space of six months. Well, that's what they did, – or rather, that's what they thought they had done.

For my part I did my level best. I accepted uncomplainingly

the unfamiliar routines, the bullying, the lack of privacy, the harsh military discipline, the indignities of 'medicals', the coarseness of language, the pack-drill, the foot-slogging (Oh! those Army boots and blisters), the poor food, the hard beds, the spit-and-polish, the cold and the wet. (Most of the time we seemed to be plodding through a foot of snow on those North Yorkshire moors.) I say I accepted the hardships uncomplainingly, like most of my comrades, – but deep in my heart I hated it all.

However, they hadn't asked me to be a soldier; I had volunteered, so why should I grumble?

Towards the end of my training someone discovered that at school I had achieved 'Matric' standard in Mathematics. Thereupon they sent me for a three-week intensive course on matters highly technical. If you look up the meaning of the word 'ballistics' in your dictionary you'll get an idea of what it was all about. I 'sailed' through the course and achieved top place in the class. As a result I was raised to the rank of Corporal, became technically a 'Specialist', and was entitled to wear a brass O (for 'Observer') with laurel leaves above my two stripes. The combination of all the above made me a B.C.A., – that is Battery Commander's Assistant.

After twenty-four weeks they reckoned they had finished their job, namely to change the raw, soft boy-recruit into a competent battle-hungry artilleryman. I had gained nearly a stone in weight, toughened up physically and been inspired with the nobility of patriotism. Their chaplains had convinced us of the righteousness of our cause and assured us that God would grant us the victory we deserved. They had preached to us that it was His will that the Germans, – those fiends in human form, – should be destroyed. I believe I really did think that I and my friends were protecting our sisters and our sweethearts from fates worse than death! So, inoculated against this, vaccinated against that, indoctrinated against any treasonable thought, I was ready for war.

The monotony of service training was broken only by the occasional leaves I was able to obtain. One short '48-hour pass' I remember well. It was in mid-December and bitterly cold. There was an hour's tramp through snowdrifts to Richmond (Yorks) station to begin with, followed by seven hours of standing in corridors before I arrived home. My week-end there lasted from 8 a.m. till 5 p.m., during which time I had to see my parents and have a meal with them <u>and</u> go along to see Ella and spend a precious two hours in her company before taking the long, long trail back to Catterick. I didn't consider even that too high a price to pay for such a brief reunion.

I was stationed in various parts of the country during my half year of training, – Catterick, of course, Mansfield in Notts, Chichester, Farnborough, Aldershot and finally near home at Lydd, where we did gunnery practice. I managed about a half-dozen brief trips to see my sweetheart before I was posted to the unit with which I was to serve until the war was over.

35 Windsor Road
Bexhill-on-Sea
Sussex

Jan 22nd 1917

My dearest Ronald.
I must apologise for not writing yesterday (Sunday), but Muriel asked me to go and have tea with her, so of course I couldn't refuse, as I always tell her I am going somewhere when she asks me.

To-day for the first time this year, we have had a little snow. I do wish we could have a jolly good snow storm, so that there would be some fun after it.

Mother heard from Mabel and Chrissie this morning & they wanted to know how you were getting on, & asked whether you could spare them a photograph of yourself in khaki, as all the girls have photographs of different friends serving in the Army.

Horace is still here, I don't suppose he will go until they fetch him now, dearest. I really don't know what else to tell you so will close with kindest regards from all & heaps of love and kisses.

I remain,

your own loving,

Ella

On 17 March I was granted the customary fourteen days Overseas Leave. Two weeks before, Ella had reached her sixteenth birthday; my nineteenth had been the previous December.

At Ella's home we were granted one privilege that had previously been denied us. We were allowed to be together unchaperoned in the front sitting room. Even so we made sure that the silent intervals between our spells of music-making didn't last long enough to cause concern to the remainder of the household.

It was gratifying to be told that I looked very smart in my uniform. Ella had grown prettier than ever during the six months of our friendship. I noticed a little change in her manner too. Her gaiety and vivacity were still there but were somewhat subdued and her spirits were not quite as high as they had been.

She was not only growing up, she was growing more and more fond of me. So why I should have felt the first pangs of jealousy during that leave-time isn't easy to explain.

On second thoughts it is. This is how it came about.

Our seaside hotels and boarding houses had been turned into hospitals and convalescent homes for wounded service men. There had been appalling casualties on the Somme and other war-fronts and we had evidence of this fact in the numbers of men recuperating in our home town. Their presence was a continual reminder that war is not a game, that men get hurt, and that many who weren't present were missing because they were no longer alive.

Ella's parents, like mine and many others, extended their sympathy to these men in the most practical form, – by inviting those who were 'mobile' into their homes. Ella talked to me about some who had visited hers. I was selfish enough not to like the idea at all. As I have said, she was growing into a most appealing and attractive girl.

Of course I was jealous, but not jealous enough to cloud the happiness we enjoyed in each other's company. In any case, I knew Ella's Mum and Dad were on my side.

Half way through the holiday, – on the eighth of my fourteen days' leave, came a telegram:– 'Rejoin unit at once. All leave cancelled.'

My unit was 239 Siege Battery, R.G.A., and while I had been on leave they had moved to Codford St. Mary on the edge of Salisbury Plain.

I only had a few hours to say my farewells to my parents, my little brother and my sisters before hurrying down to Ella's house. I said goodbye to her in the room where she had enchanted me with her singing. As a parting gift she handed me a splendid silver cigarette case with my initials engraved on it. I hadn't anything to give her. There hadn't been time to buy a present. She was very brave and didn't shed a tear. Neither of us was to know that it would be nearly two years before our next meeting.

Ella's <u>father</u> accompanied me to the station! (She didn't want to see me go.) As I was stepping onto the train he handed me <u>his</u> gift, saying, 'Good Luck, Ronald. Look after yourself.'

It was a silver-plated miniature horseshoe, correct in every detail, about three inches across. I was proud and honoured to receive it. I little realized how desperately I was going to need every bit of good luck it could bring.

It was a difficult journey to Codford and I reached Salisbury just too late to catch a rail connection. Oh well! I thought, we're not going to lose the war because Corporal S. is a half-day late.

It was market day and very busy. I have told you about the little horseshoe and the cigarette case so perhaps you'll guess what happened next. I walked down the High Street and looked in the jeweller's shop-window. Yes! I should be safe if I chose <u>that</u>. I knew enough about my sweetheart's taste in jewellery to be sure she would find <u>that</u> acceptable.

The assistant was certain my fiancée would be delighted with the gift. She would have liked a pearl necklace like that herself, she said. She found me a small card on which to write my message. (I wonder what it was; probably 'To My Darling with love. We'll meet again soon.') Then she placed the necklace in its case, and with the card packed it ready for me to post.

As I left the Post Office I felt there was something 'final' about my action. I don't mean the end of our little romance. I knew I would love Ella till I died. No, it was the final page of a chapter in our book of life.

I found myself entering the cathedral for the very first time. I have visited Salisbury Cathedral several times and have always felt saddened by its interior. I find its grey stone cold and stark. Maybe it's because the weather has been so overcast each time

I've been there; perhaps if I saw the sun's rays coming through its stained glass I would think it as beautiful as Winchester. But I never had doubts about its <u>exterior</u>. When I saw it from the banks of the Avon, the position from which Constable painted it, I thought its marvellous tapering spire the most beautiful thing of its kind in all England.

I knelt and said prayers for my family and Ella's family, and asked that I should come home safe and sound when the fighting was over.

Ella at fifteen and a half. Ella doesn't like this picture because the photographer's poor lighting has made her light brown hair look black. But I liked it; it accompanied me everywhere I went.

CHAPTER TWO

My War

*'Active Service. Saturday, 5.30 a.m. Dearest. Have just crossed
quite safely & am now on the "other side". We had a stormy
crossing but I was not ill as I slept through most of it. Bought
this from a little French boy who came on board early this
morning. Yrs ever R'*

I have now reached the difficult part of my story, the period of my war service. Hardly any of it have I ever talked or written about. Some of my experiences were pleasant, many were not. Yet I must include accounts of both, for they had such a profound effect on the development of my character and personal-ity that to omit them would make the whole of this 'book' a waste of time. My biggest problem will be what to include and what to omit.

I say this is to be the difficult part of my story. I set out with the intention of writing an account of a schoolday love affair that developed into an enduring partnership. It was to be OUR story, but from the day I went to France until our reunion Ella had less and less a part in it. There were just _her_ letters and _my_ thoughts of her that kept us together.

We parted, having made no promises of fidelity to each other. I knew there would only be one girl in my life. Ella tells me that all the time I was away – and that was nearly two years – she never took any other boy's friendship seriously. Considering we were little more than children and our 'courtship' had lasted only ten weeks, I think we can claim to have been a rather remarkable young couple.

Censorship

One of the first hardships we both had to endure was the _censoring of letters_. It is hardly inspiring for a love-sick youth to sit down and write of his secret longings knowing that some dolt of a subaltern is going to read every word – and no doubt get a kick out of doing so.

There were three kinds of letters. The first was the 'easiest' one, the field post-card. This had a printed formula in which you struck out the sentences you did not want:–

- I am quite well,
- I am coming home on leave,
- I received your letter,
- I have been wounded, etc.

The second was an ordinary unsealed letter. The officer on duty would read every one and destroy it if it revealed a military secret, or black out any indiscreet or non-permissible information, e.g. _where_ you were, what was happening, etc. Ella received many letters, especially in my very depressed period, when hardly anything remained except 'Ella Darling — — — — — All my love, Ronald.'

The censoring officer had to put his signature on the envelope. Ella says there was only one, a Lieutenant Salisbury, who ever had the decency to let one of my letters get through entire and with no deletions. But then he was a decent chap.

The third was a great privilege; it was known as the Green Envelope. We got one of these every other week except during very 'tough' times. It was the only chance one had of writing the things one really wanted to say.

The first letter I received from 'Blighty' was from Ella to tell me what a delightful surprise my gift had been. I was truly happy to hear of her pleasure and to feel that the distance between us was not really so great as I had imagined. After all, letters were a kind of bridge, the only communicating medium we had.

Now I shall get on with my story. I have just one fear: that before long the story will take over from me.

The Crossing

My overseas leave need not have been shortened at all. We were kept at Codford for over a week after being fitted out and kitted up ready for active service. We did little more than kick our heels with impatience.

Then came the day when we entrained for Southampton. There were no bands to play us off, no Tommies singing 'Tipperary', only drenching rain and a howling March gale as we filed aboard the *Mona's Queen*. She was an antiquated old bucket of a paddle steamer from the Isle of Man, masquerading as a troopship. She must have loved islands for she anchored off the Isle of Wight and rocked and rolled in Spithead for twelve solid hours before we got under way.

Like the other 999 men on that old tub, I felt we had lost the war before we got half way across the Channel. There wasn't room to sit anywhere in comfort, and anyway we were too busy being ill!

It was dawn on 1 April when we stepped onto the quay at Le Havre. We were marched through depressing streets, four inches deep in mud, to a camp miles outside the town. We spent two nights under canvas in bell-tents. The rain never stopped. The first evening, opening a tin of bully-beef rather carelessly, I cut my thumb badly. It bled on and off the whole night.

Just one other thing about that April Fool's Day. We learnt afterwards why we'd been kept waiting for twelve hours off Portsmouth. The enemy submarine that was waiting for us got the poor old *Mona's Queen* on her way back. Perhaps I <u>was</u> going to be glad of my silver horseshoe.

Siege Batteries

So now, at last, I was a fully fledged soldier of the King's New Army. Officially I was 120331 Corporal Skirth, J.R., B.C.A., C. of E.,[1] 239 Siege Battery, Royal Garrison Artillery. A battery in the Royal Regiment of Artillery is the equivalent of a company in the Infantry. The R.F.A. (Royal Field Artillery) had the sort of light horse-drawn guns still used by tradition for firing ceremonial salutes in Hyde Park. They fired 18-pounder shells on a fairly

1 To inform whoever it might concern that I should be buried according to the rites of the Church of England.

low trajectory. The R.G.A. had the 'heavies', 6-inch or 9.2-inch calibre (diameter of shell), which fire at a higher trajectory so that their shells drop nearly vertically on to their targets, e.g. into trenches. Our battery was equipped with four 6-inch howitzers – stubby fat-looking monsters weighing two tons each – which were towed by tractors and then manhandled into position. Our projectiles each weighed 100 pounds and had to be humped on shoulders and loaded into the gun by hand. I was thankful I wasn't a member of a gun crew.

The complement of a battery is from 110 to 120 men. The Officer Commanding holds the rank of Major, his second in command is a Captain and the remaining dozen or so officer personnel are assorted subalterns, i.e. First and Second Lieutenants. Then come the Warrant Officers, Senior N.C.O.s (Non-Commissioned Officers), Junior N.C.O.s like me, Corporals and Bombardiers (two-stripe and one-stripe men respectively) and, lowest in rank of all, the gunners.

When the battery is ready for action the four guns are placed in well-camouflaged positions 200 to 500 yards behind our troops' trenches, not necessarily in line and anything from 20 to 200 yards apart from each other. To ensure that everyone knows what's going on each gun-site is linked to the O.C.'s 'post' by telephone lines.

The gun crews, each a dozen or a score of men, do what you would expect, viz. load and fire the guns. The most important member is the Gun Layer, who after receiving the data he requires has to align and elevate the weapon so that it is trained on to its chosen target.

It would be most exceptional for any member of a gun crew to be able to see the target he's shooting at. The 'eyes' of the battery are either in the air, in an open basket suspended from an inflammable bag of gas, or in a front-line O.P. (Observation

Post). They also had to have telephone communication with the Command Post. They would watch enemy movements and direct our fire.

As Battery Commander's Assistant, my job was quite complex. Sometimes I would be 'observing' in the Forward O.P. but most of my work would be done under the same roof as the Commanding Officer. I was the mathematician who had to co-ordinate all the information supplied from the Royal Flying Corps, the Royal Engineers Meteorological Section and stacks of printed tables on my desk. Before action could begin I would have to work out from my maps such details as target distance and height above sea-level, and then combine this with the MET and other data. The MET details came by dispatch rider every day, – sometimes more than once a day, – and were all in cipher.[2]

2 The cipher or code was one of the simplest to use and the most difficult to solve (difficult because it could be changed hourly if necessary). It was based on this formula:–

Take *any* word of preferably six letters or more. Only use each letter once and then arrange the alphabet in two halves, one below the other, after it.

E.g. 1 Code Word: 'DRAUGHTS'

D	R	A	U	G	H	T	S	B	C	E	F	I
J	K	L	M	N	O	P	Q	V	W	X	Y	Z

To use code, take the letter over or under the one needed.

Message ZERO HOUR MIDNIGHT would appear as IXKH OHMK UZJGZNOP.

E.g. 2 Code Word: 'EASTER'

E	A	S	T	R	B	C	D	F	G	H	I	J
K	L	M	N	O	P	Q	U	V	W	X	Y	Z

Same message would be JKOR XRDO SYUTYWXN.

Of course you had to know the code word for the day. There was a similar one for numbers.

This meant I had to decode them (the code was changed daily) before I had the figures available. I had to know ground and air temperatures, wind direction and velocity, humidity, barometric pressures and all the other factors which affect the trajectory of a flying shell. The final operation was to put all the 'pieces' together and calculate angles of sight, elevation, etc. to be handed to the O.C. for transmission to the guns. Every gun had to have separate figures compiled.

Oh yes, it was very complicated! Nowadays I'm sure somebody presses half a dozen buttons and the whole process is done by a computer in a flash.

The work demanded 100-per-cent accuracy in calculation and 100-per-cent high-speed thinking. It was a position of tremendous responsibility to be placed on the shoulders of a teen-age B.C.A. (I believe I was the youngest serving on the Western Front but I have no way of proving it.) Why the office didn't qualify for a commission I never knew. Of course, Corporals are cheaper than Lieutenants, so that must be the reason! All my calculations were supposed to be 'vetted' by one or other of the subalterns before being passed to the O.C. But as most of them understood the whole process about as well as they understood Greek there was an awful potential for error. 'Awful' because if through some inadvertent miscalculation the Gun Layer received the wrong figures, shells might (and sometimes did) fall on our positions instead of those on the far side of No Man's Land.

I often had two assistant B.C.A.s, who I trained to do the routine work. This enabled the three of us to work a two-hour 'on' and four-hour 'off' rota round the clock. But because I was on call during all 'alerts' I was accorded privileges none of the higher-ranked N.C.O.s enjoyed. I was excused parades, 'fatigues' and, best of all, shell-humping. They didn't like it because I was the only one they couldn't terrify with their bullying and authority.

Comrades in Arms

Within a few days of landing in France I had made three special friends who were to influence the development of my character considerably. I was still in my teens and easily the youngest of the quartet.

We were as odd an assortment of fellows as you could find anywhere. Chance threw us together but, apart from the common bond of fellowship brought about by fears of the unknown, what held us so closely together I really cannot explain. Between us four there grew up a camaraderie which resulted in the only pleasant recollections of my active service period that I can recall. And, alas, the saddest.

I suppose this was the one period of my life when contrary to my natural bent I was a good mixer. It lasted for about six months.

Bill and Geordie

You will notice that the name I have used appears as Geordie instead of Georgie. There's a good reason for this. Every Tynesider from time immemorial has been called a Geordie by anyone not hailing from Tyneside.

Bill and Geordie were cookhouse orderlies and you can't have more useful pals than the 'Grub-Up' boys. Except when duty spells parted them, they were inseparable. Had you seen them you would have guessed them to be twins, so alike were they. Shortish, dark-haired, stocky, perpetually grinning and turning every possible remark into 'smut', they were as unlike me as chalk from cheese. They spoke a language which for weeks was totally incomprehensible to me. (If you've ever met a real born-and-bred-working-class Geordie you will understand.) Their vocabulary would have turned a Billingsgate porter green with envy.

Shocked at first, then accustomed and eventually amused, I was their target. My naivety made me easy game. But their irrepressible good humour and the complete absence of malice in their attitude made me grow enormously fond of them.

At first I was seen as rather suspect. I should say it was for the following reasons:

a. I wore two stripes on my sleeve,
b. I talked 'posh' (– so they said), and
c. I was barmy enough to read poetry!

Well, cause (a) was to be removed in a very short space of time. (You will hear how later.) Cause (b) they got themselves accustomed to, and cause (c) they had no option but to accept.

I think their main interests in life could be listed as follows:

1. Girls (big and young)
2. Beer
3. Girls (small and young)
4. Girls (any age or size)
5. Football

Now at that time my knowledge of the so-called facts of life was rudimentary, based principally on the frightening details I had gleaned from the doctor's book years before. Theirs was (apparently) the result of years of painstaking research and experiment. I don't suppose they were more than twenty-two or twenty-three but they were a decade ahead of me in worldly wisdom and their familiarity with every detail of the female anatomy.

But don't think their coarse vulgar talk corrupted me in any way. After the initial shock I found it all very amusing. It did me no harm to have windows opened onto a world which I never knew existed in circumstances where I was subjected to no temptations.

I grew very fond of these slovenly, foul-mouthed Tyneside 'twins', – mainly because never once did they make any suggestive remarks as to how my sweetheart should be treated when we were eventually reunited. They knew I was 'barmy' anyway, – the poetry reading proved that, – and the fact that I could love a girl without the physical familiarities which to them were the only reason for girls' existence only confirmed their opinion. On top of which I had reached the ripe old age of nineteen without ever having <u>had</u> a woman; <u>that</u> was incredible and made them wonder what sort of stuff 'South Country' lads were made of.

However, they admitted I had a point when the parcels came from Blighty. (They never had any; they never told me of anything of their home lives and I never asked.) They considered Ella's cakes the best they'd tasted. So they thought there might be a bit of sense in marrying a girl for her cooking, provided she also . . .

Poor Geordie, poor Bill. Born delinquents I should say. Never did any two pals go together through trials and tribulations with such optimism and zest.

Jock Shiels

What can I say about Jock? Only that he was the best friend I ever had.

He was a six-foot-tall red-headed Glaswegian who had left his work in a ship-yard to volunteer for the Army. He was the Scottish amateur boxing champion of his weight class. He excelled at everything I saw him do. It's because of Jock's strength and initiative that I am able to write of him to-day. He pulled me out of a gas-filled shell hole at Ypres in which I would have died a painful death.

He was about thirty I would guess and missed his wife Jeannie and the two 'bairns' terribly. We seemed personally acquainted with each other's loved ones through exchanges of snapshots. Jeannie was a pretty young woman and their boy was four and the girl two. It's curious how one remembers details like these for fifty years afterwards.

In my wallet I carried a photograph of Ella at fifteen in the spotted white dress she wore the day I fell in love with her. She looks uncharacteristically severe and pensive and the first time Jock saw it I remember his words:

'She's a bonnie lass a'reet. But watch your step, laddie. She'll have a mind of her own, ye'll see!'

Jock wasn't a bad character reader, actually!

I had to train him to be my deputy when another of our little group was gassed. He was very quick to get the hang of things and I never regretted my choice. To my great satisfaction I discovered he had literary tastes too. Bill and Geordie raised their eyebrows in mock horror at finding two poetry lovers in their billet.

Of course for Jock there was only one writer worthy of the name of poet. My favourites were Keats, Shelley and Byron. Jock regarded all three as of no account, far too 'aristocratic'. But Robbie Burns now: he was a man of the people.

I remember once handing him my *Golden Treasury* (– one of the three books which kept me company through the whole of the war; the other two were Belloc's *Path to Rome* and *Alice in Wonderland!* –) and asking him to read me one of Burns's poems. He chose, – and I'll write the title exactly as it is given in the *G.T.*, – 'To A Mouse. On turning her up in her nest with the plough, November 1785'.

In his inimitable Scots accent he declaimed:

> 'Wee, sleekit, cow'rin' tim'rous beastie,
> O what a panic's in thy breastie!'

Even Bill and Geordie sat up and took notice. Then he reached the lines: –

> But mousie, thou art no thy-lane [alone]
> In proving foresight may be vain –
> The best laid schemes o' mice an' men
> Gang aft agley
> And leave us nought but grief an' pain
> For promised joy.
>
> Still thou art blest, compared wi' me!
> The present only toucheth thee;
> But och! I cast my backward e'e
> On prospects drear!
> An' forward tho' I canna see
> I guess an' fear!

The pathos in those lines brought tears to my eyes. I had to admit that none of my trio of authors could have written that poem.

So there's a motley crew for you. Geordie, Bill, Jock and me: the Four Musketeers of 239. Comrades in Arms, united in some mystic way I can't hope to explain – except in our common hatred of (a) rats and (b) Major Snow!

Rats

These we dealt with in various ways. We lined up suitable missiles nightly at our bed-heads to 'bung' at them when they became impudent enough to walk on our feet. If there was a 'colony' we blasted them out of their burrows by burning sacks of cordite. Cordite looks rather like chopped up spaghetti and is put into the gun behind the shell and ignited to explode and project it into the air. We shoved cordite down a hole, plugged it and then lit a fuse. The acrid white smoke drove the rats out of every hole for a hundred yards around. At one time we had a stray fox-terrier as a splendid assistant!

Major Snow

We hated him as much as the rodents. Unfortunately we couldn't do anything about <u>him</u> for a long, long time. And that brings me to my last and least pleasant character, the person I grew to hate more than any of my country's enemies, the Commanding Officer.

Many units of the British Army were commanded by officers who by their example, their courage and the encouragement they gave to their troops were respected and even loved. I mention this lest I give the impression that our C.O. was a typical Commanding Officer any more than I was a typical Corporal.

First Captain, next Major, then Lieutenant Colonel and finally Colonel were the ranks he held during my association with him. From this you will gather that the Army's 'Top Brass' held a much higher opinion of him than I did. The Generals promoted him three times, awarded him the D.S.O. (Distinguished Service Order) twice while I served under him and for all I know made him one of themselves eventually.

Like Jock, he was a six-footer, but unlike Jock he was as lean as a bean-pole. I would guess him to be between forty and forty-five. He wore a close-cropped steel-grey moustache and a permanent scowl, on a face desiccated into parchment by the tropical suns of India and Aden.

When he was on duty you would always see on the table in front of him the three major necessities of his life: a bottle of Buchanan's 'Black and White', a beaker to drink it from and a 200 (or was it 250?) box of Abdulla No. 9 Cigarettes. He chain-smoked them, drank his whisky neat and apart from official documents read only stuffy magazines mailed to him from some snooty club in Pall Mall. When he ate he did so in private behind a screen formed of an army blanket suspended from a wire.

He was a hard-bitten monolithic die-hard from the Regular Army. To him all of Kitchener's men and all we 'New Army' boys were so many unskilled amateurs. He had no time for any of us.

Everyone from senior officers down to the humblest-ranked gunners feared him. I never saw him smile. I never heard him utter one word of praise to anyone. I never saw him perform one act of kindness. I never saw his face register emotion of any kind, – until one terrible day at Passchendaele.

As for me, I was a perpetual embarrassment to him and a necessity at one and the same time, for I was his B.C.A.

I was a necessity because the authorities only supplied one B.C.A. to each battery; an embarrassment because of the social gulf that existed between us. In every conceivable aspect we were direct opposites: he the Public School, Camberley Staff College 100-per-cent professional officer, me the Grammar School 100-per-cent amateur; he the oldest soldier in the entire battery, me the youngest. Moreover, he the gentleman, me no better than a worm. In the whole of the British Army Overseas there could never have been a more undesirable, incompatible partnership.

In every way possible he sought to humiliate me. He could rarely demean himself to speak to me directly even when only the width of a table separated us. He solved this sticky problem in two ways. If a junior officer or senior N.C.O. were present, his orders would be given to the 'middle man' and then passed on to me. If we were alone, he would put them into writing and push the paper across to me with his pen.

Under him what little pride I was justified in taking in my special job soon disappeared. My vocabulary had to be limited to a monotonous recital of Yes, sirs, No, sirs and Very Good, sirs as each occasion demanded. But I had one crumb of comfort, one advantage over the senior N.C.O.s and the junior commissioned officers:– I was able to do my commander's 'sums' for him and they could not.

So, worm I might be, but an indispensible one. I was the calculating machine upon whom he depended. Not one shell could be fired accurately from a single gun until certain mathematical operations had been completed with 100-per-cent accuracy. Those calculations were made by me (– and later to a lesser extent by my trainee deputies).

Major Snow had all the qualities the bone-headed Generals[3] of the time admired. He never questioned the sanity of the orders they issued, even if they involved certain death to the men under his command. He was completely devoid of feeling, imagination and conscience. These qualities enabled him to send men to almost certain death with as little compunction as I felt for the body lice I roasted alive by running a candle flame along the seams of my underwear.

Only one man knew him better than I: his batman. Jones was as taciturn and hostile as his master. He went about his thankless task with clockwork precision, as though he were a puppet wound up twenty years before and incapable of running down. (Had he been gifted with any imagination he would have shot his master dead, 'accidentally' of course, years before.) He lasted until the first week of Passchendaele, when he was killed by a 'crump' outside the Command Post, emptying the 'slops'. A pretty ignominious end, really.

Major Snow, more than any other person, was responsible for the shaping of my character in my most impressionable years.

---

3 Ordinary soldiers had no confidence in their supreme commander Field Marshal Haig. Generals such as Plumer and Gough were admired, one reason being that both came personally to see the conditions on the front line. Haig never came within miles of it until the Passchendaele holocaust was over. I am told (– though I have never seen it in print –) that when he saw the abandoned battlefield he broke down and wept. If he had seen it before, the attacks might never have taken place and perhaps a hundred thousand lives would not have been unnecessarily sacrificed.

Our own commander was General Gough, fiery but popular. I was acquainted with the telephonist at Army H.Q., who saw what Gough did to the sealed orders instructing him on how the battle should be fought. He scribbled 'IMPOSSIBLE' over the first sheet, 'BLOODY IMPOSSIBLE' over the next and across the 'time-table' paragraphs, 'BULL——'. These comments, in thick blue pencil, were dispatched back to Haig. The result: Gough was sacked and superseded by Plumer.

But in all that time never once did he utter the simple words that would have rewarded the efforts of a youth young enough to be his son coping with a complex job in the face of unimaginable difficulties: 'Thank you, Bombardier.'

Of course war demands discipline, ruthlessness and inhumanity on the part of those whose duty it is to conduct it. I suppose he was heir to a tradition. He lived up to standards they had set for him, standards that a person with my upbringing, background and personality could never, never accept. To put it into a nutshell: – he was the old solider. I wasn't, and never could be.

I think I'll conclude by trying to thrust aside the bitterness that has been in my heart for half a century, – to forget that he was the personification of everything which I detested, – and say that I sincerely hope that when he died, someone somewhere was sorry.

Now we'll abandon this unpleasant character and turn to topics it will give me more pleasure to write about.

Sing-Songs at the *Estaminet*

Looking back, the only comparatively happy period of my war service in France and Belgium was during the months of April and May 1917. We were stationed in a quiet sector of the Front a few kilometres from Armentières. Whenever duty rotas allowed, we would visit a village about 3,000 yards to the west, i.e. behind our position, Erquinghem-sur-Lys. The village had barely a dozen inhabitants remaining and was considerably damaged by long-range gunfire.

The proprietress of the local *estaminet*-cum-farmhouse had stoutly resisted all efforts to evacuate her to a less dangerous region and continued to run both farm and bar. From her chickens and home-grown potatoes she produced eggs and chips for the scores of Tommies and *Poilus*[4] who longed for the taste of home cooking. Everybody loved her and she was affectionately nicknamed Chère-Mère (Dear Mother). She had a stern, unsmiling face and never wore anything but black, – plus white apron, – but had a heart of gold. Only her eyes would betray the fact that she thought us quite a nice lot really. If we turned up without a centime between us because pay hadn't come up, she would serve us just as generously and forget to make any charge. (We would make it up to her later of course.)

There were three other attractions at Chère-Mère's establishment: two daughters and a harmonium. When it was discovered that I could play the ancient instrument I became very popular indeed.

Mère saw to it that no undue liberties were taken with the two daughters. The elder, Marguerite, was in her twenties, buxom and vivacious and well able to look after herself. The younger was Georgina, who was sixteen. I think it must have been Easter time because she was holidaying at home. She and I exchanged schoolboy French and schoolgirl English conversations (interrupted by her waitress duties) over my one or two glasses of *vin blanc*. Her *Lycée* was somewhere beyond Amiens in a safer area to which she had been evacuated.

She was a tall, slender, quiet and placid girl and I found her company extremely pleasant. (The one thing lacking in male company is gentleness.) But she wasn't half as pretty as Ella and would never have been able to rival <u>her</u> in my affections. I showed her the photograph; she said, '*Très belle fille.*' I felt very touched when, on my last visit, she gave me a tiny Roman Catholic Saints Day Diary with her name and address in it. I

4 French equivalent of 'Tommy'.

believed it to be a Good Luck Charm. She wished me '*Bonne chance*' and a safe return to my '*jeune fille*' in Angleterre.

Our greatest enjoyment came from the sing-songs. Everyone joined in. The harmonium was a wheezy old instrument but at home I had sometimes acted as assistant organist at our church and I succeeded in grinding out accompaniments to the songs, solo and/or choral, which would have been heard for miles around if there had been anyone to hear them. They were typical of the time and place: – none of your 'Land of Hope and Glory' stuff, but the real defeatist ditties that the rank and file of the B.E.F. loved, such as:

> *We are Fred Karno's army*
> *What bloody good are we?*
> *We cannot shoot, we cannot fight*
> *No bloody good are we.*

or:

> *I want to go home*
> *I want to go home*
> *The coal-box and shrapnel they whistle and roar*
> *I don't want to go to the trenches no more*
> *I want to go over the sea*
> *Where the Kaiser can't shoot bombs at me*
> *Oh! my!*
> *I don't want to die*
> *I want to go home.*

These concerts would inevitably end with a variation on 'The Mademoiselle from Armentières'. It would start off like this:

> *Mademoiselle from Armentières,*
> *Parlez-vous?*

Mademoiselle from Armentières,
Parlez-vous?
Mademoiselle from Armentières,
Hasn't been kissed for years and years,
Inky-pinky parlez-vous.

Then ask, 'Oh madam, have you a daughter fair? [three times, interspersed with Parlez-vous, etc.] / With bonny blue eyes and golden hair?' and then go on to describe and extol that mystical daughter's allure in great detail. The ditty could continue almost indefinitely depending on the inventiveness of the company present. Of course the longer it went on the bawdier the words got. (Luckily the French women's English was not advanced enough for them to suffer embarrassment!)

Naturally, there were less frivolous interludes when sentimental songs were in demand. On one of these occasions I heard Jock sing 'Annie Laurie' and 'Bonnie Mary of Argyle'. That was something I never forgot.

A massive weightlifter type from our neighbouring battery also turned out to be a singer of no mean talent. It was quite a surprise to discover that such a light, liquid, almost hushed voice could be produced by such a giant of a man. He sang, – unaccompanied – a little Elizabethan ballad I had till then never heard. Its last lines came into my mind more and more often as my absence from Ella grew longer: 'I did but see her passing by / And yet I love her till I die.' The contrast between the tremendous bulk of the body and the delicacy of the song was quite unforgettable.

We were boisterous and light-hearted then, no doubt because lurking beneath the surface was the ever-present fear that our fun couldn't last, that it was a 'toss-up' whether our lives would, and that they might as well be merry ones while we had them.

For six months after our last visit to Chère-Mère's establishment

I never set eyes on a single civilian. For us four musketeers service life got tougher as time went on, and little by little the unpleasant realities of war drove away our memories of Erquinghem.

From now onwards my story has to take on a more sombre note. Subsequent events sorely tested the joie-de-vivre of our little band, and the sense of humour and light-heartedness which had kept us so close was so severely tried that it too became only a pretence.

I must be sincere and truthful and write as I felt at the time of things which I saw with my own eyes. I have to tell of war's realities as I witnessed them. I have omitted much and included little, but of that little I have written in detail. I am not writing a novel, a play, nor a film script, but of the small part of a Great War in which I participated. What I did, what I saw and how it affected me. War, by definition, is tragic. So as the Clown sings at the end of *Pagliacci*, 'The Comedy Is Ended.'

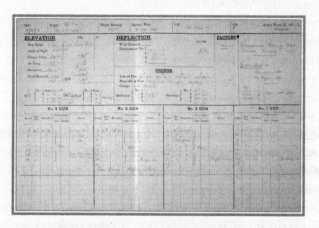

Every 'shoot' had to be recorded in detail. Here is a sample entry. Considering it is fifty-three years old it has worn pretty well. I retained it as a souvenir – quite illegally of course.

CHAPTER THREE

The Road to Disillusion

French Country House. After two and a half years of war still undamaged by the Germans but reduced to a shambles by 239 Siege Battery, R.G.A.

Wars – and How to Win Them

The first task I was given outside my official 'office' duties was a rather bizarre and, to me, distasteful one. If a child had later asked me, 'What did <u>you</u> do in the Great War, Daddy?' I don't think I would have selected this little event.

It is concerned with a small 'chateau' situated about half a mile to the rear of our gun positions. Its former occupants had locked and shuttered it and moved out of the danger zone. Its exterior showed no signs of war damage.

I had orders to march my squad of ten or twelve defaulters (each twice my age, – but then I had two stripes and they had none!) – to this building and 'occupy' it. Each man was armed with a shovel or a wooden or iron bar.

And what do you think 'occupying' it meant? The Battery Sergeant Major had been quite explicit. I had to break in, smash all the ground-floor windows with the exception of those belonging to the 'best' room, and pile furniture against the window openings. Then I was to proceed to the upper floors and do the same, barricading the window spaces with bedsteads and mattresses.

The men unashamedly enjoyed every minute of licensed vandalism, but it grieved me no end to witness such pointless destruction. It wasn't as if the house and its contents were likely to fall into enemy hands. The Battery Sergeant Major had informed me that the C.O. was having the building 'prepared' for conversion into a Divisional Headquarters. (Hence the preservation of one 'comfortable' room.) Our own battery would be using the attic room as its O.P.

Well, several weeks passed before our unit was moved on. Not a single Colonel, Brigadier or any other high-ranking officer ever came near the place. And as for the attic, one couldn't see 300 yards ahead for clumps of huge elms. What an observation post that would have made!

Some time later, alone in the Command Post, I took down the box file marked 'Secret' from our stationery shelf. It was for O.C.'s use only, but nobody had considered it warranted a padlock. Among the assortment of Roneo-typed papers I came across a 'Synopsis of Military Law'. One clause was directly applicable to the operation I had carried out. If a building had been severely damaged (it didn't specify by whom) it was legitimate to 'seize' it and put it 'in a state of defence' without consulting its owners or any civilian authority. So this was the way Wars are Won!

No, I would be ashamed to tell a child of mine, 'That's what they made Daddy do in the Great War.' To me, the amateur soldier, two words described it: Wanton Destruction.

That day, I took my first step along the road to Disillusion.

How to Lose a Stripe

For a month or so 239 Siege Battery was stationed in one of the less active sectors of the Western Front. We were bedded down on straw in a partially strafed[5] barn belonging to a ruined, unoccupied farm. Our guns, well concealed by netting screens and overhead covers, were about 600 yards behind our front-line trenches. Beyond them, on the far side of 250 yards of No Man's Land, was Fritz.

We hadn't been in this position more than forty-eight hours before we had our baptism of fire. The first direct attack came from the air when a Fokker monoplane (we only had bi-planes) bombed us, – without causing damage to anything but our nerves. Then, after our position had been spotted and passed on to the enemy batteries, we were shelled at irregular intervals by our opposite numbers.

We had casualties, but nobody was killed. Not so the horses of the R.F.A. Battery. My first heart-searing experience of war was when the barn where their animals were stabled was hit and caught fire. We ran to help the drivers save the poor frantic creatures, – but I'd rather not tell you the end of that episode.

5 Strafed: word borrowed from German, meaning shelled (literally 'punished').

Instead I'll write of an event in which I was more personally involved.

One April day I was enjoying my four-hour off-duty spell, sitting beneath a large tree writing and thinking. (The latter occupation was to ruin my career as a soldier!) I was trying to trace some lines of a Browning poem which begins 'Oh! to be in England / Now that April's there' and then contains the beautiful line 'The wild thrush; / He sings each song twice over . . .' (A thrush <u>was</u> singing in the branches above me.)

I was writing, of course, to Ella and I wanted to include the poem in my letter.

I was dreaming too, of Collington Woods near Bexhill, where the summer before she and I had wandered together. The primroses would be out by now. We hadn't been sweethearts in spring-time.

My reverie was rudely interrupted by a runner. I had to report to Battery H.Q. immediately.

The C.O. gave me instructions: I was to conduct a visiting subaltern to our Forward Observation Post and act as his B.C.A. and Observer for a 'shoot'.

I looked at the sub. He wore only one pip on sleeve and shoulder, <u>but</u> he had a red band and gilt braid on his cap. Second Lieutenant, maybe, but a Staff Officer. Obviously considered himself a somebody. I collected what I needed, slung on my respirator and binoculars, and we set off.

We had just passed the R.F.A. Battery of 18-pounders when they 'let fly' suddenly. I instinctively ducked but, recognizing the cause of the blasts, almost immediately recovered my composure. But Second Lieutenant Pilkington lay face downwards in the roadside ditch, apparently expecting the next moments to be his last. (The ditch, fortunately, was dry.) I had the temerity (and tactlessness) to go over to him and say, 'Nothing to worry about, sir. They're ours.'

He pulled himself up and replaced his braided cap. It cannot be easy to look either dignified or important crawling out of a ditch, but he did his best and with a look of contemptuous condescension said, 'When I want your comments, Corporal, I'll ask for them.'

'So that's the sort of fellow you are,' I thought! 'Bet you've never been near the front line before.'

We continued the journey in silence until we reached our support trenches and the front line. The O.P. was situated in a bay of the front-line trench, and was well enough sandbagged to be safe from anything but a direct hit. I lifted the first gas curtain (– we had two –) and in we went.

Mr. Pilkington spread out the map he had brought on the planchette (a sort of draughtsman's drawing-board). Now his lordship had to speak. He took out his fountain pen and made a small red circle round a point on the map he had brought and said, 'That's the target, Corporal. We are firing twenty-four rounds and I want a good shot. Understand?'

'I think so,' I replied.

'You do not say "I think" to a superior officer.'

'No, sir?'

'You do say "sir".'

'Yes, sir!'

'Then get on with your bloody job.'

'Very good, sir.'

I took all my 'gear' from my haversack, – dividers, slide-rule, pencil, map-scale measure, etc., – and placed them in position, then opened my book of range tables. This was a kind of ready reckoner and of extreme importance. It allowed me to make calculations to be submitted by telephone to the Battery Commander, who would give orders to train the guns on the target.

I studied the map carefully. Then I peered through my binoculars across No Man's Land, to the low ridge beyond and in the further distance the factory chimneys of Lille. The red ring on the map marked a building near the outskirts of that city.

I was taking my time, but accuracy was essential. Mr. Pilkington was getting impatient.

'Damn it, man, get on with it.'

'I'm sorry, I can't,' I replied.

'Why the hell not?'

'This map is no use to me, sir.'

His face turned the colour of the ribbon round his cap.

'Are you being insolent, Corporal?'

'I don't think so, sir.'

'You don't have to think anything. Get on with it.'

'Yes, sir. May I ask a question?'

'No, you may not. If you can do the job, do it. If you can't, I'll report you for incompetence.'

I paused for a moment, then continued: 'This map uses metric measures. All our calculations are based on distances in yards and elevations in feet. This map gives me ranges in kilometres and heights above sea level in metres.'

Trust our High Command not to know that French maps wouldn't use yards and inches! We'd only been in the war about three years.

'Then what do you propose to do about it, Corporal?'

Sarcasm now. O.K. Two can play that game.

'Nothing, sir. I am under your orders.'

There was a sudden silence. Then, very meekly, I said that I could make conversions but it would take time.

I could see he was fuming. That pleased me so I asked, 'Shall I go ahead, sir?'

'For God's sake, get on with it.'

It took a good quarter of an hour to plot my graph of conversions.

Eventually I was able to evaluate the range (i.e. distance) of the projected target in yards and its height in feet. The meteorological data I had brought with me. I entered the details on the form used for that purpose. (You can see one of these on see p. 51.)

At last I was ready to focus the glasses on the target. I looked down at the map, then back at the building we were to fire at. I double-checked. There was no element of doubt.

Mr. P. was pacing up and down all the time.

'Sir,' I said at last, 'I think there has been a mistake. The target you have ringed is a church.'

'What the hell has that got to do with it?' His face registered incomprehension.

'It's the tower of a church. There must be a mistake.'

'There's no mistake. Give me the figures,' he said.

'Sir,' I replied, 'that is a church. Only the Germans destroy churches.'

'What the hell are you talking about?'

'Churches are consecrated buildings. I wouldn't want to take part in destroying one.'

Pilkington came nearer and gave me a look that should have shrivelled me.

'Are you a bloody conchie?'

I paused before replying. 'I don't know . . . Perhaps I am. I don't think—'

He wouldn't let me go further. 'Listen, Corporal, I am your superior officer. What you think has nothing to do with it. I shall report your insolence to your Commanding Officer. If you add insubordination to insolence you'll bloody well wish you'd never been born. Hand me those figures. That is an order.'

I did so. I had no option.

The only other words I uttered were 'Yes, sir,' 'No, sir' and 'Very Good, sir.'

In the light of after-knowledge I was able to see what that exercise was all about. It enabled Staff Officer Pilkington to claim that he had served in the battle zone, had been under fire and had distinguished himself as a competent gunnery officer. This no doubt fitted him for instant promotion among the Big-Wigs back at base. I am pleased to record that contrary to his report stating that the target had been obliterated, I know that not one shell fell within 250 yards of its target. My calculations must have been very inaccurate!

The next day, our Battery Notice Board displayed the following announcement:

As from April 23rd 1917, Corporal Skirth, J.R., reverts to the rank of Bombardier as a disciplinary measure.
R.A. Snow, Major.
Officer Commanding 239 Siege Battery,
Royal Garrison Artillery.

So that red-ribboned popinjay <u>had</u> reported me, – and I had not been called on to give any explanation or offer any defence. This, I supposed, was military justice.

I had to lose a stripe, prestige and sixpence a day in pay. But worse than all these was the penalty which did not appear in print. It was communicated to me with great relish by the battery's prize bully, Sergeant Major Clinch: I was to be relegated to the foot of the leave rota.

Leave was the one tangible thing to look forward to. Losing it was the part of the punishment which hurt me most.

Partly from pique, I renounced the privilege of 'messing' with the N.C.O.s. I told my three friends that from then on I would 'muck in' with them. If in future any of them addressed me by rank (which had been their way) I'd kick him in the shins! 'My name is Ron,' I said. 'Not Corporal, of course, and not bloody Bombardier.'

Straightaway Jock said 'Ronnie' was the name he'd use – 'You jolly well won't,' I said. (I hated people calling me that.) 'O.K., laddie; then what about Robbie?' 'Fine,' I said.

From that day on I was blood-brother to Geordie, Bill and Jock. From that day I was proud to be called Robbie.

That episode proved one thing to me: Army discipline mustn't be challenged. Pilkington was right: you didn't have to think, only obey your superiors. It doesn't matter how right you are, unless your officer thinks the same as you, he will be more right when it comes to the crunch. The two stripes on my sleeve meant something to the gunners who were my inferiors in rank, but nothing to the chap with one pip on his.

Well, I was learning the craft, – not the art, – of soldiering by slow painful degrees, but I had some way to go yet. The trouble was the process was taking me further and further along the road to Disillusion.

It wasn't long before the Established Church of England contributed their bit!

The Church Militant

I have already described the 'Christian' environment in which Ella and I grew up. I suppose that fifty years ago most children had some sort of religious upbringing. Nearly all the elementary schools were owned and controlled by the Church. The education we received was sectarian to the nth degree. Nowadays they would call it indoctrination.

Whatever its faults, we willingly accepted the standards and ideals set for us. We knew the Church Catechism by heart, even if the words 'conceived and born in sin' didn't make sense to us; the Ten Commandments were recited without fail every Friday morning in the presence of the vicar or his curate. We thought we did pretty well not breaking any of them. We honoured our parents, we didn't kill or steal (– not often anyway –) and we certainly never coveted our neighbour's wife, nor his ox, nor his ass. I could be pretty smug about that one, for my neighbour hadn't got an ox or an ass and if you had seen his wife you would understand how easy it was not to covet her.

But, joking apart, we did derive enjoyment from being brought up in this environment. I don't think we grew into prigs, though we had our snobbish opinions and petty prejudices. Obviously the Church of England was the <u>right</u> religion or it wouldn't have been patronized by royalty and all the best people. Chapel-goers were rather lower class and as for the Roman Catholics, they were absolutely beyond the pale, – they thought Mary as important as Jesus, burnt candles to saints and said prayers to statues. But all those things were superficialities. Outside school we played with the lot, – irrespective of what place of worship they attended.

Now, that digression over, let's get on with the story of the one and only time I witnessed the Church in Action.

It happened just after the All Quiet phase came to an end. We were more and more frequently in action and were almost daily retaliated upon by the enemy. As the weeks went by we became less and less the amateur Kitchener's Army types and more and more professional. By experience, which they say is the best of teachers, we learnt to recognize and distinguish between the differences in pitch, intensity, whines, roars and whizzes that approaching shells would make and could usually estimate whether they were going to fall short, pass overhead or cause us to take prompt evasive action. Sometimes this meant just falling flat on one's face and pressing close to Mother Earth.

Now one 'quiet' Sunday morning in early May orders came round that all C. of E. men were to parade. About thirty of our chaps turned up, – all pretty disgruntled-looking types, I must admit. On reaching the 'parade-ground' (a field!) we saw a strange sight. From a light General Service lorry a longish trestle table was being unloaded. A priest in clerical garb took it from the driver and, helped by an assistant padre, erected it in front of the lorry, and spread a suitable cover over it to convert it into an altar. A gilded crucifix was placed on it, then a chalice and containers for consecrated bread and wine. All was set for our first al-fresco Holy Communion. (By now the group of waiting communicants had dwindled to a dozen.)

The silence was broken by an enemy plane approaching, flying not overhead, but near enough to divert our attention. We saw it to be a Fokker and guessed straightaway what its pilot's mission was. Yes, we were right: he went straight towards the blimp anchored about a mile behind our gun positions. He fired a burst of incendiary bullets into the sausage, wheeled away (– no doubt watching the two Observers bail out safely; they had their parachutes strapped on open in readiness –) then circled a second time to make sure his task had been completed successfully and roared away low over our heads back to his base.

A blazing blimp is a magnificent sight, – when you're at a safe distance. (Once I was directly under one when a Fritzie got it and I didn't see any fun in it then.) We were entertained most days by raids of this kind, usually followed by a similar strafe of the German balloons by our Royal Flying Corps. I never saw a shot fired at the parachuting Observers. I think the two Air Forces had a kind of gentleman's agreement about shooting sitting, – or rather, falling, – ducks.

After this entertaining interlude I was able to collect my thoughts and put myself into a more devotional attitude. Then I realized there was only one communicant left, – me.

Well, thought I, I had better make the padres' journey worthwhile, so I started walking towards the improvised altar. As I was doing so I heard another quite familiar sound, – the rhythmical whirring of approaching shells. They were travelling at higher than average altitude and aimed, I guessed, at the marshalling yards in the rail-head station five or six miles back. But as in peace, 'Safety First' is a good motto, so I rushed to the foot of a big elm and crouched low against its trunk. My estimate was pretty good: they went over at high velocity, I counted the seconds and then just as I expected, one-two-three-four deep-voiced 'crumps' meant poor old Baillent station had received another packet.

I looked across the field at the open-air 'church' just in time to see three figures crawling out from under the lorry. Now, I thought, perhaps we can get on with my Holy Communion.

Not a bit of it! As I started towards the altar, the trio, – two in surplice and one in khaki, – whipped their ecclesiastical gear off the table and had the site cleared in thirty seconds flat. The two padres scrambled over the tailboard, the driver leapt into his seat and the lorry made the quickest standing start I had ever seen.

I stood gaping at the fast-disappearing wagon, hardly able to believe my eyes.

Those two priests, dressed in the cloth which advertised their faith, had fled at the first inklings of personal danger! They, God's agents on earth, had considered the safety of their skins more important than the spiritual health of my soul. They had given us their blessings when we went off to war, told us God would grant us the victory our cause deserved. Then at the very approach of danger, their faith was so slender, their trust in

God so feeble, that they scuttled away like rabbits into their burrows!

I think I was morally shattered by this exhibition. For the first time in my young life I used the word 'bloody' as a real oath. I shouted in their direction, – they were out of ear-shot, of course, – 'You bloody hypocrites!'

The Home Front

Before my sweetheart disappears completely from my story I should record that our correspondence continued in spite of all obstacles and tribulations. Ella kept me informed with home news throughout the whole of that terrible period. She remembers how sadly she missed me during the first few months of our separation but her happy home life and large circle of friends made the days pass pleasantly. I was delighted to hear that she had taken up singing seriously and was having professional tuition. She had also struck up a close friendship with my seventeen-year-old sister Elsie-May, so, among other topics, they had me as an object for discussion!

I heard that Evelyn's Horace was still in 'Civvy Street'. 'They' still hadn't come for him. He was alleged to be engaged in a work of national importance, viz. plumbing.

As time went on and the weeks became months and the months a year or more, Ella was subjected to well-intentioned but somewhat cynical remarks from older girl-friends (– not my sister, though!), – who were getting engaged or rushing into war-time marriages. 'He's having a good time over in France with all those fast girls. Why don't you get out more? Find yourself another boy,' etc., etc. Ella laughed such comments off.

But the longer the separation lasted the more difficult things must have become for her. The war showed no sign of ending and often she must have wondered whether I was being as faithful to her as she was to me and whether our friendship had any real future in store.

Fortunately for me, – and I hope for Ella, – her parents were 'on my side'. She has told me how, when she had delayed writing to me, on more than one occasion her father said to her sternly, 'If you don't want to wait for him, write and tell him so!' Then Ella would feel contrite, reach for the writing-pad and get to work, but the fateful words 'I'm not waiting for you any longer' never went on to paper. She needn't have worried about topics to write to me about. All I wished to see was 'I still love you, darling.'

Some time during that summer I had news from her which she thought I would find disappointing, but strangely enough I didn't. A few weeks before she had been due to take her Pupil Teacher Entrance Exam she had been taken ill. As a result she missed her chance of becoming a teacher. She wasn't sorry because her experience as a monitress had convinced her she would not be happy in my chosen profession. She had therefore decided to take up a business career and had enrolled at 'Night School' to take a bookkeeping and secretarial course. Until this was completed she intended to continue her apprentice teaching.

I wrote to tell her how glad I was at her decision. I didn't really think we wanted two teachers in the family (– if there ever is a family, I thought ruefully –), and anything which brought her happiness would make me happy too.

Earlier I stated that I should experience difficulty in the selection of topics for inclusion in the war section of my story. After a great deal of memory-searching I have decided to describe two only in detail.

I write these accounts fifty-five years afterwards. That's a huge span of time to elapse and a hazy memory may play tricks with truth. It would be an impossibility to recreate with complete and absolute accuracy the thoughts, feelings, opinions and reasoning of more than a half-century past. But I have made an effort to do so.

In part it is not so difficult a feat to attempt. In many respects those opinions, feelings and convictions have remained with me unchanged through the years. I feel as strongly to-day that war is futile, that it settles nothing, that it is uncivilized, cruel and wicked, as I did in 1917 and 1918. So I am confident that the remainder of what I shall set down is as honest and truthful a record as I can make it.

By virtue of my job, I had to live in a sort of No Man's Land. I belonged neither to the officer clique nor to the rank and file. My work segregated me from the latter and made me associate with the former, Of course, that gave me privileges denied to my fellows, such as spending my on-duty hours in officers' quarters, usually the Battery H.Q. I am not attacking the officer clique but they had the 'cushier' life. They rarely suffered the miseries and hardships of the rank and file. They saw our war, but didn't live it.

War Story No. 1: After the Battle, Messines

The little journal in which I managed to keep a record of my adventures gives a detailed account of the events of 8 June 1917. I wrote it during one of the few quiet intervals which followed. From it I am extracting the essentials so as not to oversensationalize what is already a gruesome story. I tell of what I saw and did on one of the two most terrifying days of my life, the day when for me the REAL war in all its horror began.

The Battle of Messines was a preliminary to the Third Battle of Ypres. Before it opened the Messines Ridge had been subjected to the heaviest and most intense artillery bombardment ever seen in war. My battery did its share, firing continuously for three days and nights.

Underneath the enemy front-line trenches at the base of the Ridge were 500 tons of high explosive. At 3 a.m. on 7 June, every one of our guns opened fire, providing a barrage of exploding shells behind which our infantry could advance. Simultaneously the subterranean mines were detonated. This was Zero Hour.

I felt the ground rock beneath my feet although we were over a mile from the scene. It was heard in Kent and Sussex a hundred miles away and was the biggest man-made explosion before Hiroshima.

When the day's fighting ended the entire Messines Ridge had been captured, together with thousands of prisoners. The artillery's job was done and for the remainder of that day our battery was silent.

I saw some of the prisoners stream by. But for their grey-green uniforms and strangely shaped helmets they might have been some of us, viz. ordinary very scared human beings, – extremely unlikely to be the baby-killers and rapists our propagandists had told us about. Many I saw smoking cigarettes handed to them by their captors. War, I realized then, is a funny business: the nearer you are to the 'enemy' the less you hate him. I believe that on the field of battle hatred only exists in moments of panic and desperation. The soldiers on both opposing sides are in the same boat, – not victors and vanquished, but victims,

– victims of forces completely beyond their control. That is why the first reaction of any Tommy to a captured Fritzy was, 'Have a fag, chum.' Unconsciously he feels, 'There, but for the grace of God, go I.'

I come now to the day after the battle. There was an uneasy silence; everyone knew it was the lull before the storm reopened. Inevitably there would come a counter-attack, – the question was when.

Before your infantry attack, you first have to 'silence' the enemy's batteries. This is a polite expression meaning that you seek out their positions and then blow their guns and men into smithereens. Then they can't fire shells at your infantry. This is what we had done the day before, – in theory at least. Some German batteries were certain to be active and many others would have replaced the ones put out of action. The counter-attack would start with the shelling of our gun positions and those of all our neighbours.

For various reasons, information about the whereabouts of our infantry had failed to reach us. We were well camouflaged beneath trees, and the screen of wooded ground between us and the old front line prevented us seeing the actual battleground. It was essential to find out our infantry's new positions. Until they were carefully plotted on our maps we could not fire a round without endangering our own chaps' lives.

Major Snow sent a party of four to collect the required information and lay a telephone line from his Command Post to the new front line. The four were a Lieutenant Hedges, Bill and Geordie, whom you already know, and me. (We had no idea when we set forth what the expedition's aim was. I only discovered subsequently.)

Bill and Geordie weren't telephonists at all, – they had never laid a line in their lives. The officer in charge was a newcomer. He had a map in his pocket but very little know-how under his tin hat. I had a carrier pigeon. Nobody told me why. I asked Mr. Hedges, but he didn't know; he assumed I had been told.

The least fortunate of the four were the two Tynesiders. In addition to normal battledress and equipment they were lumbered with the heavy accumulators which provide power to the telephones, weighty coils of wire and a wooden box of tools.

With Mr. Hedges leading, map in hand, we reached our old front-line trenches and picked our way between the shattered barbed wire and huge shell holes into No Man's Land, which was here about 200 yards across. In the middle were the only scraps of green vegetation visible. Beyond, leading to the foot of the gently rising Ridge and up its mile-long slope, was a landscape that was unearthly. Not a blade of grass, not a tree stump more than a few inches high, not a solitary building, had survived the days of concentrated shelling. It was, with the deathly silence all around, a lunar landscape come to Earth.

Here and there between the thousands of shell craters were greyish heaps of dust which had once been human habitations. I could not help wondering what 'cover' we would have if Fritz started shelling now.

Mr H., a little fusspot of a man, kept stopping and calling back to us to hurry. Geordie and Bill simply could not do so with the burdens they had to carry. I was midway between him and them when we reached the site of the enemy's old trenches, under which our mines had exploded the morning before.

It was a ghastly sight which met our eyes. I can't attempt to describe what shapes and colours things which were once human bodies assume after they have been blown sky high. Some looked like bluish-green replicas of the Michelin Tyre-man, – only inflated to twice life-size. Others were . . . incomplete . . .

Hedges, with his fingers to his nose, stumbled through and over these objects. I did the same, – for a short distance, then nausea overcame me. I had never set eyes on even a peacefully dead person before. I had the utmost difficulty in forcing myself forward, – over and between what lay there. But Hedges was yelling like a man possessed and I made myself follow. I turned my head to see where my two pals were. One was being violently sick. As far as I could see, ahead, to left and right we were the only living creatures in that nightmarish landscape.

I followed the Lieutenant up the cratered slope, averting my eyes as best I could from things I didn't want to see. But there was one figure, a few yards from the track we were following, which I could not pass without taking notice. The officer's shouts fell on deaf ears. I clambered across a heap of rubble to take a closer look at it. Then I knew I was about to faint. I crouched and pulled my head low between my knees. That little bit of remembered Scout lore prevented a black-out.

All of a sudden the silence was broken. A rumbling as of a not-very-distant thunderstorm was followed by the roaring of shells. They passed overhead, on the way to our battery's positions. More and more followed and we heard the crump, crump, crump of their explosions. We were unable to see where they fell because of the wooded terrain where our gun sites were hidden. I expect they were two and a half to three miles behind us.

Then shells began falling shorter. We hurled ourselves into the nearest shell holes heedless of what they contained. I was lucky for mine was empty. For several minutes there was a 'scatter' bombardment, with shells falling indiscriminately over the whole area.

This was the first time we had been under direct fire away from the battery. There, when shell-danger threatened we had reasonable protection; here there was no cover whatever.

In the short intervals between bursts of shelling we made some progress. A dozen times we had to flatten ourselves or jump into a shell hole. Then Fritz decided to switch from using H.E.s[6] to shrapnel. In our shell holes we had been protected from side-blast, but shrapnel shells are timed to explode in the air, – anything from ten to a hundred feet above your head, – showering death-dealing metal all around. Your only protection is your tin hat and you can't get all your body under that.

Bill and Geordie, line-testing, found communication with the Command Post cut. That meant retracing their route until they found the cause. Mr. Hedges emerged from his burrow furious at the delay. I was scared myself, but not half as much as he appeared to be. He went a short distance further, calling to me to follow. I didn't. I was in a deep, dry shell hole and I wasn't moving out of it until I had a very good reason. I lay with only my head above ground level.

Without any warning a shrapnel shell burst in the air almost immediately above him. I ducked and pressed myself as close to the slanting side of the shell hole as I could. For several minutes all hell seemed let loose. Shells of all kinds whined, whistled and screamed, exploding in the air above us and all around. Flying clods of earth and fragments of steel pelted down on my helmet. Something struck me hard at the back of my knee. Then the racket stopped – as suddenly as it had begun.

I was sure I had received a serious leg injury. I felt apprehensively along it, moved it nervously and found it still all in one piece. It must have been a lump of Messines clay that had given me the thumping wallop! I was so thankful I forgot my fears for a moment.

6 High explosive shells plunge into the ground before exploding, unless fitted with an impact fuse.

I was aware of some shouting and screaming and raised my head to look.

Something horrible had happened to Mr. Hedges. I saw him running down the slope towards me making incomprehensible noises, with blood streaming down both sides of his face. There was a hole in his shrapnel helmet. I had no idea what I should do and climbed out intending to meet him, but there was the screaming of another shell approaching. I flung myself back-wards instead. It was another shrapnel. The lethal bits of red-hot metal rained down. I heard the horrible singing noise they make as they whirr downwards and there were two sharp 'pings' on my helmet to remind me not to be brave and take unnecessary risks. I stayed throughout the next brief lull and prayed.

Silence again. Where were Bill and Geordie? There wasn't a sign of them. Nor of Mr. Hedges. I must do something.

I scrambled to where I had last seen him. I looked all around. There were hideous things to be seen – but none of them was Mr. Hedges. I never saw him, or heard of him, again.

But what of my old pals? I wouldn't be able to live with myself if I didn't find them. I hurried as best I could towards where they had been repairing the line.

I did find them. And how I wished I hadn't. They were past my help, or anybody else's. I burst into uncontrollable tears. I remember crying, 'Oh God! Why couldn't you have let them die less horribly?' I tried to console myself with the thought that I had been spared the mental agony of watching helplessly while they died. I don't think I could have stood that. But I felt that something inside me had died too. I was heart-broken.

(I remember a biblical sentence coming into my head: 'And in death they were not divided.' How ludicrously inapt it was! For they had been most grotesquely and obscenely divided.)

I was still partly stupefied when I stumbled into a shell hole some distance away. Suddenly the fact registered that I was still carrying the pigeon basket. Again I thought, I must <u>do</u> something, but I hadn't been told what the object of our expedition was. Somebody should have given me instructions to follow in an emergency. But they hadn't. I was on my own.

The significance of the carrier pigeon came quite clearly to me now. It was our means of communication if all else failed. But with whom was I to communicate? And about what? I could only guess what my position was. If I went forward I would presumably reach our new front-line trenches. But they might be one, two, or even three miles beyond the crest of the Ridge. And suppose Fritz's counter-attack was let loose soon, I wouldn't stand a chance: I'd be blown to bits by the artillery barrage, and if not by his, then by ours. (I was midway between the two armies, both resting and licking their wounds, as it were.)

I remember feeling very shaky, not so much with fear, perhaps, as hunger. We had brought no rations with us. I didn't think I had stamina left to struggle upwards towards the summit of the Ridge. Downhill would be less exhausting. Besides, a retreat into our own territory, – assuming I could find the way, – wouldn't require as much courage as an advance into the unknown. Whatever decision I made, I would lose if the shelling restarted. My luck couldn't hold out much longer.

One thing I could decide at once. What to do with the pigeon! Where would its 'home' base be? It wouldn't fly to our battery, I knew that. Divisional H.Q. perhaps. Or Army Corps H.Q.? I'd better get a message ready. 'Report three of our party killed; I'm attempting to return to 239 S.B.' I hoped the paper they gave you was big enough. You fold it up small and put it into a little metal container and attach it to the bird's leg. How? I fished around in my pockets. Damn! I hadn't brought a pencil with me. Never mind, there would be one in the basket.

I unfastened the straps and opened the lid. There wasn't any pen, pencil or paper. Only a dead pigeon.

Strange, isn't it? how some of life's little problems solve themselves.

Of course, like Ella, you will think it strange that I hadn't already been aware of the fact because of the absence of wing-fluttering or noises from the basket. But I hadn't. I had been extremely pre-occupied with other matters. Anyway, it was a very docile pigeon. It had never fidgeted from the very start. Perhaps it had been dead all the time.

I was desperately afraid. I am not ashamed to admit it. As the daylight waned and the mists grew thicker my imagination ran riot. It was my loneliness as much as my fear that made me see those ghastly swollen parts of bodies somehow assembling themselves into horrific evil beings. Evil things about to take revenge on me for what had happened to them.

I found my way back, eventually. I sang almost every hymn I knew as loudly as I could, thinking perhaps to keep the evil spirits at bay. It seemed impossible that I could be the only living human being when, within five miles, there were thousands of concealed men of both armies, all as silent as the dead. But so it was. I have never in my life before or since been in such mortal terror.

Perhaps some of my feathered comrade's homing instinct had been bequeathed to me; perhaps my prayers to God to guide me had been answered: just when I was sure I hadn't strength left to crawl any further, I caught sight of the partially screened flashing of hand-torches. A minute or two more and there were Jock and Windy hauling me up over the tail-board of a lorry, – and Jock's voice: 'Where the hell have ye been, Robbie? Ye bloody near missed the bus!'

As we drove off, the shelling re-started. We were moving out

of the line because the Big White Chiefs considered we'd finished our part in winning the Battle of Messines and they had
generously granted us a three-day rest. We didn't know it, but
that was the last 'rest' we were to have for five long months.

As we jolted along, in between the snatches of conversation,
in between the little prayers of gratitude that, unobserved, I
offered to God, I pondered over the day's events.

I wish I could have seen the tragic-comic element in it, – the
traipsing into and out of battle with a bird in a basket, – but of
course I couldn't. All I could think of was that a young officer's
life had been thrown away and two of my closest friends had
been blown to pieces.

For what? For whose satisfaction? For King and Country,
surely! If they were ever found, if they were buried, their tomb-
stones would tell how they gave their lives for both. For a King
who'd never heard of them and a Country full of war profiteers.

But I must return to something which exercised a terrible fascination for me.

A hundred things shocked me beyond imagination that
dreadful day, but it was this one that made the deepest, and as I
found subsequently, the most lasting impression.

It was a sight I would have liked to avoid, but there was a compulsion to look which I could not resist. I have told you already
that I had to fight an inclination to faint as I stepped around a
crater's rim to take a closer view.

What I saw might have been a life-size wax model of a
German soldier. He was in a posture I can only describe as half-
sitting and half-reclining. Resting his body on the edge of a
smaller shell hole he had leaned back against a mound of
thrown-up earth. But for his complete immobility you would
have thought he had assumed that position quite deliberately

and, overcome by tiredness, had fallen asleep. Everything about his posture looked perfectly natural and normal, – except that there was a something you don't see, you feel. An aura of death.

There was no bloodstain, no bruise visible either on his person or uniform. Leaning back, his helmet had been tilted upwards revealing his face. It was the deathly pallor of that face which shocked me beyond my powers of description. Part of a lock of blonde hair was resting on his forehead above the two closed eyes. I thought Germans wore their hair closely cropped, – but not this one. There was the suggestion of a smile on the pale lips, – a smile of contentment.

I fought down my initial revulsion and went closer still. This figure was my enemy. He <u>had</u> <u>been</u> my enemy, perhaps, but he wasn't <u>now</u>. For this man I should feel hatred, not compassion.

This man! He was, or had been, no man. He was a <u>boy</u> who, but for the colour of his hair and uniform, must have looked very like me. I was nineteen, he probably younger still. What could he possibly have done to deserve <u>this</u>?

Whatever killed him, it couldn't have been one of our mines, – otherwise his body would have been inflated till it had burst open to look like those . . . those other things. No, he must have died of shell shock.

One hand still held the open wallet he had been looking at before death struck. There were two mica windows with photographs behind them. One must have been of his parents. The other had '*Mein Hans*' written diagonally across one of the lower corners. It was the picture of a young girl who could have been Ella's twin sister.

I was sick with shame and pity. <u>That</u> was the sight at which but for the first aid treatment I'd given myself, I would have fainted.

Things hardly ever seemed to work out for me the way my elders thought they should. No doubt they would have expected me to be filled with implacable hatred towards any man in a German uniform. To be glad to see one of my country's enemies dead. To vow revenge against them for the wrong they had done to Geordie and Bill. But it was not so. To me, all three were killed by the stupidity of others. Hans had died as uselessly as Bill and Geordie. And when the thought came to me, as it did, that it might have been the blast from one of our shells, one of my shells, which killed young Hans, I felt a sense of guilt almost over-shadowing my pity and sorrow.

On 8 June 1917 war for me changed from being an abstraction to a personal problem. From that day forward it became my war. I, not others, was responsible. I would have to live my life with a troubled conscience.

And only ten months before, I had been a raw scholar sitting in his classroom at school.

My adolescence ended that day. Henceforward I had to live and think as an adult.

The Fifth 'Musketeer': 'Windy' Clark

Windy wasn't one of our little band of brothers, but after Bill and Geordie had gone he became my trainee telephonist. He was so unaccustomed to it that he always handled the receiver as though he expected it to blow up at any moment.

I'd guess he was about thirty-five years old. The only fact I ever gleaned about his private life was that he had been called up just as his little grocery business in Otley (or was it Bingley, or Batley or Ilkley?) had begun to make a profit. His missus was having to cope with the problem of 't' bloody Co-op', who, he said would do their bloody best to bankrupt him while he was away.

All Clarks in the army are 'Nobby', – with the exception of ours. The battery already had <u>two</u>, – so, having discovered that his parents had christened him Windsor, we corrupted that into Windy. That word was also a derisive adjective (– 'getting the wind up' meant showing funk –) but our Windy knew it was a term of affection and not contempt.

Windy was a grey-complexioned, dark-eyed character, perennially pessimistic about everything and everybody. No one ever succeeded in getting a smile out of him. In every respect I can think of Windy was the opposite of the two boys whose place he took. When our two Tynesiders boasted of their triumphs in the art of seducing girls, Windy would give them looks of pity and bewilderment. 'Women!' he would say, looking for somewhere to spit. 'Women! You can have the bloody lot!' Which, in a way, were Bill and Geordie's sentiments exactly!

Of course he should never have been in the Army at all. With his chronic bronchial cough and adenoidal voice it should have been obvious to the most brainless nitwit of an M.O. that the first whiff of poison gas would kill him. Jock and I agreed that nothing would have given us greater pleasure then than to encounter personally the quack who had graded Windy A.I. – provided we had had a horsewhip handy. But that pleasure never came our way.

Windy gave me a piece of advice which, although the phraseology is peculiarly that of the West Riding, has far more practical sense in it than selfishness: 'If thee iver does owt for onny body, do it f' thee-sen.'

I've made him out to be a taciturn, morose, uncompanionable devil, haven't I? He wasn't anything of the kind. I'm sure Jock and I loved him as much as he loved us.

And as for that Yorkshire motto of his, – we knew it would be instantly thrust aside in an emergency. He would have laid down his life for any of us if the necessity ever arose. It didn't, but he laid down his life just the same.

At Ypres, some months after he came as a replacement for Geordie, there were two successive nights of gas attacks. On the second night it was my turn of duty. Jock and Windy were asleep in elephant-iron shacks under a hedge a few minutes' walk away from the Command Post.

For these attacks the Germans used the almost odourless mustard gas, much more deadly than the chlorine and phosgene used earlier. Gas shells fall with a sort of phut! phut! sound as they hit the ground; the case just splits quietly open to discharge its poisonous contents.

I think I dreaded gas even more than high explosive. I got caught once, not getting my mask on quickly enough. It set up nothing worse than occasional chest pains and fits of dry coughing. I was lucky.

The second night-spell was half done when I heard the dreaded phut-phutting. Nobody had sounded the gas alarm. I hurriedly pulled my respirator on and dashed to Jock's 'bivvy'. I woke him up just in time to prevent disaster. Then together we sought out Windy by torchlight.

By the time we found him it was too late. I didn't dare shine the torch on his face for more than a fleeting moment. I knew what chaps who had been badly gassed looked like. All we could do was get back to the Post and send for stretcher-bearers.

26 July 1917
Ypres, Belgium

Looks like another big 'push' coming soon; there's a big pile-up: guns, ammo, stores. We're now just outside Zillebeke – not much of it left standing though. Dug-outs reasonable. Strafing sporadic.

Ypres city is about two miles east. M.P.s have placed it out of bounds in daylight. No one goes there unless they're mad like me. This p.m. broke rules and went to take closer look. Approached via Hell Fire Corner. Fritz balloons visible low over horizon. Expecting strafe any minute.

What a scene of desolation! Ypres has been shelled night and day for months. A miracle anything still stands. Somebody called it a martyred city. Fritz keeps it under bombardment so we can't use it. But what would we do if we could?

I'm walking over heaps of rubble towards what's left of Cloth Hall. Not a living being in sight. Yes there are. Rats! They scuttle for cover as I approach.

I'm in what must have been City Square. Stone-paved, but plenty of shell holes. Piled up debris either side of a track like a snow-plough makes. There's a smell of decay and death. Wonder how long before Fritz opens up. I'll go and look at cathedral ruins then bolt for home. On the way see there's only fragments of central tower and outer walls of Cloth Hall left. In 1914 'twas the pride of Belgium, they say.

Am 'inside' cathedral now. No roof, no windows and only one third of walls remain. Hardly a sign of where high altar would have been. Suppose chancel would be at east end, – here! Now just a home for rats. The loathsome creatures are everywhere. God! What makes them so fat?

Only one completely recognizable feature. In one corner there's a Madonna of plaster in her niche still intact.

I look from the rubble-strewn floor and up to the blue sky where the roof once was. I think <u>our</u> church could be like this. Or Winchester Cathedral! I don't know whether I still believe in God or not, but I kneel to say a prayer for myself and my loved ones so I can't have become a total unbeliever.

Now there's a hammering sound outside. It makes the rats run out of some holes and scuttle into others. I feel scared and shudder. There's something unearthly about the place. I hurry outside, and what do I see? Two Australians in their Bush Hats with chunks of rock in their hands bashing the heads off the only two remaining sculptured saints on the ruined outer wall. Whatever was that vandalism for? To cart them 12,000 miles to Sydney or Melbourne and stand them on a mantelpiece perhaps?

Better get back before my luck changes and Fritzy opens up. On outskirts of city turn to have a final look. Yes, martyred is right.

Just in time! He has opened up. I can see his shells exploding where the Menin Gate used to be. They can't do more damage than they have done, except just turn rubble into finer rubble. Red dust hangs in the air for minutes after each crump explodes. Wonder if those two Aussies got caught!

I'm back. Nobody has noticed my two and half hours' absence.

Between War Story No. 1 and War Story No. 2 stretch five long months of almost unrelieved misery. I do not intend to dwell on the details: I used to think sometimes that the lucky soldiers were the dead ones.

Throughout the months of July, August, September and October my battery was almost continuously in action. We probably had a few two-day spells of rest out of the firing line but I don't remember them.

We suffered grievous casualties. What a useful euphemism that word is! It covers such a multitude of horrors: men blown to bits, machine-gunned, disembowelled, gassed, maimed, blinded, deafened, drowned, shell shocked and sentenced to death (for so-called cowardice). Except for the last, we had our share of each.

By the end of October only a score of our original company

had survived. Every man's capacity was now stretched to its uttermost limit. Morale was at breaking point.

A humane commander would have had his battery withdrawn from fighting until it had recovered its broken spirit and could be brought up to strength. Not Major Snow. Pride demanded that he ordered his handful to fight on and on. By the first of November only one heavy battery was engaged in the Passchendaele area, – all others had been withdrawn. You can guess which battery it was.

I said the men's morale was breaking. I suppose I should include myself. I had long since lost any desire to continue as a fighting soldier. Idealists and cowards aren't of much use on a battlefield and I was a bit of both.

At nineteen I found my standards of conduct obsolete, my ideals shattered. I had lost all faith in institutional religion. My Church had authorized me to break the sixth commandment in the name of patriotism. 'Blessed are the Peacemakers'? No! Not in 1917. Blessed are the War Winners. Blessed are the Munition Makers. Twice blessed, for they lined their pockets and kept their skins intact at the same time.

These were the thoughts that I couldn't dismiss from my mind during those dreadful months. I wouldn't have stuck a label on myself then, but I know now what I had become. It's a word that is distasteful to many: Pacifist.

I still believed in God, though I was being assailed by doubts. I prayed daily. Prayed that He would stop the war going on, and end the misery it caused. Soon it became obvious that He wasn't going to, for the longer it went on the worse the horrors of it became. I had been taught 'God is love'. Rubbish! I couldn't help thinking. If He loved us, if He were omnipotent He could put a stop to it to-day. But then, I thought, perhaps He isn't omnipotent.

Eventually I worked it out, – at least for myself. God was all right. It was we who were wrong. Why the hell should He care what happened to us lot? We had brought this War Evil into existence, not God. The reason Evil and Ugliness were triumphing over Goodness and Beauty, why Pity and Compassion were considered weaknesses, and Ruthlessness and Cruelty regarded as noble, – the reason for all this was the wickedness in ourselves and not the indifference of God. That was why the more murders you committed, the bigger the Hero you became. That was what made your superior officer slap you on the back and say 'Splendid, old chap! Jolly good shooting!' when your shells had destroyed in minutes the beauty which craftsmen had toiled lifetimes to create.

Disillusion is very, very bitter when you are young, thoughtful, imaginative and sensitive.

Apart from my friendship with Jock, I had one ray of brightness which illuminated my gloom, – my continuing love for Ella. It is true she was becoming more and more remote. Our months of separation seemed like years. As less of my time could be devoted to thoughts of her she became almost an idealized image created by my fancy. Snatches of that little song I'd heard at Erquinghem would sing in my head: 'I did but see her passing by / And yet I love her till I die.'

Ella did become flesh and blood to me with every letter or parcel which reached me in those dark days. There were only two of our little band left to share her cakes now.

As for me, I wrote as frequently and cheerfully as possible, concealing the unpleasant facts of life, – which would have been struck out by the censoring officer anyway, – and assuring both my family and her that all was well. (Everybody was concealing the truth, so I was aiding and abetting in a way, – but not for propaganda purposes.) I told Ella I loved her more than ever, even if it was the idealized girl of my hopes and dreams rather than a human being that I worshipped. What did it matter then, anyway?

Passchendaele

I write more than half a century after the events occurred. Memory plays tricks, but the happenings of that particular day are so indelibly impressed in it they could never be forgotten. I have never spoken or written of them till now.

The story opens in the early hours of a day in the first week of November 1917, a day which dawned fine and sunny. That in itself was memorable, for the autumn had been the wettest in living memory. Equally notable was the fact that it followed a night of only sporadic enemy shelling over a battlefield which had been a stinking, raging hell night and day for weeks past.

239 Battery had been ordered into its position just over the crest of Passchendaele Ridge a few days previously. Why? Nobody knew but Major Snow. No commander in his right mind would have chosen such an exposed position. Others must have refused, for we alone were there.

Fritz had 'surrendered' the few hundred yards of mud and withdrawn into the cover afforded by Houthulst Forest, most of which still stood as recognizable woodland. We had 'advanced' into the mud the enemy regarded as untenable after weeks of incessant bombardment. Their Observers could watch every move we made from their kite-balloons over to the east.

I was convinced by now that our C.O. had taken leave of his senses.

Our new Command Post was a captured 'pill-box'. Pill-boxes

were little fortresses made of impenetrable concrete and were dotted about the former German front line. They were partially sunk into the soil with about three feet of their walls raised above ground level. Machine-gun 'slits' faced westwards. They were Fritz's solution to the problem of defending terrain so waterlogged that you couldn't dig down more than a few inches without coming to water.

The post, on the day of which I am writing, was manned by just three men, – Major Snow, Jock Shiels and myself. The first task that had confronted us was the building, under fire, of a sandbagged blast wall in front of our vulnerable entrance. (The pill-box had been built with its doorway on the wrong side from our point of view.) A small working party had come up along duck-board tracks two nights previously with pack-mules laden with filled sandbags and with their help Jock and I made a pretty good job of it. Snow, of course, hadn't lifted a finger.

The pill-box had a separate compartment for the 'Old Man' to retire into, a sort of bed-sitter-cum-lavatory. Until his batman had been killed the week before, Jock and I had been in contact with him only when action compelled him to take command. We took turns of duty as and when we could, trying to snatch an hour's sleep when sleep was possible and growing wearier and wearier with exhaustion and frustration every day. Poor old Jock, being the lowest-ranked, now had to perform humiliating batman duties as well.

When things were quiet enough and Snow took a turn of duty in his retreat, we both slept (after a fashion) on the floor. Heavy British shelling before it was captured had failed to crack the structure but had tilted it enough to cause water to flow towards one wall. We could usually find a reasonably dry part of the concrete on which to spread a groundsheet and blanket. Apart from that, we had no beds or bedding.

We were dirty and lice-ridden because we hadn't taken off our clothes for weeks. When we were out in the rain, – and as I've said, almost every day of that autumn was wet, – our tunics and trousers got soaked. We would take them off and replace them with our greatcoats, unless they were even wetter. We had no means of drying garments other than the heat of our own bodies. It is miraculous that we escaped pneumonia. Many of our comrades didn't. Of course we had no washing or cook-ing facili-ties and I can leave to your imagination what had to serve as sanitary 'amenities'. You just couldn't catch diarrhoea, – or if you did you had to restrict its attacks to the hours of darkness!

Our food was standard iron rations: bully-beef, biscuits, pork and beans. (I don't think I've referred to that delicacy before. It was a tin of haricot beans with a greasy lump of fat about three quarters of an inch square alleged to be pork, floating on the top of the gruesome fluid which kept the beans moist.) We got half a loaf of bread every second or third day; the rest of the time it was biscuits. (No dog ever had the chance of refusing those squares of hard tack.) Chaps from the old Command Post would bring us dixies of tea, but they had to wait till darkness fell before they could venture out. Of course the tea was cold long before it reached us.

Oh! I forgot to mention that our O.C. was fed reasonably well, – on cold beef or ham, fruits and Thermos flasks of hot tea. And, of course, there was the ever-present bottle of Black and White to keep up his spirits and give him the Dutch courage our situ-ation demanded.

Around us stretched the most horrific landscape ever seen by men. The whole area as far as the eye could see was a vast morass of flooded craters, the rim of one touching that of the next. I won't dwell on the contents of those shell-holes.

Transport, or any form of movement, animal or human, was impossible except along duckboard tracks, destroyed daily by enemy guns and/or planes and reconstructed nightly by the Royal Engineers, – until there were no more left. (No more engineers, I mean.)

When my mind goes back to that scene and I recall the ghastly horror of the sights and smells that we had to live with I am still amazed that I, sensitive and squeamish as I was, could endure them for so long without losing my reason. (Jock was built of tougher material than I and I don't think his mental suffering was as great.)

We communicated with our rear-ward Post (– the one we had left two days before –) by telephone, – at least we did when the lines weren't cut; most of the time, a 'runner' had to take his life in his hands to deliver any urgent messages or take ours back. He had to be as sure-footed as the mules we depended on so completely for our supplies (horses were too nervous for this). The duckboards were always slime-covered and almost every other shell hole contained part or all of one of those unfortunate beasts who had slipped.

Major Snow, alone of all the heavy battery commanders in our sector, had ordered our men to advance our gun positions to sites about a quarter of a mile behind our pill-box. They had only been able to man-handle the two-ton guns into some sort of operational state by first constructing roads of ex-railway sleepers laid across the foul swamps. The men were on the verge of mutiny, stretched to their furthest limits, physically and mentally. Of our original company of 120 I doubt whether 30 remained. Yet our O.C. resolutely refused to inform our Corps Commander that 239 Siege Battery was no longer a fighting force. Blind pride and obstinacy, complete indifference to the plight of his men and a brain that would not accept defeat even when it stared him in the face made him in my eyes the personification of all the evils of war. My hatred was so intense that had I possessed a suitable weapon I would have had no hesitation in using it on him. That was the only time in my life I ever wanted to kill another human being and the only time in my life I would have been capable of doing it.

Only a lunatic would have believed that a battery of four heavy guns could be operated by a handful of men at the end of their tether with exhaustion and lack of sleep. Four guns, – in theory anyway. One had already sunk irretrievably up to its axles in the Flanders mud; Snow didn't even go to look at it. Another had received a direct hit from a 'five point nine' [7] which wiped out its crew at the same time; Snow didn't want to know about that. A third had been loaded with a faulty shell, made by one of our patriotic profiteers, which blew up before it left the gun and killed all its crew. The fourth, actually our No. 1, could have been used, – had there been any fit men left to operate it. (Let me remind you that every shell had to be lifted manually, that they each weighed 100 pounds and that at every shot the recoil was so tremendous that the gun's 'tail' buried itself in the soft ground and had to be dug out before another round could be fired.)

I have listed these facts so that you can judge whether a sane Battery Commander would do anything but ask for permission to withdraw. Of course he wouldn't. I doubt whether he would even ask. He would do it, permitted or not.

War Story No. 2: Tragedy at Passchendaele

Now, at last, I am able to relate the happenings of that November day.

---

7 German 5.9-inch calibre gun. The counterpart of our 6-inch howitzer.

I begin just before 5 a.m. It was my spell of duty and quite dark. We were down to our last two candles fixed in bottles. I was sitting at the table below the machine-gun slit we used for observation purposes. Cumulative lack of sleep and physical fatigue, coupled with the lull in shelling, prevented me from keeping my head erect for more than a minute or so at a time. It was only the alternating banging of my head backwards against the wall and downwards on to the table that kept me from complete unconsciousness. Snow was asleep in his cell and Jock on the floor near me, dead to the world.

Suddenly, quiet as things were, I found myself wide awake. A thought had shot into my brain. The day before I had acted as runner to the old H.Q. at dusk when there was still enough light to see over the battlefield. I had been so intent on keeping a foothold on the duckboards and hurrying to complete my mission before Fritz started another bombardment, that I had failed to answer the questions which had come to mind:

a. Why was our battery in such an isolated position?
b. Why were none of the R.F.A. light batteries near? (They were usually ahead of us; we fired over the top of them.)
c. Most unusual of all, where were our infantry?

Somehow these slumbering queries had woken me up. I came to a conclusion which I could only prove right or wrong one way. That way meant committing the soldier's one unforgiveable sin: leaving his post without his officer's permission.

If I were caught I would be in trouble up to my neck. There was already one black mark on my conduct sheet. 'What the hell!' I thought. 'If I do nothing, I'll only go mad.'

Yes, I must get over to No. 1 Gun Site. I couldn't risk phoning. I might waken Snow. It would have been useless, anyway: the line had been cut the day before.

My plan could only succeed if Fritz co-operated: in other words if he continued inactive.

Quietly I donned my respirator and helmet and got safely to the vestibule between the gas curtains. I waited a second or two to make sure I hadn't disturbed Jock.

It was still dark but I knew I shouldn't lack illumination for my trip. Our lads would send up Verey lights [8] quite frequently and between them and Fritz's parachute star-shells (flares) I would have more than enough light for my needs.

I went along the wooden track on hands and knees, keeping motionless whenever a star-shell lighted up the area around me. Before I reached No. 1 Gun I knew the answer to Question (c) on my list. There weren't any Verey lights going up, therefore there weren't any of our infantry in front.

No. 1 Gun Site was another ex-German pill-box. I reached it unharmed. As I scrambled through the curtains I felt dizzy – probably with the tension, added to my physical fatigue.

Inside it was pitch-black. I fished out my matches and struck a light. The place was empty.

'My God!' I whispered to myself. 'They've bolted.' No, I thought, they couldn't have. They must have been ordered out. Ordered to withdraw! By whom? And why hadn't we received the same order?

There was the stump of a candle left on a box-top. I lit it, sank to the floor and tried to grasp the situation. Again the dizziness threatened to overcome me and I forced my head downwards to the floor and waited for it to go.

I concentrated as hard as my strength would let me and in a few minutes had made another decision. If only my luck would hold out another half-hour!

8 Flares fired from a special type of pistol.

I had to first get back to Command H.Q. without being sniped at, waken Jock and whisper my plan to him. I could count on Jock's support, I knew. But I would be sunk if Snow had woken up and was there awaiting my return. Time was against me too. In a half-hour it would be daylight.

My luck was in. Snow wasn't to be seen. Jock listened intently while I whispered.

'I'm in this with you, Robbie lad! Go ahead!'

I poured out the details of my whole crazy scheme. First, I said, he must take over my duty and brave the Old Man's wrath when he discovered my absence. 'Tell him I've gone outside for . . .' You'll guess what I meant.

I set off. 'Good luck, laddie,' Jock whispered as I hurried away.

I had a twenty-minute crawl-cum-walk ahead of me. Whatever happened I mustn't slip into a shell hole this time. There would be no one to haul me out.

I felt better already. Doing something is always better than doing nothing. I knew the least dangerous duckboard route, – I'd done it several times before. (I wouldn't ever let Jock out as a runner, not because he wasn't brave enough but because he'd got Jeannie and the kids back home and I'd only got me.) The only fear I remember experiencing was that another dizzy spell might come on. If it did I would end up drowned and poisoned.

Still luck was with me. I reached the old Command Post in record time.

Our second in command, Captain Jordan, was the man I wanted to find. He wasn't there, – but Harry was, with a sergeant I'd never seen before. (Harry was the Gun Layer there and a sensible, level-headed chap.) There was a hubbub and bustling, the noise of tractors and lorries on the move, which told me all I wanted to know. The troops were pulling out.

'Where the bleeding hell is the Old Man and your mate?'

Harry asked. I told him. He opened his mouth, and instead of saying what he was thinking invited me to have a cup of char. Pouring it from the can into a mug he said, 'We've been detailed to wait for you three bleeders. If you hadn't turned up by seven, I had to bleedin' well go and find out why.' I looked at my watch, it was 6.15.

After swallowing the mug of stewed tea I felt better. I emptied my water-bottle outside and came back to fill it with the rest of the tea. It would be stone cold by the time I got back to Jock but cold char is better than none.

I'd got to do some quick thinking. 'Try the line again, Harry,' I said, thinking Snow might have ordered Jock out to repair it. Harry pressed his button, buzzed and buzzed but got no reply.

'It's been bleeding "dis"[9] all night,' he told me.

'I know,' I said.

Harry told me what had been going on. He'd overheard Captain Jordan's conversation with the other Battery Commanders. (Jordan had taken charge of 239 as Snow couldn't be contacted.) All batteries had been ordered to withdraw immediately, abandoning immobile guns, stores and ammo. The salvaged ammo was stacked up nearby, ready for transport.

'We've put all your bleedin' gear on the G.S. Wagon. We're supposed to take you, your mate and bleedin' Snow with us. The old bastard must—'

I was nodding, nearly dozing off, but I pulled myself together when I realized what Harry was telling me: he himself had brought the dispatch to Snow.

'When was that?' I interrupted.

'Earlier to-night. When you and your mate were having a kip.'

'Good God!' I said. 'The bastard's cracked.'

9 Disconnected.

'Bleedin' cracked all right,' Harry went on. 'The old bleeder took the envelope from me and refused to sign for it. I stood there while he opened the envelope, read the bleedin' orders, tore them into bits and chucked them out the winder. The bleeder's an effing maniac, if you ask me.'

'Hell!' was all I could say.

I was off along that duckboard trail as fast as I could go. It was getting light. Another half an hour might be too late.

So I was right. We had a raving lunatic in charge. He, the old invincible, the old rock of Gibraltar, wasn't taking any second-hand orders, from Captain Jordan or anyone else. He'd move when Haig told him to and not before.

How do you foresee what a lunatic will do? A grown man wouldn't be sure. I was a nineteen-year-old boy; my enemy twice my age at least.

I, who had 'lost' my religious faith, found myself praying for strength to fulfil the mission I had in mind. When you're desperate you find you have to believe in God. There's no one else to call on.

I had reached the tricky, slippery part. Here I couldn't hurry, I couldn't take risks. Then came that dizzy feeling again. I crouched down. It was half-light now. I dug my hands under the duckboard edges so that I shouldn't fall sideways if I fainted.

I remember standing up suddenly, feeling O.K. again. I remember looking all around at that fantastic twilight landscape of unending shell holes, nearly all containing horrific things that had once been parts of men or animals. I remember shouting across that desert of filthy death, 'All right, lads. It's all over. The bloody war's over. We can all go home!'

I came to my senses before I did anything suicidal, thank God. Once more I collected my wandering thoughts and resumed my crawling run along that wooden track, estimating I had only three or four hundred yards to go.

Suddenly like the crack of doom the silence was broken. Fifty, perhaps a hundred, shells came hissing, whining, plunging and exploding all together. 'Oh God!' I exclaimed. 'Isn't the war over after all?'

So Fritz was going to blow my plan and the three of us sky high. 'Well,' thought I, 'we'll see! I haven't had the one with my name on it yet. I'm still in with a chance.'

The sudden bombardment ceased. I was still in one piece. What I had to hope now, – apart from covering the last lap safely, – was that the din hadn't woken Snow up.

It was full daylight when I re-entered the pill-box. Fortune was still with me: Jock was at the duty table, Snow nowhere to be seen.

'Thank Christ, Robbie,' he whispered. 'I didn't think you could do it.'

'Sh!' I hushed him, handing over my water-bottle. He uncorked it and swallowed the concoction with as much relish as if it were a fresh-brewed cup of Lipton's best.

Quietly, I said, 'We've got a bloody maniac in there.' I pointed to the 'cell'. 'If we stay on he'll kill the pair of us. If we don't, Fritz'll get us. We're done either way.'

Jock nodded. He watched me take two field post-cards from the box on the table. I passed one to him. On mine I deleted all the printed sentences except 'I am quite well' and 'I am coming home on leave' and added 'darling Ella' after 'leave'. I pencilled her name and address in the space provided. Jock followed my example, completed his card and handed it to me.

Just then the Old Man appeared from behind his partition. He almost froze me with a frown. But again the silence was broken by a roaring low overhead and before he could speak a salvo of shells all burst together. The combined crashes were followed by a series of rapid crumps and muffled explosions and then one vast crack that made the pill-box quiver.

'My God!' I called to Jock. 'That's our ammo gone up. Harry's there with—' I didn't finish for I was watching Snow's face. Shelling or not, the showdown was coming. Whatever happened I mustn't lose my head. Jock was depending on me.

More shells burst close outside, making the pill-box floor tremble. Fritz was making up for lost time now.

Our commander had been taken aback by the suddenness of the outburst. Now he stepped towards me, glowering. I must let him make the first move. Desperation, or near-madness, dispelled all my fear of the madman I was facing. I felt no anger now, only a chilly contempt for this monster who for eight months had intimidated and humiliated me. I steeled myself, determined to make the stand I knew was necessary. I turned myself into a sort of spectator, watching and listening to another nineteen-year-old youth defy his Commanding Officer.

'Bombardier, why did you leave your post without permission?'

'I thought it necessary, sir.'

'That is an insolent remark.' More shells were flying over. They were falling and bursting nearer.

'Sorry, sir, I can't hear with that damn noise going on. I wish to make a report.'

'This is insolence. If I want a report from you I'll ask for it. Get up, Gunner Shiels, the Bombardier will take over.'

'Do as the O.C. orders, Jock.'

Jock left the table and moved towards our sleeping area.

'Sit down.'

From sheer force of habit I obeyed, removing my helmet and placing it on my end of the table. Then, suddenly realizing I was faltering in my intentions, I pushed the chair back and stood up defiantly.

'I said <u>sit down</u>! That is an order.'

(Standing.) '<u>I</u> said I wish to report to you that—'

'Damn it, man. This is insubordination! Have you taken leave of your senses?'

'Perhaps, sir.'

'<u>That is</u> insolence!'

Snow thrust himself into the chair, picked up the dead telephone to No. 1 Gun and buzzed. No reply, of course. I remained standing. Snow, fuming now, turned to Jock and shouted, 'This line is cut. Get outside, trace the fault and repair it.'

'Better obey orders, Jock.' (He picked up his box of repair gear.) 'Wait for me, I'm coming too, in a moment.'

'You will not leave your post, Bombardier. I am giving you an order: SIT DOWN.'

(Still standing.) 'Gunner Shiels will <u>not</u> repair the dead line, sir. It is unnecessary. There are no men at No. 1 Gun. Repeat. <u>NO MEN</u>. <u>That</u> is what I am reporting.'

'I am placing you under arrest.'

'No, sir. You can't, sir. There are not enough men present for you to arrest anybody.'

Outside there came more roaring and more deafening crashes. I was amazed at my temerity. I still felt like an onlooker, – not a participant.

Snow rose from his chair, his face paler than I had ever seen it. I lifted my helmet from the table and put it on. Jock reappeared. He had been waiting and listening between the gas curtains. Over the din we could hear Snow raving – 'Disobeying orders . . . death penalty' etc., – none of which threats meant anything to me then. My eyes were following the movement of his hand towards the holster at his hip. <u>This</u> was a development

I hadn't foreseen. So we'd not only got a lunatic but a homicidal one. Jock had seen the danger, pulled the candle out of the nearest bottle and grasped it by its neck. (I remembered a demonstration of unarmed combat we had seen at Aldershot; I knew exactly where to put the boot in if Snow drew his pistol.) Jock and I backed to the doorway. His tin hat and respirator were on, the bottle ready for hurling. I gestured to him to get out. Then I stepped back.

At the gas curtain I shouted, 'My pal and I have had enough of you, <u>and</u> your bloody war. We're getting out of it. Understand? <u>We're getting out</u>.'

I don't think he was able to grasp the full significance of the words he heard or the evidence of his eyes. I am certain it was the first time in his military career he had encountered open defiance from his men.

My final words to him were 'Call it desertion, if you like. Call it cowardice if you like. Call it any bloody thing. Jock and I are off.'

Jock's final message to him was 'And go to bloody hell!'

Snow's hand was still on the holster when we left.

It wasn't until we were outside that I realized how quiet it was. The shelling had stopped.

Together we ran from behind the blast wall to the blind side of the pill-box. We crouched low and close against it, waiting for our enemy to emerge. Nothing happened for minutes. Cautiously Jock peered round the corner. 'O.K.,' he whispered.

Blast! More shells coming. Safely over our heads, thank God.

As I lay huddled against that low wall I found myself shaking from head to foot. Not so much with fear of the consequences of the crimes we had committed but because the other Me, the one who had defied the mad tyrant, had been replaced by the cowed being I normally was.

But it was I who had got us into this mess and there was no going back now. I heard Jock whispering 'Robbie, what's the next move?'

I made the effort and shook off my weakness. I went over my plan in my mind again. Then I explained it to Jock.

My scheme was, Fritz permitting, to scramble by the wooden tracks from pill-box to pill-box, taking advantage of what scraps of cover were available: a few splintered tree-stumps here, a pile of brick-dust there, a series of shell holes not too watery wherever possible.

I had covered most of those tracks before, communicating with our former gun positions. Jock hadn't. The whole adventure seemed now to be taking on the aspect of a mad dream. Here was I, usually the quiet one, doing all the talking, and Jock almost as silent as the grave. Come to think of it, this was a graveyard that we were in. And it was going to be ours if my plan failed.

The first problem was the most difficult to solve, – how to cross the 300 yards of exposed ground between us and No. 1 Gun. For all I knew we might be within sniping range of a German sharpshooter. It was broad daylight now. We could see the observation balloons going up behind their positions.

If we could get to No. 1 we might stand a chance. If we had the luck of the devil we could reach the crest of the slightly rising ground optimistically called Passchendaele Ridge. What was to happen after that I hadn't begun to think.

Without any warning, Fritz solved Problem No. 1 for us. With a deafening roar he put down an artillery barrage on what he thought would be our infantry's new positions, 500 or 600 yards ahead of us.

The barrage produced a smoke screen more effective than we could have hoped for. Jock suddenly came to life. 'Robbie, this is our chance, let's dash for it.'

How good it was to hear Jock take the initiative! 'Making a dash' wasn't quite the right expression as we had to take great care with our footholds, but we reached No. 1 Gun safely.

From behind the blast wall we watched the bombardment. I thought, 'You're wasting your ammo, Fritz. Those chaps were all dead before you opened up. You can't make them any deader.'

We sat on a couple of sandbags by the pill-box entrance, so that we could dash inside if the barrage lifted. Again I had that feeling of weakness coming over me.

'Are you all right, Robbie lad?'

I managed to raise a smile, unbuttoned one of my side pockets and extracted a tin of condensed milk. I had picked it up when telling Jock about my scheme, before Snow had appeared. I knew now why I was feeling groggy, – it wasn't fear, cowardice, guilt or anything like that. I hadn't had any food for over twelve hours.

I unclasped my jack-knife, stabbed two holes in the top of the can and said to Jock, 'Will you join me?' He couldn't stand the stuff and made retching gestures to indicate the fact. I raised the can in a mock toast and let the creamy liquid stream into my mouth.

It did the trick. My queasiness passed off and I felt ready for the next move. I stepped inside the pill-box. There had been a change since I was here a few hours before. Fritz must have been testing some armour-piercing shells, – the three-foot thick roof had been shattered, – but we had bits of walls as some sort of protection.

We thought we'd better wait awhile until Fritz made up his mind about the barrage. If it lifted we would be in serious trouble. I looked at my watch. 'Ten minutes,' I suggested. Jock nodded.

The hellish racket went on.

*

Before we had set off on this ill-fated venture I had explained to Jock what might be the consequences. Not that he needed telling really.

'I'll be the one to get it in the neck, Jock, because I'm an N.C.O. I'm guilty of insolence, insubordination, cowardice in the face of the enemy and God knows what else! That's enough to get me the firing squad. On top of that, I'm a deserter. So are you.'

'Too true, laddie.' Jock grinned ruefully. 'But if oor lot get us, we're suffering a wee-bit shell shock, aye?'

'Aye, Jock,' I replied: 'We'll be so damn shell shocked we can't remember a bloody thing!'

Before the ten minutes had expired, the shelling ceased. All was quiet again. An immense pall of smoke hung to the eastward. This was our chance to make for pill-box No. 2. It was about 200 to 250 yards away, I should guess.

I had just swallowed the last of the milk when Jock's beloved Robbie Burns came into my mind: 'The best laid schemes o' mice an' men / Gang aft agley.'

I didn't dare say it aloud.

The sun, damn it, was shining through the smoky sky. Why couldn't it rain? It had done so every day for months when we didn't want it. Now it would have dimmed the visibility.

There wasn't any point in creeping or crawling. The smoke had cleared sufficiently for Fritz's Observers to see every move we made if two solitary figures were of any interest to them.

I had just said 'Now, Jock' when we heard a salvo of shells heading straight towards us. We flung ourselves flat between the chunks of broken concrete. One shell went over our heads, the second fell short and the blast from the third nearly lifted us off the ground. Lying still, we waited for the rain of falling bits of clay, iron and stone to cease.

Jock was first up. 'Robbie,' he called. 'Look!' Over the Command Post there was a cloud of black, brown and whitish dust; the sandbag blast wall had vanished. It had received a direct hit.

'That's settled the old bastard,' was Jock's comment.

Another salvo of shells was coming. 'They've spotted us and got our range,' I thought. Once again, one shell went over our heads, one fell just short. I grabbed Jock's arm and yelled, 'Run for it!'

We bolted along the track. We were only fifty yards away when shell number three came. It got the ruined pill-box as we were diving into the nearest shell hole.

In circumstances such as these you don't have time to choose your shell hole, you fling yourself into the nearest one and hope for the best. A couple of dead mules did more good to us in that crisis than they were ever able to do in their lifetimes. They saved us from rolling into a ghastly poisonous slime. But oh! the stench. We crawled against the sloping sides of the crater, – it was a really big one, – our feet giving us purchase as we pushed them against the foul-smelling carcasses.

Shell number four hadn't arrived yet; we waited, our hearts filled with fear. The silence was more unbearable than the din.

'Got a fag, Robbie?' Jock gasped. I fumbled for the cigarette case given me by Ella. I hesitated a second as another thought came. She'd never get that card in my pocket if Fritz got us first. Nor would Jeannie get hers. Who would tell them about us then?

In the case were two cigarettes and the little saints' day calendar. I lighted one, passed it to Jock and then lit mine. He lay back, took one luxurious deep draw and watched the blue smoke slowly rise in the still air.

I had just replaced the case and buttoned the flap of my breast pocket when it happened. We both heard the terrifying scream of number four.

They say that the shell that's coming straight at you is the one you never hear. It's not true. You hear its approaching shriek with its terrific crescendo of noise, – just for a second. Then you're dead. You can't tell anybody anything.

I had just time to cry out 'Please God, don't, don't let me—' when the shell exploded with an ear-splitting crash. Everything inside my head seemed to break. I was conscious just long enough to feel myself blasted out of the crater on to something wooden; just long enough to know that Jock was dead.

Months later, when my mental faculties were working normally again, I was able to complete my unfinished prayer.

But not with 'don't let me be killed', which are the words I would have used had I remained conscious long enough. Instead I made a request: 'Please God, don't let me ever be ungrateful.'

CHAPTER FOUR

The 'Lost' Months

'Miss E.M. Christian, 35 Windsor Road, Bexhill
o/ Sea, Sussex, Blighty. 21/12/17. Just a p.c. en route to let you
know I am still A.1. Will write letter at first opportunity. –
Happy Xmas. Best love & x's Ronald.'

From 6 November to the end of March there are only isolated happenings which I can remember. Those I do recall come to mind most vividly, – like a short film suddenly projected in a darkened cinema, followed by a lengthy black-out.

During this 'twilight' period I had lucid intervals. These were the times when I wrote home. Ella tells me my letters were very heavily censored at this time, probably because I expressed either depression or unpatriotic sentiments or both.

You will want to know how I came to be rescued after being

thrown out of the shell crater by the explosion that killed Jock. I just don't know.

All I can say is that some fellows had the courage to go out and bring me to safety before I was blown to smithereens. Whoever they were, – Harry and the sarge perhaps, – I owe them my undying gratitude, for they certainly saved my life.

Now, this is the way I intend to tell of my life during those extraordinary 'lost' months. As soon as a recollection comes to mind I shall jot it down. One train of thought usually leads to another and a sort of chain reaction sets in. Then I shall have to do some sorting out, rather as if a child had thrown the pieces of several different jig-saw puzzles on to the floor and had to find not only which pieces belong to which puzzle, but how each individual puzzle fits together. Already some of the 'pieces' I have in my note-book are fitting together. Some things which have mystified me for a couple of generations are coming together to make a recognizable pattern.

So now I'll continue.

Trying to Remember

It was the suddenness of the jab that woke me up. Anti-tetanus again, no doubt.

Where am I? I can't recognize the place or any of my companions.

A voice is saying, 'Get up and take those puttees, boots and trousers off.'

I feel 'swimmy' as I swing my feet to the floor so that I can sit on the edge of the bed. The light is very, very bad and I have sharp pains behind the eyes. 'Oh God! I'm not going blind, am I?' I put my fingers to my face and panic-stricken feel around my eyelids. They seem all right. I blink the eyelids up and down. They seem all right too. Then why does everything look so blurred and so dim?

I stoop to unfasten one puttee and see the gash in my trouser-knee. The puttee is sodden with a half-dried, sticky reddish slime. It's blood. But I have only a <u>little</u> cut in my knee so the blood can't have come from that . . . Oh God! It must be Jock's blood . . . I'm overcome by a fit of coughing . . . gas . . . then I faint.

This isn't the same place. A doctor has just dug a piece of shrapnel out of my neck. I can't see him but he's saying 'A little souvenir for you.' He comes from behind. He's wearing a grey coat . . . or is it a white coat that looks grey to me?

He is holding something in front of my face. It is the 'souvenir'. I have to force my eyes into focus to see what lies in the palm of his hand: a jagged scrap of iron the size of an acorn. I watch him fold a piece of paper into four, drop the shell fragment into one of its corners, fold it over again and hand it to me. 'Only skin deep,' he adds. 'You're damn lucky!'

'This yours?' An R.A.M.C.[10] orderly is holding up the cigarette case Ella gave me. I lean over to look closely, nod and take it from him. There is a deep dent in the engraved front. 'The bit that did <u>that</u> got away. Saved the M.O. the troubled of hunting for it inside your chest.'

I'm sick again. Then comes another fit of coughing. I can still smell the gas that started it, – or think I can.

*

10 Royal Army Medical Corps, or 'Rob All My Comrades' according to your point of view.

What am I doing here? Someone is asking 'What's your first name, mate? Lucky?' He is holding up the little horseshoe. They've emptied the contents of my kitbag on to a table. There's some spare clothing too which I recognize as my tunic and forage cap. I look down and find I am wearing fresh trousers, puttees and boots. Someone is telling me to put the tunic on. 'Check this lot here,' he says, 'and sign for them.' I do it, – like an automaton incapable of thought.

I'm wearing a new undervest and shirt. Who put them on me? I don't know any of these chaps. Who are they? And where's Jock got to?

Crash! My brain woke up from its torpor. 'Jock's dead. It's all your fault. You gave him a cigarette, remember?' Oh God! I'll never be able to smoke a fag again without thinking of him. Why didn't I die too?

'Hey! Are you Bombardier Skirth?' A sergeant is waking me up from a dream. I nod. He is holding a paper. 'Your number's come up. Show a leg! You're on the Christmas leave list.' I pull myself up. Christmas leave? I feel dazed.

'What's the date?' I ask.

'The tenth,' he replies.

'Tenth of November doesn't sound much like Christmas to me,' I say sarcastically.

He stares hard at me. 'Are you bloody mad? It's the tenth of December.' He gives me the look of helpless despair one would give to an imbecile, and stalks off.

The tenth of December? Then to-morrow's my birthday. I'll be twenty. A big boy now, out of my teens.

I sink down on the edge of a hard plank bed. Where the hell am I? Am I in a camp? A hospital?

My memory just doesn't work. The harder I try the bigger the blanks become.

I was knocked out at Passchendaele? Right. Jock was killed at the same time? Right. Then there's five weeks to account for . . .

An orderly comes in with some papers he lays on the table. I call out to him, 'Where are we, chum?'

'Buckingham Palace,' he replies sardonically.

I think hard. Mustn't take things too seriously.

'And you're George the Fifth? Pleased to make your acquaintance, your majesty.' I extend my hand humbly.

It seems to have been the right answer. 'Well, if you must know, Abbeville,' he confides, then disappears.

Abbeville! That's in France, not Belgium. Some way behind the line. There's a hell of a lot been happening in the last month that I don't know about!

Over the bed next to mine there is a small piece of looking glass on a shelf. I reach for it and take it to the hut door. I stumble, surprised to find my left knee tightly strapped. Then I notice there is a bandage and some strapping round my left wrist.

Outside the sun is shining but the light seems funny, like when there's an eclipse. I hold the mirror up to examine myself. I look a pretty ghastly sight. They've taken most of the hair off the left side of my head and there is a plaster dressing where the shell splinter had been. My cheek and neck that side are the colour of gun-metal.

I replace the mirror and stretch out on the camp bed, feeling empty and lonely.

Blighty for Christmas! Ella, Mum and Dad, turkey and Christmas pud! A hot bath!

I ought to be frantic with joy. I've waited months for this news. But I can't go home looking and feeling like this.

I'm scared about something else too. They must have got my conduct sheet. Snow would have put it all down in writing: insolence, insubordination, desertion. They'll probably court-martial me and it will be my word against Snow's, a Bombardier's statement against a Major's. There's no doubt which one <u>they</u> will accept.

Remember, I tell myself, that pill-box got a direct hit. It must have at least concussed Snow. Perhaps killed him outright! That was my hope. Dead men tell no tales. But, <u>if</u> he had survived and I was put on the carpet I must lose my memory. Yes! That was it. Shell blast did funny things to men. 'I can't remember a thing.' Oh hell! I can. Why do you forget the things you want to remember and remember the things you want to forget?

They've sent for me. Got to accompany Sergeant to the Guard Room. I'm for the high jump all right.

Why do they give you a medical first? I must play up the shell shock bit for all I'm worth. The gas cough ought to help; that's real anyway.

R.A.M.C. orderly says, 'Get on these scales.' 'Do they usually weigh you before they shoot?' I ask, trying to be funny. 'Dunno,' he replies. 'Haven't shot many lately.'

There's a miserable-looking little squirt of an officer at a table with a bottle of booze and a half-emptied tumbler in front of him. 'Nine stone one,' mutters the orderly and writes it on my card. ('So I've lost a stone,' I think.)

'Who's he?' I point to the squirt, who seems to be dozing off.

'Who the hell d'ye think? The M.O.,' he mutters. 'Drunk half the time. Gets five bob per head for passing all walking wounded A.I.' I have a fit of coughing (genuine). 'That's no bloody use,' says the orderly. 'He's deaf as well as drunk.'

Now I've got to have an eye test. I tell him I've been having trouble with my sight, – 'Like looking through smoked glass all the time.'

'What a bloody shame!' he exclaims in fake sympathy.

'See that test card over there?' he asks.

I say, 'Yes, but—'

'O.K.' he says, 'as long as you don't say <u>what</u> card? That makes me bloody angry.'

He ticks off another square on my card. My sight's good enough to see it's headed with my number, name, rank and unit. 'You won't work your ticket with him, mate.' He nods to the squirt, who appears to have fallen asleep. 'If you've got two legs, two arms, one eye, – and can stand up without holding on to a chair, he'll grade you A.I. and back you go up the bloody line!'

Gradually it was seeping through into my fuddled brain that this was no court-martial procedure.

The orderly laid the completed card in front of the M.O., who pulled himself up with difficulty, took a one-second look at me through bleary colourless eyes, pulled his fountain pen from his pocket, marked a bold A.I. on the card and emptied his glass.

There's a blank now. The next thing I can recall is travelling somewhere in a horse box.

See Europe by Train

Klik-klok, – klik-klak . . . klik-klok, – klik-klak. The rhythm of the train wheels gets on your nerves. We've been in this damn truck for hours and its speed has never exceeded that of a push-bike.

Klik-klok, – klik-klak . . . klik-klok, – klik-klak. At this rate we'll be lucky if we get New Year Leave, let alone Christmas . . . We can't be heading for Boulogne or we would have been there hours ago. So it will be Le Havre . . . Or Cherbourg perhaps? Wish I had a map . . . Wouldn't help much though; none of the stations we pass through have names . . . probably removed for security reasons.

Klik-klok, – klik-klak . . . klik-klok, – klik-klak. All the fields are covered with greyish snow. We're freezing . . . Hope there's another hot dixie of char at the next stop.

The four other chaps in this truck play pontoon or solo whist day and night. Lucky we've got enough candles. We don't have any windows. It's a horse box really, no seats, only straw on the floor. The only time light comes in is when we slide the door along, then the icy wind comes in and it's cold enough to freeze a brass monkey.

They don't care much for me, because of my stripe, I expect, – they think I'll start throwing my weight around soon. They needn't worry. I didn't come through Passchendaele to sit on anybody or be walked on by anyone. It's too much damn trouble ordering blokes about.

'Hey lads,' I say, 'where are we going?'

The nearest one swings round and replies, 'Beggared if I know. Don't you, Bombardier?'

'Don't any of you know?' I ask.

'Not a bloody thing,' is their answer.

'Isn't this the Blighty leave train?' I enquire.

'Is it hell? You must be joking. Nobody here's going on leave.' They all look at me incredulously.

'What's the matter, Bomb? You must have been having a kip when they shouted "All leave cancelled." Don't you remember?'

*

I return to the 'doorway'. I have it open just wide enough for me to sit on the floor and dangle my legs. I cover my knees with my greatcoat. One advantage of being the only N.C.O. is that they can't order me to shut the bloody door. I want to know what's going on in the outside world.

Klik-klok, – klik-klak . . . klik-klok, – klik-klak. Another blinking stop. What for this time?

I lower myself to the track . . . still have to be careful of that groggy knee, though the kneecap seems to have stopped sliding about . . . I look along the train . . . it's the longest I've ever seen, – with open gun-carrying wagons hitched behind the engine, followed by what looks like half a mile of cattle trucks.

Every one bears the same legend as ours stencilled on its side:

HOMMES 40
CHEVAUX 8

Let's work that out . . . If 8 horses = 40 men, then 1 horse = 5 men.

Ours is the very last one. I'm damn lucky . . . don't have to share with thirty-nine other chaps or even seven and four-fifths horses! Only four fellows and a load of crates.

I trudge through the snow to take a look at the loco which has to haul this colossal load. It's a monster, – looks as though they've borrowed it from a Wild West railroad film . . . Has everything, including bells on the top and an immense cow-catcher-cum-snowplough in front.

There's a queue forming to obtain hot water. The driver presses some magic knob and boiling water hisses out from near the wheels into the dixies of tea-leaves. By the time I get back my truck-mates have already brewed up.

*

The train's on the move again. I look at my wrist to see the time, forgetting that I haven't got a watch there. Of course I haven't, – they took bits of watch-glass out of me.

Klik-klok, – klik-klak . . . klik-klok, – klik-klak. Maximum speed now, a steady twelve miles an hour. Most of France seems to be uninhabited. Everywhere we've been, everywhere we go, it's flat and covered with this greyish snow . . . or do my eyes just think it's grey? I doze off.

We're in a siding now. The pontooners have wakened me because 'grub is up'. Chef's Special again: bully stew, pork and beans followed by hard rice grains in tepid water . . . Hell! When shall we taste real food again?

Klik-klakking along once more. Now it's dark . . . Candles (– we've found a box-full –) in bottlenecks are lit . . . cards are dealt . . . I'm too weary even to watch . . . Don't want to read either . . . Fall asleep, thank God.

Daylight again . . . was that the first, second or third night? What does it matter, anyway? One of the cardplayers tells me we passed through a big town just before daylight . . . He couldn't see any name.

I doze off once more and when I wake the train is stationary again . . . Push the door open quietly because the chaps are asleep.

I look down at the rail-track, still snow-covered . . . I blink my eyes and look again. The snow is <u>white</u>. I'm overwhelmed with joy for a moment . . . then shut my eyes and open them slowly to make sure. I am wide awake now. I glance back inside to make sure my companions haven't been disturbed, then jump carefully down. I look along the train. No one else is stirring.

There is a broad river on the far side of a snow-covered field. Beyond it— Oh God! I thought my eyes were all right and now I've started seeing things.

I seem to see an island floating on a silvery white ocean. Mists are slowly clearing and revealing a fairy-tale city. It stands far away on a rocky height. There are battlemented towers, roofs of houses, spires, and on the summit of a high church a statue of a saint or god.

The mist which had made it look like an island is gone. All the buildings are snow-topped and, as I watch, the tiled roofs, the castle, the tower with its statue all turn from white to silver and then from silver to gold. The snow lying on the field has become golden too. I do not know whether to cry, or pray that I have not gone out of my mind.

I turn away from the fantasy city and, rounding the corner of the truck, am nearly blinded by the brilliance of the rising sun. It is a dazzling half-sphere climbing from behind a distant hill, flooding the whole world with a golden radiance. I swing round hurriedly, apprehensively. The roof-tops, spires and towers change from shining gold to glowing orange, the high statue throwing back such golden brightness that you would think an arc lamp had been switched on as a beacon.

With a start, I realize that the train is moving again. I climb aboard, still not wholly convinced that what I witnessed was not an illusion. Before my brain registers the fact, the train has passed through another station. Miraculously, in a hundred yards or so it decelerates to yet another stop. I jump down and hurry to the nearest platform.

There in letters a foot high is the 'clue' I want: –

AVIGNON

I return in a trance. This can't be the Avignon! The Avignon I've read about is away in the south of France, in the Rhône Valley somewhere, far away from snow and ice.

The children's rhyme starts singing inside my head:

> Sur le pont d'Avignon
> L'on y danse, l'on y danse
> Sur le pont d'Avignon
> L'on y danse tout en rond

The men are waking now, sliding open the doors and hitting the tea-trail once again. I hurry along to where the great locomotive is discharging its hissing liquid into the waiting dixies. There, smiling benevolently, is the moustachioed driver, looking very, very French in his blue beret.

I shout up to him, '*Qu'est-ce que c'est, cette ville?*' and point in the direction of the city.

The driver's smile broadens on hearing my school-French accent.

'*Avignon, mon ami. Avignon. France-Sud.*'

I call out, '*Merci, merci,*' filled with joy at discovering the city is indeed real. Then a disturbing thought comes into my head. I run back and ask the driver our destination.

'*Pour moi, Marseille,*' he replies. '*Pour vous, je ne sais pas.*' Then, patting the side of his driving cab, '*C'est la guerre!*'

My heart and spirits sink. To me Marseille means troop-ships. Troop-ships sailing to the eastern Mediterranean. Perhaps to Palestine. Perhaps to Turkey – for Salonica, which from all accounts is another death-trap.

Back in the train again. Those four play their card games inexhaustibly. Just watching them sends me to sleep. I have asked them not to wake me for anything except food.

One of them peels off the patch from my neck to examine the wound. He tells me it has healed round the edges but there is a raw place about the size of a thumbnail. We haven't any new dressing so I get him to stick the old one back. *C'est la guerre!*

I wake up to a gentle rocking. My worst fears have been realized: we are at sea. Why can't I remember going aboard ship? Then comes the answer, a very muffled klik-klok, klik-klak. We <u>are</u> still in the train. The wheels are only just audible, the swaying of the wagon caused by the curves of the rail-track.

The air blowing into the truck feels warm. I lean out and look upward and above is the bluest sky I have ever seen, with tiny puffs of brilliant white clouds floating in it. I am seeing colours as they really are! There is no snow to be seen.

Another hour . . . We keep entering and leaving tunnels, passing through stations which <u>do</u> have names, but they mean nothing to me . . . Now we're shunted onto yet another siding for yet another long wait . . . I slip down onto the track. We are on the outskirts of an industrial town, with tall smoking chimneys and high factory buildings, and in the distance I can see the masts of ships rising from behind warehouses.

Is this Marseille?

Two Redcaps (Military Police) order me back, saying that no man is permitted to leave the train. I wait until they become involved in an argument with some others, and slip away unnoticed by ducking under the train buffers. I can see a station not a couple of hundred yards ahead.

My arrival on that station platform must have caused considerable surprise. I was quite possibly the first Tommy those passengers had ever seen.

There, plain as a pikestaff, was the name of the town:

SAVONA

Where the hell was Savona? I'd certainly never heard of it.

I go over to the kiosk and select a view-card from a display stand. (I'm afraid I didn't see the view it depicts: no promenade, no fountains, only the inside of the station and some buildings alongside the railway.)

I fish out a handful of French money and offer it to the kiosk proprietor. '*Combien?*' I ask. He looks closely at the coins and replies very slowly, '*Ici, c'est l'Italie. Ce n'est pas la France ici.*'

Italy! I gasp. Then, to my delight and astonishment he says in English, 'Il signore, you are English soldier.' I say I am, and hasten to explain why I have no time to chat. He quickly grasps the situation. I select several bars of chocolate and packets of biscuits. Oh! It seems ages since I have been able to indulge in such luxuries. I take the French notes from my wallet and put them with the coins and my new friend writes their value on a paper bag, calculates their equivalent in Italian currency, deducts the amount of my purchases, then gives me my due. (I hope he took a fair commission for himself!)

I ask him the date and with his pencil write my message to Ella. I ask about postage costs but he shakes his head, assuring me that the precious card will be on its way before noon.

I rejoin the train, no one any the wiser. No one, that is, but me. For I have discovered from my first Italian acquaintance that we are forty-five kilometres west of Genoa and heading for that city.

And what a colourful scene there is as we klik-klak slowly through Genoa station. Smiling girls dressed in brightly col-oured clothes stand on the platform with baskets of fruit and flowers. As we go by they throw oranges and sprays of golden mimosa into our carriages. The news of the arrival of the first British troop train in Italy has reached them before we have. We lean out, waving to them as they blow us kisses.

After so many months of stark ugliness, this little episode glows like a jewel in my memory. And to think that this summer-like scene took place on 21 December! I feel cheered up enough now to take out my sewing gear and mend the slashed tunic pocket. I polish my boots, shave (in cold water) and generally spruce up my appearance, feeling that the least I can do for our Italian Allies is to look presentable.

By that evening we found ourselves travelling into what looked like a different country and what felt like a different climate. The sun was setting behind a mountain range on our left, which meant that we were now going northwards, away from the Mediterranean coast. Evidently we were climbing, – our speed became a permanent 'dead-slow'. The temperature dropped rapidly and, as darkness fell, it began to snow.

With the return of the snow my spirits sank. How I was beginning to hate it! I don't think it was so much the snow's fault as its association with the man who bore the same name.

I remember very little of the last stage of that week-long journey. It had begun in a cloud of muddled impressions and it finished similarly. In the early dawn of 23 December 1917 our thousand-mile train journey came to an end. We had arrived at Verona, northern Italy.

A Little Bit of History

As these events happened so long ago it might not be out of place to interpolate a few paragraphs of background information to explain why we were in Italy at all. Not that we knew then, – we hadn't the slightest idea.

In the autumn of 1917, following the collapse of Russia (then fighting on our side), the Germans had been able to transfer troops from eastern Europe to the Italian front, which for two and a half years had been a bulwark against attacks on France's rear. The front was in the Alps, stretching in an arc from the Swiss border along the old frontier between Austria and Italy and down to the Adriatic beyond Trieste.

On 24 October, the combined Austro-German forces broke through the hitherto impregnable Alpine Front at Caporetto. It was the most appalling military catastrophe in Italian history. 400,000 Italians 'took to their heels', 200,000 were taken prisoner and colossal quantities of guns and equipment fell into German hands.

The remaining Italian armies retreated eighty miles across the plains beyond the flooded River Piave, almost due north of Venice. It looked like the end of the war for Italy. On the Western Front, Haig (G.B.) and Foch (France) got together and decided that reinforcements must be sent before the Italians surrendered altogether. My battery was on the first train sent to Italy.

By the time the Anglo-French divisions arrived, the Italians had reorganized and halted the enemy by their own efforts. Our contributions to the defence of Italian territory, and to the advance a year later which resulted in victory, were so insignificant as to be negligible.

A War-Time Christmas

23 December 1917

Breakfast (–ugh) in Verona station siding. Stores, equipment, and men loaded into wagons and transported along snow-covered roads to small town an hour's drive away: San Martino. Very quiet. No civilians walking streets. Some large detached houses all shuttered and empty.

Personnel parade in paved quadrangle surrounded by cloisterish buildings. (School or convent perhaps.) We're being sorted into regimental units. R.G.A. men number about four dozen. They can't make a battery out of that!

They're all complete strangers to me. Where are our officers?

Somebody yells, 'Grub up,' and there's a stampede. Then comes an announcement . . . Sorry, no food yet. Supplies haven't come through. All dismiss.

We, the R.G.A. group, are shouted at by a B.S.M. (Battery Sergeant Major) in a new uniform. We're led into the forecourt of a large faded-looking villa: 'Casa Bianca'. Was lucky enough to get a picture, poor though it is.

Inside the house we see a fine entrance hall with stone staircase leading to upper floor. B.S.M. shows us our quarters: one vast stone-floored room devoid of furniture. He bellows orders – no other part of building to be used except 'bog' downstairs, garden out of bounds, etc., etc.

'Oh yes?' I think. 'We'll see about that!' Outside in the forecourt a lorry has arrived. We file down to each collect two blankets and one palliasse (canvas sack stuffed with straw) and hump them up staircase. Decide for yourselves where you sleep, shouts B.S.M. There's no effing beds.

All very polite and hospitable, – the true Christmas spirit! Perhaps he'll come and sing us a carol or two later.

I was confronted with the one situation I most wanted to avoid, being one of a crowd. More than anything I longed for solitude and seclusion. For fifteen long months I had been deprived of it.

I stood by the doorway watching the men choose their bits of floor. They weren't active service men. My guess was they were all recent 'call-ups' of the 35–40 age group. I might be only half their age in years but compared with them I was a veteran in soldiering.

A short little fellow with a puckish wrinkled face was nearest. I went over and asked him where he came from.

'Peckham,' he answered.

'That's London, isn't it?'

'You bet it bloody well is.'

He was just the type I wanted. 'Have a fag?' I offered.

'Haven't had a bloody drag all day,' says he. 'Ta very much, Bombardier.'

I had several packets of Red Hussars in my pack. I'd been saving them up.

'What's your name?'

'Sparrer. Alf Sparrer.'

'Listen, Alf. Take these.' I handed him the packet. 'I'm finding a billet for myself. Not up here. I don't want anyone to know but you. Do you take your rum ration?'

'Do I take—'

'All right,' I interrupted. 'You can have mine every time rum's up. No charge. That is, if we make a deal.'

'Carry on, Bombie,' said Alf.

*

I began my unauthorized tour of exploration. Under the left-hand stairway (it was one of those grandiose double-flight affairs meeting on a landing) I discovered a door with its key still in the lock. I opened it.

At the end of a short passage was a large doorless store-cupboard, lighted by a ceiling window. I took possession there and then.

When the men upstairs had all wandered off I brought my two kitbags, blankets and other odds and ends into my retreat. Then I returned to the landing and helped myself to a good handful of candles from a box lying there as well as an extra, third blanket.

I took the key from my door and locked myself in, lit a candle and examined my hermit's cell. The tops of the large boxes stored there were all nailed down but one made a splendid table. There were some objects stacked upright against the dark wall. I pushed some cases aside and what did I find? Two camp beds! My luck was unbelievable. I lifted one out, tested it for stability and strength and graded it A.1. To complete my comfort I returned upstairs and collared a couple of palliases to lay on the bed. It was as good as the Ritz.

While there was still daylight I explored further. Another door led into a large scullery-washhouse. At the far end was an outside door, also with a key in it, which opened on to an enclosed back garden the far gate of which gave access to an alley leading to the main street. I would be able to arrive and leave unnoticed.

I had observed the *padrone* of the local café, the Trattoria Garibaldi, getting ready for business. (It isn't every Christmas that 250 thirsty men arrive in your village from a foreign country.) So there was <u>one</u> civilian in our street, and a jolly useful one too!

*

I made my pact with Alf. If anybody upstairs made enquiries for me he was to say I'd just gone down to the 'lav' (which, by the way was another indispensible amenity, not being the one the 'mob' were using), then come down and give three taps on my door. If it was locked he'd know I'd gone out.

Now all this scheming was the beginning of an 'operation' I had thought out in my more lucid moments on the train. From the very first opportunity (– and this was it –) I was going to fight the war my way. I couldn't <u>stop</u> the war, it is true, but nor could they stop me from doing what <u>I</u> wanted, <u>if</u> I kept my head. I would co-operate superficially with my Yes, sirs and Very good, sirs, – while doing the very opposite if I wanted to.

I had made a good start. Luck, and Alf, were with me. My hideout remained undiscovered during the whole of our stay in San Martino.

I said earlier that more than anything I yearned for privacy. At last I had secured it, at least for a while. Rightly or wrongly I was convinced that the only way I could work out my regeneration was to have opportunities for contemplation. (Nobody had heard of yoga in those days.) I had to devise a philosophy of living, or else go to pieces completely.

I had gone through an unimaginable set of experiences. I had denied my God and lost faith in my religion and my fellow men. At Passchendaele I had virtually been killed. Now, in Italy, I had to bring about my own resurrection. How to do it was a problem I couldn't hope to solve surrounded by people with whom I had nothing in common.

Christmas Day 1917

No church bells! . . . Suppose they're prohibited by war regulations . . . Am feeling a bit depressed.

Look through the scullery window. It's a white Christmas all right . . . well, a greyish-white one. Cheer up . . . Happy Christmas!

Ella and her parents will be at Communion, I expect. I know Mum will be. Then they'll all have a busy morning preparing the Christmas fare. Wonder if food has got scarce at home.

8.30. Breakfast up. Good thing there's a striking clock within earshot as I haven't a watch. Splendid Christmas breakfast: slices of bully fried in what tasted like axle oil but with actual <u>bread</u> instead of hard tack. And plenty of tea made in the posh Sir Thomas Lipton style. Hooray!

An announcement: all personnel to attend special Christmas Parade, 11.00 hours. Commander-in-Chief to address first contingent of B.E.F. in Italy. <u>Also</u> pay has come up. (Item No. 1 booed, item No. 2 cheered.)

C-in-C appears, accompanied by an assortment of Brass Hats. Looks to me a bit like an inflated Charlie Chaplin, with a moustache like Kitchener's (points clipped). Lord Cavan of something or other. Now he's talking a lot of tripe about our gallant Italian ally's call for assistance. How we've rallied to their call, how we are ambassadors of Britain and liberators of the Italian people. I just manage to suppress the urge to vomit until the parade is over.

When Dr. Stokes got married, my family moved to a home opposite a public house in the older part of town. At the time, work on a new sea-defence scheme and a new Promenade had attracted scores of 'navvies' to the area. On Saturday evenings they would gather in the forecourt of our tavern, drinking, singing and brawling until they had drunk the place dry. On hot summer evenings the foul odours of stale beer and sweat would hang in the air and penetrate into the rooms where we ate and slept. The combined effect produced in me such a loathing for alcoholic drink that I never touched a drop of it until I joined the

Army. After landing in France I acquired a liking for *vins blancs*, but as for spirits of any kind I think I would rather have drunk petrol!

So back to the story of my first war-time Christmas. It seemed that this was the one day of the 365 when I should come out of my hermit's cell and seek some company. I made, for me, a very bold decision. I would join the crowd in the trattoria opposite and, for the first time in my young life, get gloriously drunk.

When I entered it was packed to capacity, – and every customer was wearing a British uniform. Alf Sparrow and some others were nearest the bar. I pushed my way through to join them. I treated them to anything and everything they fancied while I, not to be outdone, sampled almost every drink on offer.

I was fascinated by the array of vari-coloured bottles. They produced in me a glowing sense of *joie de vivre* I hadn't experienced since the days of the French *estaminet*. I joined in the songs: all my worries and depressions drowned in the medley of Heaven-knows-what I swallowed.

Alf helped me stagger home and, first making sure no one observed us, came with me into my retreat. I dimly remember him throwing the key on my table after straightening me out on the camp bed.

That night I went through hell. For hours I suffered agonies of nausea, colic and diarrhoea. I had never felt so ill in all my life.

Experience, as I have written earlier, is a grand teacher. If that was the Dolce Vita, it wasn't for me.

I believe our 'Christmas Dinner' was served about 3 o'clock the following afternoon. I don't know whether there was roast turkey with cranberry sauce as I wasn't present. All I recall having that day was:

a. several dixies of tea which good old Alf brought me,
b. a splitting headache and
c. more sickness.

The hangover worsened the effects of shell shock, and the head pains continued for several days. No painkilling drugs were available so there wasn't much I could do.

On the Carpet

A few days later I was ordered by the B.S.M. to report to the O.C.'s office. 'And smarten your bloody self up,' he added, as sweetly polite as ever.

A feeling of panic came over me. Something must have come through about the Passchendaele affair. I tried desperately to calm myself and collect my thoughts. 'You're for it all right,' I told myself. 'It was bound to come. But one thing they can't charge you with is desertion. Here you are, still wearing the King's uniform, still with your unit. You've got to keep cool. Say "Yes, sir," "No, sir," or "I cannot remember, sir." Whatever you do, you don't say you remember Snow, Jock or anything else about that day.'

I walked to the Battery Office, stepped smartly up to the table and saluted. After a short pause ex-Captain, now Major, Jordan asked me to fetch a chair and sit down. I breathed a sigh of relief. Surely you weren't asked to sit to hear the charges against you.

Next to Jordan was a First Lieutenant I'd never seen before.

As the major spoke he was turning over papers on the table in front of him. He said my regimental number, name and rank – apparently reading from the top sheet. All I had to say was 'Yes, sir.'

Suddenly he glanced up from the paper in his hand and said, 'It seems you had a tough time before being knocked out at Passchendaele?'

I couldn't think of a suitable reply so I nodded weakly, too bewildered to do anything else.

Then he did an extraordinary thing. He took the papers from the table, tore them into small pieces and threw them into the waste-paper basket.

As though from a distance I heard him giving me orders: 'You will continue as B.C.A until the reorganization of the battery has been completed. You will be given duties, mainly clerical, which I shall rely on you to perform efficiently. You will be excused parades; instead you will report to me or Lieutenant Salisbury', – he pointed towards his junior officer, – 'daily at 0900 hours. Any questions, Bombardier?'

'No, sir. Thank you, sir.'

'That will be all.'

I saluted and left.

I could hardly believe my eyes and ears. I hadn't been able to see the papers on Jordan's desk but I was willing to bet that one of them was my conduct sheet.

A Half-Day Excursion

New Year's Week, 1918

My first mission for my new employers! Lieutenant S. hands me an envelope containing official documents to be delivered personally to R.T.O.,[11] *Verona. Light van waiting. I'm required to bring back sealed envelope and package from said R.T.O.*

11 Railway Transport Officer.

The driver's an R.E.[12] *man and a miserable-looking one at that.
'Driving on the right's a bloody nuisance,' is his opening remark.*

'You'll get used to it,' I reply.

Depressing conditions . . . snowing or slushy roads beneath, steel-grey skies above, and as bloody cold as Catterick. We've been in Italy a week and haven't seen the sun yet.

Verona. R.T.O. is, as expected, self-important and pompous. (Why does every chap with a red band round his cap and a bit of gold braid think he's God?) He signs receipt for documents I've brought and informs me that the ones I have to take back won't be available (– stops to look at his wrist-watch –) for two hours.

I buy two post-cards and a writing pad. I notice an Italian–English phrasebook and a pocket-sized dictionary. Just what I'm looking for; have to learn some Italian now.

From the station there's a broad avenue flanked by 'posh' hotels and shops. I take a side turning that looks more promising. The buildings are all arcaded so you don't see there <u>are</u> shops until you're under the arches. The snow is now falling thickly so I'm glad of the protection the arcades afford.

Ah! Here's a tiny watchmaker's shop. Doesn't look too expensive. The proprietor is very understanding, though he has no English. I choose a nice-looking Swiss watch with luminous hands and figures.

Next door is a chemist's. I want some cough mixture and a roll of plaster. The chemist's face registers astonishment when he sees an English soldier. I ask him to examine the sore spot where my tunic collar chafes. It feels like a boil coming up.

The chemist seems unduly concerned about such a trivial injury. He disappears and returns with a box of white ointment, applies some to the wound and fixes an adhesive dressing over it. Shaking his head he tells me, 'Should see doctor . . . It is not good.'

12 Royal Engineers.

He offers me the ointment, together with a roll of bandage and a packet of lint. Then, after all his kindness and trouble he refuses to accept any payment. I say I am offended. He still refuses, saying, 'Signore . . . Me . . . I am more offended if you pay!' I thank him very sincerely and we shake hands, parting like friends of long standing.

Nearby there is a caffè *(in Italy they have two 'f's). I munch rapturously on some fat bread rolls filled with slices of salami and pickle, drink two cups of real coffee, and eat croissants, dipped in the cup in imitation of the locals who all crowd around me. I point in my phrasebook to the Italian for 'I do not speak Italian!' They are amused and slap me on the back.*

The food and drink taste heavenly and once more I have the greatest difficulty in paying for my purchases. I slip a note of the value I imagine the bill to be under a plate and leave.

The snow has stopped. I hurry down the main avenue and reach the bridge over the river. It's a big city, extremely picturesque. I look at my watch . . . Gosh! It's past 2 o'clock. No more time for sightseeing. There's a war on, you know.

I hurry back to the stazione, *sign for and collect sealed envelopes from his highness. Driver is waiting, not quite as charmed by Verona as I: 'Bloody stinking hole . . . Couldn't get a glass of beer anywhere.'*

The following day I had reason to feel considerably less cheerful myself. While alone in the office, making copies of our daily increasing Nominal Roll, I examined one of the papers enclosed in the package I had brought from Verona (not intended for my eyes of course):

Message from Major R.A. Snow, Officer Commanding 239 etc., etc. to Major D. Jordan temporarily i/c of aforesaid unit . . . It is hoped that Major Snow will resume command on completion of reorganization and/or expiration of his present term of leave.

The Turning Point

I believe it is possible to reach a depth of dejection from which there are only two ways of escape. Either one becomes insane, or by some means or other one lifts oneself out of it. I had reached that depth shortly after Christmas of 1917. Physically, of course, I was unwell. Mentally, very disturbed indeed.

I was in a new country. I felt friendless and alone. The three splendid friends I had become so fond of and the one whom I had loved like an elder brother were dead. I couldn't help thinking that but for me Jock might still be alive.

It is easy to be wise after the event, especially so fifty years later. At the age of twenty I knew nothing of psychology, – not that I know much about it now, – so how was I to understand that the cause of my mental malaise (is that the word?) was my burying a sense of guilt deep in my subconscious where it was slowly poisoning my personality?

There are just two more events from that time which I am able to call to mind. They occurred in the first week of January and almost every detail is firmly implanted in my memory. As to what happened afterwards I can only make guesses, – but more of that later.

One afternoon I felt a sudden urge to inspect the church opposite our White House. (You can see it in the viewcard of the Casa Bianca on p. 139.)

I crossed the road, noticing the somewhat unusual statues at the foot of the broad steps. Some boyhood prejudices against Roman Catholic superstitions and 'Popery' came into my mind. I looked up to the summit of the church's façade and observed yet another sculpted figure on its highest point. It was a very imposing edifice for such a small town.

The sky, which seemed to have been heavily overcast for weeks past, had brightened slightly; weak rays of wintry sunlight were beginning to slant down through small gaps in the clouds.

At the top of the steps I kicked the snow from my boots, lifted the latch and pushed the heavy timber door open. There was no porch: I stepped straight on to the stone flooring, then paused to allow my eyes to accustom themselves to the dim light. The first thing I realized was that the church was empty. (It was a curious thing, but I think of the whole village as being empty, – except for the military.) When at last my eyes had adjusted themselves, I took a few steps forward and, holding my breath in astonishment, looked around me. I was standing inside the most beautiful place of worship I had ever seen.

My thoughts went back to my own church at home, – and then to the cathedral at Winchester. The latter was a dozen times the size, magnificent in its vast Gothic splendour. You could have put the church of San Martino inside it and there would have been room to spare. My church of St. Barnabas was an austere red-brick barn in comparison: gaunt, bare, cold and lifeless except during service times.

This building was alive, a living poem of adoration and thanksgiving, a picture-book in stone, mosaic and paint, created as a thanks-offering by the artists, masons and sculptors whose work surrounded me. I stood overwhelmed by its beauty.

I am not ashamed of the feelings I am trying to recall. You must remember that for a year I had been deprived of the one thing that to me was as precious as life itself, my love of beauty. Nothing is uglier than brutality. War had nearly dehumanized me, so much so that I had thought all the joy I had once derived from music, art and nature had vanished for ever, – that never again would I have the opportunity or desire to gain happiness from them. I was glad I had the church to myself for I wouldn't have wanted anyone to see my tears as I sank to my knees and said, 'Thank you, Lord.' I felt like a blind man whose sight has been miraculously restored.

In my mind's eye I can still see the shaft of pale sunlight that shone through the upper window and projected a primrose-coloured circular patch on to the floor. There were no chairs in the central area. You had only to look downwards to see why: it was a picture-book of mosaics.

On either side of the central space was a row of round arches supported by marble pillars, heavily gilded. The spaces above and between the arches, and between the circular windows above, were ornamented with glittering mosaics and paintings, – and above all this, completely filling the wide circular ceiling, was a glorious representation in paint of the Ascension.

I seated myself on one of the chairs in the side aisle. At the far end I could see a statue of the Virgin Mary. Below, half a dozen candles of various lengths were burning. So there had been worshippers here, and recently too. When I looked up I noticed how their flickering light illuminated the under-surface of the arch above. It appeared to be gold-ornamented. I stayed there in the silence for a long time, thinking.

Suddenly I heard the door being opened from outside, followed by the noise of booted feet on the stone floor. I turned and watched a soldierly figure, helmet in hand, stride towards the altar steps, kneel upon one and cross himself. He was wearing the green uniform of the Italian army. An officer, evidently. He bowed his head as he prayed.

Below the altar steps there was a railed tomb, which from where I sat was somewhat obscured, and beyond it in a niche was a statue. The soldier rose from the steps, genuflected and then stopped in front of the sculpted figure. I saw him kneel again and pause, then taking two candles he fixed them on their brackets, lit them and dropped some coins into the nearby box. All the time he was completely unaware of my presence.

I followed him with my eyes as, his devotions completed, he walked back towards the entrance. Just before reaching it he halted, brought himself smartly to attention, looked upwards and gave a military salute. Then he opened the door and quietly disappeared into the street.

What was there, I asked myself, in an empty church that he could regard as an officer superior to himself? I rose and went to see.

The dimness was relieved by another ray of pale sunlight coming through that rounded window. It gave sufficient illumination for me to receive the answer. Above the doorway, suspended by bronze chains from the roof, was a near-life-sized oaken carving of Christ on the Cross.

The soldier's humility and dignified piety affected me more than I can say. I had come into a Roman church ready to sneer. But a cynical unbeliever would have found it hard to express derision in the face of such sincerity. Like someone in a quotation I only vaguely remember, I came to scoff and remained to pray.

Before leaving, I went to examine the tomb and the sculpture in the niche. They commemorated the same person. Lying on the tomb was the marble effigy of a knight in armour. But this knight was an unorthodox character. He was holding his sculpted sword the wrong way round, with its broken blade in his hand and the hilt lying across his chest. The weapon of war had been transformed into the cross of Christianity. Cut into the marble of the kerb surrounding the tomb was an inscription: 'Beati Pacifici.' My Latin wasn't up to much, but I could translate that without effort: 'Blessed are the Peacemakers.'

In larger Roman lettering at the foot of his tomb was his name. Of course! The knight was San Martino. You didn't need any knowledge of Italian to know what that was in English: Saint Martin.

This was where his remains lay, – this was his shrine. This magnificently decorated church had been erected in his memory and the village which had grown up outside had taken his name.

Where else had I heard of this saint? The pathetically ruined cathedral at Ypres, where those oafs were decapitating the little statues, – that was St. Martin's Cathedral. And, of course, London has its St. Martin in the Fields.

I walked slowly and thoughtfully away, wondering who, or what, he could be patron saint of.

It was not till much later that I realized that that experience marked the turning point in my young life. In the church of San Martino in the first week of 1918 I reached the end of the road to Disillusion. In fact I had already turned the corner and begun to take the road back.

I spent most of that evening taking a good look at myself. I was glad of the seclusion of my hermit's cell. Before I went to sleep that night I had got some things that had been disturbing me pretty well straightened out.

The following day I paid a second visit to the church. There was something very important I had to do.

A young woman was lighting a candle in front of the Virgin's statue. I concealed myself and waited quietly until she had left. It was essential that the church should be empty; I wanted to be alone.

I moved to a seat closer to the tomb of St. Martin and studied the sheet of paper I had brought with me. I had written a sort of summary of my reflections of the evening before. It was headed 'What I should be thankful for' and underneath was a sort of catalogue:

- That I am still alive.
- That I still have my sight.
- That I only pretended not to believe in God.
- That I have been brought from the Hell of Passchendaele into a peaceful Italian village.
- That it's possible the papers recording my military offences have been lost.
- That, though I hate the Army and the war, I have been given a job worthy of my ability.
- That I still have my love for Ella and she still loves me.

I had written a P.S. which read 'I am not to ask any favours, – only for forgiveness and moral courage.'

I folded the paper, put it into a pocket, knelt and whispered the appropriate prayers. Then I went over to the Virgin's shrine. Someone had placed a bowl of silvery-green Christmas roses on the table beneath. I looked again at the statue. I couldn't tell whether it was modelled in plaster, wood or marble. It was beautifully enamelled and gilded. The face had a more terrestrial beauty than a celestial one, as though the sculptor had copied one of the girls from a Botticelli painting. She looked very young too, – much too young to be holding a baby of her own. I suspect the designer's thoughts to have been anything but spiritual. Why were my thoughts straying in such an irreligious direction? Only because the face of the statue reminded me so forcibly of the girl I loved.

I regained my composure, took three candles and fixed them

on the little spikes provided, then lit them with the taper. I knelt, said, 'Thank you, Mary, you helped to make me very happy,' and passed on to the altar steps. I knelt again and once more expressed my gratitude for the preservation of my life, my limbs and my sight.

St. Martin had three candles too. After I had lighted them I placed some money in his box as I had in Mary's. I wasn't quite sure what to say to him so I just said, 'Thanks for having such a beautiful church built around you.' Finally, I walked to the doorway and gazed up at the hanging figure of Christ.

I didn't salute like my Italian confrere. I knelt and said just three words: 'Thank you, Lord!'

Then I made my vow. That is what I had really come for. I vowed to God that in return for his gift of life to me I would never, never knowingly again help to take a human life.

It wasn't going to be easy, I knew. But from somewhere or someone I would gain the moral courage to carry out my resolve.

Since writing about this episode I have investigated the St. Martin/San Martino legend. No, not legend, for he was a man of real flesh and blood.

He lived in the fourth century A.D. He was the son of a wealthy French nobleman and took up soldiering as his career. He was fond of the good things of life, particularly liquor. In spite of this, he distinguished himself in battles and won many awards for bravery.

One day it was revealed to him that killing, even in battle, was sinful in the eyes of God. Thereupon he left the Army, gave away all his earthly possessions and entered the Church. The rest of his life was spent preaching the gospel of peace throughout France and Lombardy.

But here is the most interesting bit. He is the patron saint of (1) all who are persecuted for their beliefs and (2) all reformed drunkards!

By pure chance, from the host of saints that might have been available, I had chosen the one most likely to understand me!

So now to the final event I can recall.

It started a day or two before the happenings I have just described, when shaving hurriedly in the morning I cut myself just below the left ear, where some reddish blotches had recently appeared. I had some difficulty staunching the bleeding but with the aid of a piece of the plaster I had bought in Verona I eventually succeeded. I got to the office on time and set about completing some written work unfinished from the previous day.

Mr. Salisbury came in. He was a pleasant-looking, somewhat nervous and completely inoffensive chap of about thirty, not ex-public-school-and-Sandhurst in the least, but one of the New Army types who were now being conscripted into the forces at home. He probably knew rather more about me than I would have wished, having had to censor my letters home. (This was the time when, as Ella told me later, most of what I had written was deleted.)

He observed the plaster and the red spots and asked me about them. In his opinion they should be looked at by an M.O., but as we had no M.O. nothing could be done. To tell the truth I was surprised he thought the matter important enough to comment on.

That afternoon with the aid of my shaving mirror and an extra bit of looking glass I was able to examine the sore area fairly closely, particularly the part behind the razor-cut. It was swollen and tender and it looked as though the shallow shrapnel wound which I'd believed to have healed was festering. In addition small red sore patches were spreading upwards into my hair. I still wasn't too worried, but I spread some of the antiseptic ointment the chemist had given me over the affected area, put the plaster back and tried to forget all about it.

The next day the blotches had become scaly and had spread another inch or so. When Major Jordan saw my condition he evidently suspected something contagious and instructed me to find a billet where I could be isolated from the other men. I confessed I already had one, whereupon I was sent 'home'.

The next morning a Red Cross Ambulance van drew up. I was told to collect my kit and go. The driver was a decent-looking young fellow a year or two older than me. I slung my gear into the van and climbed up beside him. We drove for half an hour or so along the snow-covered roads before reaching the outbuildings of a large hospital on a hilly slope on the outskirts of Vicenza. I was led into a civilian hospital. I don't remember seeing any nurses, only white-coated doctors and their auxiliaries. One of these came to inspect my rash. He was English-speaking, – at least <u>when</u> he spoke, which wasn't often. He gave me an injection and some evil-smelling preparation to apply to the neck wound and blotches. Then I was allowed to go, with instructions to return two days later.

The ambulance driver and I found a canteen nearby where we enjoyed some remarkably good coffee before he drove me back to San Martino. By the time we arrived I knew that he was English born, had a father in the diplomatic service and a Swiss mother, and that he was called Raymond Raggett.

Two days later I reported back. This time an Italian doctor examined me, did a certain amount of tut-tutting and gave me another injection and a different ointment to apply, – all to no purpose because a boil had developed on the edge of the wound and the sores continued to spread.

Third time lucky, they say! Raymond fetched me the last time, and said he thought I looked pretty groggy.

It was the Italian doctor again. (I say he was Italian, but I later learnt that he was a German, – what the dickens was a German doing on our side?) After inspecting the affected area he instructed an orderly to give the sores a swabbing with a solution that stung like hell. Then when I believed the ordeal to be over along came the doctor with what looked like a small scalpel the size of a nail-file. I soon found out what it was for. His theory was that to cure eczema, or whatever it was I'd got, you just dug the sores up one by one rather like weeding a garden.

Now I'm not particularly good at standing physical pain at any time. At that stage I was very near breaking point. He chose this moment for his master stroke, lancing the boil. (If you've ever had one of those minor afflictions I know I shall have your sympathy!)

I couldn't see what he was about to do but when he struck, well, I don't know what it's like to be hit by lightning but my guess is it's a similar sensation. I remember the stab of pain which shot through my head. I swung round in a sudden frenzy of anger and kicked out. I don't think my boot 'went in' because I fainted.

That is the only occasion I can recall when I completely lost my temper and went mad with rage. For all I know, though, I may have repeated that little histrionic performance during the ensuing two and a half months. Because from that moment – the moment of black-out – my memory went into hibernation.

As I said earlier, I hoped that recounting these experiences might awaken other long-forgotten memories, to provide me with clues as to what happened to me during the rest of that January, the whole of February and most of March 1918. But it hasn't, – so far.

San Martino, near Vicenza, northern Italy.
My first 'residence' on Italian soil. January 1918.
Casa Bianca marked with an 'X'.

CHAPTER FIVE

Rebirth and Rehabilitation

Panorama from Bella Vista. This sketch is a miniature copy of the one I drew for the Observation Post. It was made in 1918 but not inked over till after I left the army.

I have now to continue my story without any precise knowledge of what happened during the remainder of the 'lost months'. Some light has been shed on them; as I had hoped, one recollection has brought to mind another and that has led to a third and so on. But there are still many gaps unfilled.

I shall start with a day I can clearly remember.

1 April 1918
Cittadella, northern Italy

April Fool's Day. I'm fairly sure that in 1918 it was Easter Monday. It was also twelve months to the day since I set foot on the continent of Europe.

The location: 'A picturesque medieval town 14 miles east of

Vicenza, standing within red sandstone 14th century walls not far from the outliers of the Alps. Has some fine 17th and 18th century villas lining a beautiful road leading to the city of Treviso.' (According to my guidebook.)

I should think that description pretty accurate, – the only things I can remember about Cittadella are the blood-coloured walls, the tremendous view of the distant Alps and the villa which was our Battery H.Q.

I haven't the remotest recollection of where I had come from or where I was to go to next. All I recall is that stepping out of the train at Cittadella station I was met by Alf Sparrow. I remembered _him_ all right, – though he hardly recognized me as the 'drunk' he had put to bed on Christmas night.

Alf had a small truck waiting, but before setting off we had a coffee and a chat. I learnt that the battery had been shifted from San Martino to Cittadella weeks ago and had now moved on again, – to a village twenty-five miles away.

'We haven't been near the bleedin' war yet,' said Alf. 'Not that I'm anxious. What do you think the bleeders are making us do now? Building roads! Have the bleedin' guns come? Not on your life they 'aven't. Nor have my Thornies.' (The five-ton Thorny-croft lorries he'd been waiting for since January.) 'Somebody ought to go to Blighty and stir them b——s up . . . Blimey, you don't 'arf look different . . . How long is it since you went . . . January? Staying at the Savoy, I expect . . . They certainly bin feeding you up.'

He chucked my knapsack and kitbag over the tailboard and I climbed into the van beside him.

My new quarters turned out to be in one of those eighteenth-century villas mentioned in the guidebook. At the rear was an orchard so huge it seemed to go for ever, and every tree was in bloom.

I have only hazy recollections of my stay. The first thing that struck me was the name of the town itself. It was nice to be posted to a place that had my sweetheart's name on the end of it.

I can't remember much of the work I did then. I did a few spots of translating official correspondence[13] (– who told them I could do that? –) and made several journeys out into the towns of the district, helping drivers find their way. I do remember going to Treviso, Padua and Mêstre, – three of the most important towns in the province, – usually to supervise the collection of supplies.

As for my billet, I only remember two of its rooms. It was the largest house I was ever billeted in. The 'front' room was used as our office; everything except writing materials had been taken away. My sleeping quarters were at the back, also on the ground floor. They had French doors which opened on to a patio with a sort of pergola over which a very old wisteria had twined itself. It was just coming into flower. A short stretch of neglected lawn separated the patio from the cherry orchard.

The only other unusual feature was an antique metal-framed mirror, its black and gilt ornaments faded and dust-covered. The first time I looked in it I saw myself looking so fit and so glowing with health that I hardly recognized myself. The last time I remembered seeing myself had been at Abbeville, and what I had seen then had made me weep.

Early in the evening of my first day in Cittadella, I walked in the orchard, thankful to be alone. I didn't feel ready to 'mix' yet.

13 With the help of my pocket dictionary I was able to translate from Italian into English with fair accuracy. I believe that I must have taught myself during the 'lost' months. I would have been in continuous contact with Italian-speaking people in hospital.

I laid myself down beneath one of the trees, watching the little petals fall like gentle snow-flakes. Suddenly, out of my sleeping memory, a fact came to the surface which gave me a stab of pain in the head like a neuralgic spasm. I sprang to my feet and hurried as fast as my legs would take me towards the railway station. Breathless, I burst into the canteen and there, thanks be to God, was Alf with a mug of cocoa in front of him. I asked the question that had disturbed my serenity so violently and heard his reply.

'Snow? Never 'eard of no bleedin' Snow. Our O.C.'s Jordan. Wot's the matter, Bomb? Gone potty?'

I had, – with joy and relief!

I woke very early the following day, – just after daybreak. I dressed and strolled along the Cittadella road between the tall poplars which lined the road. Pale wreaths of mist rose from the fields, then thinned as the sun began to appear over the horizon behind me.

I walked under the archway into the citadel, then mounted a flight of steps, their dark crimson stone worn into hollows by the feet of centuries. At last I stood on top of the walls that almost completely encircle the town. No one was stirring in the streets below and not a sound could be heard.

To the east, the sun was now a red-gold globe in a cerise sky, just clear of the distant skyline, the hills which separate Italy from Austria. Turning towards the south and west, my eyes roamed over the great plains of Lombardy and Venetia, here and there gently broken by low hills. The mists had gone, revealing a draughtboard of cream and green, – fruits, blossom and squares of vines, mulberries and maize.

Then I turned full circle and looked northwards.

I believe I told you earlier that one of the books which

travelled all over Europe with me was Hillaire Belloc's *The Path to Rome*. I don't suppose anyone reads it nowadays. In my judgement then it was the finest travel book ever written.

> I saw a sight in the sky that made me stop breathing, just as great danger at sea, or great surprise in love or a great deliverance from death will make a man stop breathing . . . Sky beneath them and sky above them, remote from this world, peaks and fields of intense ice, they glittered as though they wore the armour of the armies of Heaven; they stood up like the walls of Eden. I say it again; they stopped my breath.

Belloc had seen the same vision as I did that morning, – his first sight of the Alps.

The next day I discovered a pile of newspapers and magazines stacked away for disposal. Having nothing better to do I rummaged through them.

They were all American, so I assumed that before the British had requisitioned the villa for their purposes, some Americans had been the previous occupants. I was very 'hard up' for reading matter and an hour went by quite pleasantly.

I found myself interested in some articles in a paper called the *Kansas City Star*. One of their youngest reporters sent a monthly news-letter home from Italy. He was driving an ambulance for the Italian army. I enjoyed his reports immensely because he seemed to have spent most of his time in places where I had just been and I gathered he was about my age.

Before Easter week ended, I had a letter from Ella, accompanied by a small sepia-tinted photograph. It had been taken specially for me on her seventeenth birthday.[14] We had parted fifty-five weeks before. Everywhere I had gone I had carried two precious possessions with me. The first was the cigarette case, now dented, which had helped save my life in Flanders. The second was the p.c.-sized photo of her as I remembered her on the day we first met, – a schoolgirl, just turned fifteen, – the picture I carried next to my heart and in my head.

There were times when I wondered how much she would have altered. Fifteen, sixteen and seventeen are the adolescent years of change. I gazed at the new picture till my eyes misted over and I read and re-read the letter that had come with it. The only words that came into my mind were the final line of that little song: 'And yet I love her till I die'! My heart was too full for any others.

Cartography

Now I must transport you to the foothills of the Italian Alps, about sixty miles north-west of Venice.

I was there on an assignment which provided some of the most enjoyable days of my soldiering life. I was allowed to work in my own way, in my own time, unsupervised. Nobody's life or safety was threatened and it was all carried out in the midst of breathtakingly beautiful scenery.

At the end of April 1918, our battery was still at only half-strength in personnel, – and at no strength at all in armaments. The lorries and howitzers still hadn't arrived, four months after we had come to help out the poor Italians!

Our Commander-in-Chief, Lord Cavan, who had honoured us with his gracious presence on Christmas Day (and hadn't been

14 This is the picture on p. xxviii.

seen since), was suddenly afflicted with a brain-wave. Someone must have informed him that he had troops who had been in Italy for sixteen weeks without firing a shot.

This is how I imagine he must have set about putting things right:

'Colonel, spread out that map! Good! What are all those red lines zig-zagging all over the place? Good lord! Really? Trenches. And what are all these curvy lines? Contours? Oh! never mind. Where's the front line? . . . What! That lot of zig-zags! . . . Pity these Italians haven't found out how to make a decent line of trenches. Right! Look, I'm putting a X here and another X there. We'll take that section over from them . . . What? Haven't any infantry to send there? Then send the artillerymen into the front line . . . If they haven't any bloody guns it's the best place for them . . . Order that battery you told me about forward and give the lazy blighters some fighting to do.'

What we were going to fight <u>with</u> he didn't explain, for there wasn't one rifle, Mills bomb or bullet between the lot of us. As for consulting the Italian commander who had been in charge before, I don't believe such a thought had entered his head.

The outcome of this inspired bit of military leadership was that one morning Major Jordan, Lieutenant Salisbury and I were making a tour of inspection of the area concerned in the take-over bid. My presence was required because I was reputed to be the best map-reader the battery possessed.

The sector we were to take over stretched for about 6.5 kilometres, and ran most of the way along the top of a mountain ridge, which, according to my map, was at an altitude of between 1,000 and 1,500 metres above sea level.

The first fact we discovered was that there was nobody to take over from. Not one single Italian, Frenchman, Australian, or even mountain goat.

In between admiring the splendour of the mountain scenery I gathered that the O.C. and Mr. S. were getting steadily angrier. They had ample reason because the problem of selecting suitable sites for our guns (if and when they arrived) over four miles of wild mountain territory would have baffled a Napoleon. The approach road was hopelessly inadequate. Hannibal would no doubt have got his elephants up there somehow, but howitzers, being somewhat bulkier, wouldn't be quite so obliging.

Besides we hadn't got either Hannibal or Napoleon. If we had, they would no doubt have asked the same questions as Jordan and Salisbury were asking: How do we get the guns up here to start with? Where do we put them when we've got them here? And what the hell do we fire at if ever we get them into position? We can't knock the bloody Alps down.

I found all this mildly amusing. After all it was their problem, not mine. I was there only as their records clerk.

At last they arrived at two conclusions: that nothing could be done until

1. the new military road had been completed, and
2. a detailed survey and maps of the terrain had been prepared.

The maps we had been supplied with showed no military installations, – positions of forts, dug-outs, Observation Posts, trench-lines, – in short nothing of any use to an occupying force. Who the blazes was going to draw up maps for the job in hand? the O.C. asked. He hadn't an officer to spare, short-staffed as he was: moreover none of them had the sufficient know-how.

I knew of someone who would be delighted to tackle the survey problem, – though he wasn't an officer. But I was too much of the 'old soldier' now to speak until I was spoken to. I had learnt never to volunteer for anything.

Major Jordan looked hard at me. 'Bombardier,' he asked, 'could you do it?'

'Well sir,' I replied, 'I would like to have a shot at it!'

I wasn't sure whether the look he gave me was one of surprise or desperation, – as though he'd scraped the bottom of the barrel and all he could find there was me.

'Then start right away,' he said.

The half-strength personnel of the battery were billeted in and around the village of Piovene, which was a picturesque half-inhabited place surrounded by vineyards and maize fields.

From my billet near the Command Post to the heights which are the scene of my story I had a climb of well over 3,500 feet, which took me anything from two and a half to three and a half hours. Quite often, though, I was given a lift to a point only a half-hour's scramble from my destination. The descent was easy: I could 'cut' the twenty hairpins and get back to H.Q. in a quarter of the time.

All this exercise I found exhilarating. Day by day I grew fitter and stronger.

The Italian Command had maintained a First Aid Post near the summit of the road, where an avalanche-proof shelter provided cover for two light ambulances and two Fiat trucks. There were sleeping quarters for the three men on continuous duty and the post was equipped with a telephone.

I was the first *Inglese* the patrolmen had encountered and we were soon very well acquainted. In return for their companionship and help I brought them tobacco, – and if you have ever smoked an Italian cigarette you will understand why they raved over ours.

Some way above the First Aid Post, alongside the sharp U-turn of the seventeenth hairpin up, the rock face had been cut back to accommodate a wayside shrine to the Virgin Mary. Sparkling icy-cold spring water gushed from a crevice in the limestone crag and splashed into a basin it had hollowed out for itself, then overflowed to tumble in little cascades beneath the shade of the firs into the dizzy depths below. Every day I would stop here to quench my thirst and refill my water bottle.

This was the shrine of the Madonna della Fontanella, which means 'Our Lady of the Little Spring'. She was a rather forlorn-looking figure, neglected since the trenches above had been deserted.

I never passed by without a word of greeting. You may smile, but after all she was my only female companion, certainly my nearest, and she <u>had</u> been gracious enough to incorporate the name of my sweetheart into her own, not once but twice. Perhaps the Alpine flowers I sometimes placed in a jar were as much an offering to my far-away girl-friend as to her.

Cavella

This part of the Italo-Austrian frontier was defended by a system of forts, trenches, dug-outs and O.P.s strung along the mountain crests.

The defence line ran roughly east and west, except in the centre where the configuration of the mountain ridge caused it to run north to south for 300 to 400 yards. The eastern (i.e. nearer) end was marked by the Bella Vista Observation Post. It had been given that name by its previous occupants. From Bella Vista, the trenches ran roughly westwards for nearly four miles to what I will call <u>my</u> mountain, Cima San Pietro (St. Peter's

Peak), rising all the time. Here, reaching the mountain's precipitous west face, they came to an abrupt end. Hollowed out of the rock beneath the Peak was the O.P. that became my personal hide-out, unnamed when I took possession of it, but soon christened 'Cavella'. It seemed quite suitable, for it <u>was</u> a cave (– blasted out of the solid mountain rock –) and adding my girlfriend's name gave it an appropriate Italian sound.

The cave was, I would guess, about fifteen feet square, six feet high and about 200 feet below the mountain summit. It was cold-proof, hot-proof, damp-proof and bomb-proof.

As far as I was ever able to discover I was the mountain's only human inhabitant. The previous occupants of Cavella had left behind some odds and ends which I was able to make very good use of. They had left the observation table immediately below the look-out opening and on it I had mounted my map. I would have fixed an Observer's telescope above it had there been one, but there wasn't. Besides the table there were two chairs, very old but usable, a number of strong ammo boxes (empty) and, best of all perhaps, a large pile of sawn logs of every conceivable thickness plus a brazier in which to burn them.

The mountainscape seen from the Observer's window (glassless of course) was staggeringly beautiful and extensive. If only I could have brought home the panoramic sketch I made, it would have conveyed some idea of the view.

To start with, the mountain in which the O.P. was situated was the end peak of the 4,000-foot-high range running west from the Asiago Plateau. Cavella looked across the narrow Astico gorge, here over 3,000 feet deep, at a stretch of ten to twelve miles of Austrian-held territory, with row upon row of mountains towering beyond, and the jagged peaks of the snow-capped Dolomites in the far distance.

Far below, at the foot of my mountain and completely out of

sight, a feeder stream, – the upper course of which I could see, – came down from the snow-mountains in the north and made a T-junction with the Astico, and the combined waters made a sudden left-hand turn beneath the western edge to flow south-wards towards Piovene and eventually the sea.

Now in the darkest, furthest corner of the cave there was an opening not easy to see until your eyes got accustomed to the gloom, an opening into a tunnel which ran fifty or sixty yards through the bowels of the mountain, bringing you without warning into a second chamber. This was a second Observation Post and its window was in the vertical face of the mountain's western flank. It was a replica of Cavella except that it had been stripped of all equipment. The prospect from the look-out open-ing was magnificent, and it included one feature which stood out in bolder relief than anything else, – a tiny church squatting on the summit of an isolated hill. My map told me its name, – the Church of the Madonna di Castello, – the 'Lady of the Castle'. Accordingly I named the second look-out Castello.

My first patrol of inspection showed me <u>why</u> the Italians were able to leave this sector undefended in order to transfer their troops elsewhere.

It wasn't until my second or third day that I ventured out from the security of the trenches. All that time I hadn't once heard a sound to suggest a war was on. I decided to take a chance. I should at least be out of machine-gun or sniping range.

I made my way stealthily forward to the edge of the ravine. There I saw why no Italian, British or any other Allied soldier was needed to defend <u>this</u> stretch of the frontier. It was com-pletely impregnable.

I looked down on a colossal wall of rock nearly three thousand feet deep. (That's five Beachy Heads piled on top of one another.)

A few stunted trees had managed to secure a foothold here and there on rock ledges, but otherwise the near wall of the gorge was a perpendicular limestone crag. On the far side were equally unclimbable grey cliffs. At the bottom, like a silver ribbon, lay the Astico stream.

I asked the inevitable questions. Hadn't Cavan or one of his generals discussed the take-over with the Italians first? Hadn't they troubled to find out what the terrain was like? And why, in Heaven's name, hadn't they done what I had just done – come and seen for themselves?

'But then why should I worry?' I thought. If they hadn't been such a lot of bone-heads, I wouldn't have been given this job, and I was enjoying it.

Around this time, the Quartermaster Sergeant fell sick and was sent away. We assumed he had contracted typhoid because we were all ordered on an inoculation parade shortly after. We were given two days' 'excused-duty' to get over it.

The Q.M.'s job is I would say the most envied for all in the service, so there was both disappointment and consternation when I was appointed temporary, unpaid 'Quarterbloke'. I was only half the age of the average Q.M. Yet I was the obvious choice, for in spite of my lowly rank I was now the longest-serving N.C.O. in the whole unit.

The Q.M. is in charge of stores, – clothing, food, equipment and, most important to many, tobacco and rum. I think I made a reasonably efficient Q.M. Nobody ever 'drew' anything from my stores without a 'chit' bearing the duty officer's signature. Nobody, that is, except me! It didn't seem right that I should do extra work without financial reward, so I used the opportunity to look after number one. Before those two days went by I had accumulated all that I might require in the near future, and removed them from the Q.M. Stores to my own quarters.

The first necessity was a new uniform. There are varying qualities of khaki serge. If you're unlucky you get tunics and trousers that feel as though the material has been woven from wire-wool. I 'issued' myself with the softer stuff. I needed a new tunic anyway because the old one was nearly splitting at the seams. The healthy outdoor life was having a noticeable effect on my physique! I was disappointed to find there were no shorts though; you would have expected troops who would have to withstand an approaching summer of sub-tropical heat to be supplied with something cooler than heavy serge and thick puttees. But they weren't. I was able to buy a couple of pairs in the nearby town of Thiene. I didn't dare wear them in the presence of officers or when on duty at Piovene, but in my little mountain kingdom they were my everyday wear. Then on a day 'mission' to Treviso, a large town about forty-five miles away, I was able to buy some collar-attached shirts (pale blue) and a pair of light-weight boots. When clad in these purchases plus a soft green cap with a good shady peak to it I must have looked the most un-English, un-military soldier in the British Army.

Having fixed myself up with clothing, I set about assembling my other requirements, – to wit one camp bed ('officers for the use of'!), three blankets, ample stocks of tea, sugar, canned butter, tinned milk and meats, matches and candles, a kettle and frying pan. By the time I'd transported all these to my billet, it looked as though I'd require the services of Messrs Pickfords to get them to my mountain retreat.

On the second of my 'leave' afternoons I ran into my friend Giulio in the village. He was refreshing himself with a demi-litre of wine outside Mario's Caffè before running up to Fontanella with the medical supplies he had collected in Thiene. I joined him under the coloured umbrella and took a glass of Soave. It was the only alcoholic beverage I could face after the fiasco on Christmas night.

Before our little siesta was over Giulio had solved my problem. He drove his light lorry along a stony track between the vineyards so that he could back up against my living-room window. I made sure no one was about and then got to work loading all my recently acquired belongings, – if that's the word! – into it. We were up and away in five minutes.

Giulio drove as near to Cavella as his versatile vehicle could get and then helped me carry my 'goods' into my hermit's cell. I was very glad of his help, as the chattels had to be humped over a steep bluff, then down into the grassy hollow below the fir trees, where the entrance to my cave was.

I took him inside and showed him the fruits of my mapping efforts. He was considerably impressed, and more so when he saw the tremendous views from the spy-hole over the two valleys. '*Magnifico!*' he exclaimed. (He hadn't been up there before, in spite of being stationed nearby for over a year.)

I saw him off, after expressing my gratitude for all the help he'd given me. '*Mille grazie! Giulio. Ciao!*'

Of course all this was most irregular. Totally amoral too, I suppose. But it did help to strengthen one tiny portion of the Anglo-Italian Entente. And I'm quite sure Giulio enjoyed his part in the operation as much as I did.

At last the day came when I was able to report that my survey was completed. It had taken me about three weeks but as the battery was still unequipped for action there was no work for me at the Command Post.

Alf Sparrow, – still waiting for his Thornies, – drove Major

Jordan, Mr. Salisbury and me to the nearest point of approach and I guided my two superiors into my 'mountain kingdom'. (I had been monarch of all I surveyed!)

I led my visitors first to Bella Vista. I drew their attention to the large panoramic sketch I had made and, after fixing my new map flat on the Observer's table, placed the drawing upright between the far edge of the map and the lower ledge of the spy-hole. The drawing was the same breadth as the map and they showed the principal features of the landscape in matching-coloured inks. Anyone but a complete moron would be able to identify every natural feature in the territory spied on by reference to my drawing, – and find its position on the map in a few seconds.

Finally they looked at the technical information I had compiled and tabulated. Both Major and Lieutenant were favourably impressed. It was obvious neither had seen anything like it before.

By this time I expected the O.C. to have had enough, but no, he would go and inspect the other O.P. before returning to the plains. Accordingly we retraced our steps to where Alf awaited us and I navigated him to the nearest point a vehicle could get to Cavella. He muttered curses at the roughness of the route, as well he might for it was more like a dried-up pebble-strewn watercourse than a motor road, but he managed to get us there with the Fiat's springs still intact.

The two officers followed me, toiling up the steep slope of the pine-clad bluff and down the goat track which joined the trenches fifty yards from my O.P. entrance. It was their first visit to this part of our front line. They had become hot and bothered, not entirely I suspected because of the rise in the temperature, but because of the anger induced by realizing that Cavan's scheme was a pointless waste of man-power.

They again examined my note-books, studied my annotated map, and looked closely at my panoramic drawing, all set up in the same style as I had used at Bella Vista.

Before we left, Major Jordan enquired about my pre-service occupation. 'Were you a cartographer?' he asked. 'No, sir,' I replied. 'A student teacher.' He made no comment, just raised his eyebrows. He was a silent type of chap.

Unexpected News

After my mapping mission was completed, I continued to spend much of my time up in the mountains, as the battery's sole Observer. One morning I was just about to set off from the village when I was asked to report to Battery H.Q. Lieutenant Salisbury was there with news for me.

Major Jordan, he said, would be leaving shortly and so would he, though only temporarily. A new draft was expected, which would mean fresh officers taking over. Among the new arrivals would be a B.C.A., whose rank it was presumed would be Corporal. I was a B.C.A. with only the rank of Bombardier. In spite of my seniority in war service I would be the new man's inferior in rank. The O.C., Mr. S. went on, wished to avoid any embarrassment the situation might produce by offering me promotion.

He paused, no doubt to watch the effect his words had on me. I think he was a little disappointed that I didn't display more enthusiasm.

I said I felt grateful that the O.C. had taken so much interest. Then I was informed that I could choose between

a. promotion to the non-commissioned rank of Sergeant, or
b. recommendation for Officer Training.

The Major, Mr. S. told me, had been most impressed by the manner in which I had carried out my recent assignment. He was quite sure that a recommendation for Officer Training would be acted upon without delay. As a result I should have to return to England.

'Well, Bombardier Skirth, which shall it be?'

I was so dumbfounded, I didn't know what to think. 'Could I have time to consider?'

'The O.C. would like to know to-day. The sooner the better. He is leaving to-morrow.'

'May I have just one hour to think things over?' I requested.

'One hour then.'

I stood to give the customary salute before leaving.

'Oh! I nearly forgot,' Mr. Salisbury added. 'Major Snow is returning to take command. Thought you'd like to know.'

There's a proverb that says every cloud has a silver lining. Perhaps the reverse is true as well.

I had sixty minutes in which to make a vital decision. Not much time to make a choice on which your future, possibly your very life, may depend.

I walked slowly along a track leading to a bridge. I leaned over the rail and watched the pale green water bubble its way over and between the rounded boulders. I wondered how many miles the floating twigs and leaves would travel before they came to their journey's end. The river was moving gently but irrevocably to the sea. The pieces of flotsam would be carried with it, whether they wished to go that way or no.

'Heavens!' I thought. 'What has all this to do with my problem? I should be concentrating on that, not on leaves floating downriver. I'm not a twig being carried willy-nilly with the current!'

Then it came to me. If I make the wrong choice, that's exactly what I <u>shall</u> be. I shall be compelled to go with the stream. As an officer, I shall have to transmit orders from my superiors to those of lower rank. In short, I shall have to conform.

But if I choose the other option, what then? As a senior N.C.O. my position would be just as difficult. I needed help. There was only one place where I knew I would receive it. In the church.

The village Padre was leaving as I arrived at the entrance. We had come to know each other quite well. This time he was in a hurry; he just said in Italian, 'Bless you, my son,' before he mounted his ancient bicycle and rode off.

I think I was in the church for about twenty minutes, but that was enough. I knew what I had to do.

When I got back to the Villa Rosa no one was there. The only writing paper was a pad of signallers' message forms. I took one and wrote more or less as follows.

To: Lieut. Salisbury
From: Bdr. Skirth, J.R.
Message: Please thank Major Jordan for confidence he has shown in me. I regret I am unable to accept promotion for health reasons. I fear extra responsibility might produce recurrence of ill-health. I am willing to continue in present post as Bombardier.

That afternoon I spent a long time writing to Ella. The actual letter didn't take long; it was the postscript to it which demanded so much thought and so much concentration that I wrote it over and over again. It was by far the most important piece of writing I did in all my service career, possibly in all my life. My whole future depended on its wording being absolutely correct.

It is quite impossible for anyone to say after fifty-odd years, 'This is exactly what I wrote on that day.' The best I can do is to declare that what follows is as near the actual truth as I can make it. The gist of both letter and postscript remain indelibly engraved in my memory.

When I was satisfied with my efforts, I folded the letter and postscript separately and placed them in an ordinary envelope. An ordinary envelope, because I wanted its contents to be censored.

This is the letter.

> *Somewhere in Italy*
> *May 1918*

Ella darling,
Glad to report that I'm still well. We've been lucky since we arrived in Italy as they haven't sent us up to the firing line yet.
I've just realized it is a year since I wrote to you quoting a little poem that begins

> *'Oh! to be in England*
> *Now that April's here.'*

I bet you don't remember, but I do!
It's rotten luck that we've had to be parted two Aprils running. Think I'll tell them to get a move on, win the war, and let me come home.
Don't worry about lack of news to write about. Just put 'I still love you' on a slip of paper and send it to me, marking the envelope URGENT.
All my love,
Ronald
Xxx

*P.S. They have lovely wild flowers growing on the mountain
sides. It's like living in a rock-garden.*

The letter you have just read I expected to go through uncen-
sored. On separate sheets I wrote the postscript, which I knew
would never go any further than the Officers' Mess.

Ella darling,
   *I don't expect the censor to allow this part of my letter to
reach you but I hope he will.*
   *There are things I have concealed from you up till now that
I think you ought to know; things which have turned me into
a different person from the Ronald you knew.*
   *Later on, perhaps, I hope to be able to explain to you more
fully why I have just declined the offer of a commission which
would bring about my return to England quite soon.*
   *The truth is, darling: that I am a fraud. I'm a fraud
because I have to pretend.*
   *When I enlisted I took an oath of loyalty to my King and
Country. I was happy to do so because I believed our country
was fighting a just war; also I wanted to make you feel proud
of me.*
   *But gradually my feelings have changed. I have become
convinced that wars are wicked ways of settling disputes,
that in fact they don't settle anything. I believe this war is an
especially wicked one because so many <u>innocent</u> people get
killed, hurt and bereaved. The longer it continues the more
dreadful it gets and the wickedest thing of all is that nobody
in authority is trying to stop it.*
   *A year ago, almost to the day, I got punished because I
allowed my religious beliefs to interfere with my duties as a
soldier. Part of my punishment we are both suffering now, –*

the deferment of my leave which is the cause of our long separation.

I haven't told you, or anybody, of the fearful experiences I had in Flanders because I didn't want you to be upset.

I was nearly killed several times. But that wasn't the worst part. The worst part was seeing my pals die. Four of my best friends had their lives taken away from them all to no purpose. That's another reason why I think this war is so wicked and stupid, because all the terrible loss of life is <u>unnecessary</u>. Losing my pals the way I did nearly broke my heart.

Not long afterwards I had a mental illness. I had to go into a kind of hospital somewhere. But don't worry, darling. I got better and I'm fine now. I am also in a quiet part of the Front where there's no fighting and no danger.

Now I've come to the part that is the hardest for me to tell you.

Last Christmas I went into a church and I made a solemn promise. (Nobody persuaded me into doing this – only my Conscience.) I vowed that because God had spared <u>my</u> life I would never help to take away another's, – unless I had orders which I could find no way of evading. No one but me (and God) knew anything about this.

I would have transferred to a non-combatant unit like the Red Cross or the R.A.M.C. if they would have let me, but I knew they wouldn't.

So you see, darling, I am faced with a terrible dilemma: – my enlistment oath demands that I do one thing and my pact with God another. It's a conflict between my duty and my conscience.

My officers do not know the real reason for my refusing promotion, which is that I cannot accept any reward or profit

*for the part I am being compelled to play in all this war
wickedness. I believe that I could find the courage to risk my
life to save another man's; but I know I haven't been given the
right to take another's life from him.*

*People who think like me are called Conscientious
Objectors. To make it sound worse they call them Conchies.
Nobody likes them. Everyone seems to despise them, even when
they risk imprisonment or even death for standing by their
principles. I hope I never have to face that sort of test.*

*But all the time I continue to wear the King's uniform I
shall carry out the duties allotted to me as efficiently as I know
how. No one will ever have reason to doubt my loyalty.*

*Well, there it is, Ella darling. My confession! Dare I
hope that you will understand? I shall pray that you won't
condemn.*

*My conscience is troubling me no longer, – now I've told
you. From now on I shan't be accusing myself of hypocrisy. I
shan't have to pretend to be something I am not.*

Oh! Please don't think too badly of me, darling.

I love you so much.

Ronald.

The postscript was a means of conveying information to my
superiors in the only manner which seemed to me possible
then. I trusted my officers, believing that confidences written in
a love letter would be treated as private and personal. I believed
that they would be unable to discuss with me information
obtained in such a way without a breach of their codes of
honour.

I was proved to be correct. My confession was never referred
to, and nor was the subject of promotion ever discussed again. I
was treated as though my letter had never been read.

So, after all, the army censorship which I so hated served me well.

Giulio

As my friend Guilio plays quite an important part in my story I think I'll introduce him to you properly now. Although I didn't know him for long, he and I became quite close friends.

Giulio was an ambulance driver in the Italian Army Medical Corps. He was four or five years older than me, a shortish, stocky, ever-smiling fellow with the whitest teeth and the blackest curly hair you ever saw. He had a face the colour of a ripe chestnut and when stripped to the waist, as he often was on the days we met that summer, disclosed a torso equally bronzed by the Italian sun. As far as I know he was unmarried, though why some nice girl hadn't got herself affianced to him I can't explain.

The common ground on which we were able to meet was that of language. Giulio was learning English in his spare time and I was picking up Italian. His aim was to join a cousin working in one of London's plushier hotels; I very much wanted to visit his home city of Rome, – because of (among other things) Michelangelo's ceiling frescoes in the Sistine Chapel, which I had studied in an art book as a boy of fourteen.

A large number of the hours when I was supposed to be working on my mountain survey I was actually truanting at the Fontanella Post. Equipped with pocket dictionaries, phrase books, paper and pencils, Giulio and I entered into a sort of pupil–teacher relationship, – being learners and instructors simultaneously.

Like all his countrymen, Giulio was a master at 'talking' by gesture when words failed him. I can see some of his movements now. The tapping of fingers and slapping of the forehead when impatient at his own forgetfulness; the rubbing of a finger and thumb along his typically Roman nose when puzzled; the sly wink when imparting some piece of confidential information and the half-spread arms with palms forward combined with a shrug of the shoulders to signify resignation and his '*Che sarà sarà*' philosophy.

Quite often Giulio would drive me into Thiene, a bright town of about 10,000 people situated in the next valley. His area H.Q. was there, as was an (all-Italian) Service Men's Club run by the Red Cross. I was the only Tommy seen there at that time but the discovery that I could play the piano caused them to accept me straightaway. (It's a rather surprising fact that although most Italians are splendid singers, very few are pianists!)

How different were the sing-songs there from the ones at the French *estaminet*! No 'Mademoiselle from Armentières' or 'I want to go home', but folk songs such as 'Santa Lucia' and 'Sorrento' and operatic arias and choruses. (You may wonder where we got our sopranos and contraltos from. The men, of course, – their falsettos would have turned the Melbas and Tetrazzinis green with envy.) Our renderings of *Traviata*, *Butterfly*, *Pagliacci* and the rest would have done credit to a La Scala production.

One afternoon in Thiene, while Giulio had business to attend to, I went off to a shop he had taken me to earlier, where if you were lucky, and if you were liked by Carlo, the genial proprietor, you might be able to buy some real chocolate. By mid-1918 food shortages in Italy were serious and many luxuries were unobtainable. The native product was as ghastly as Italian cigarettes, – seemingly a compound of cocoa-factory floor-sweepings, brick-dust and gritty sugar, – but small supplies of the genuine stuff somehow got smuggled across the frontier from Switzerland via the Lakes.

This afternoon I was in luck. Carlo produced four bars of Peter's Milk from his hiding place and I gladly paid more than the asking price for them. I went off well satisfied, sparing a thought for my unfortunate comrades-in-arms slogging their hearts out in the sweltering heat on the mountain-side, widening the hairpin bends.

Back in the street, I heard the soft sounds of a piano coming from the open doorway of a music shop. I went closer and peeped inside.

I could just distinguish a girlish figure seated at one of the pianos. After the sunlight's glare the shop's interior seemed shrouded in a twilight gloom, but it was what I could hear which riveted my attention. The music took me back home, to my doctor-hero's surgery and my sweetheart's sitting room. (How clearly I could recall our last evening together, when she had played the very same piece!)

My thoughts were a thousand miles away when my brain suddenly registered that the proprietor was gesturing to me to enter. He directed me to a chair with his fingers on his lips in a friendly, almost conspiratorial manner.

The piece was delightfully played and at the end the girl stood up and turned to discover that she had for her audience a soldier in a strangely foreign uniform. Blushing to the roots of her light-brown hair she fled in shy confusion to the safety of an inner room. Whether or not she heard my '*Molto grazie*' I don't know, but for her grandfather's sake as well as her own I applauded politely and sincerely.

Grandpapa had no English, but with his gesturing and my smattering of Italian we managed an interesting little conversation. All this time I could see the figure of his young '*cara nipotina*' (little grand-daughter) half-concealed in the doorway, listening. I couldn't leave the shop without making a purchase, and plaster busts of Verdi being out of the question I settled for two 'miniature' piano scores of *La Traviata* and *Il Trovatore*! The Service Men's Club's impromptu concerts always included excerpts from these works and I knew the scores would find a good home on top of the club's piano.

After making payment, I was bold enough to go over to the instrument the girl had been playing. I saw her withdraw quickly into some even deeper gloom beyond her doorway but I've no doubt she was still within earshot. I looked enquiringly over to Grandpapa. '*Permesso?*' I asked.

He nodded. '*Si, si, signore. Per favore!*'

I turned over the pages of the Mozart volume the girl had been playing from, seeking the sonata which was my own special favourite. (It was the one I had heard Dr. Stokes play the first time I had eavesdropped on him.) It was exactly the same edition as Ella's presentation album.

I sat and played through the 'Andante Grazioso', the delicate little pastoral melody on which the variations which make up the movement are based. My fingers had never touched an instrument of such quality. I was out of form; accompanying sing-songs at the club was hardly adequate practice. But it sufficed.

A little later I sat sipping a cooling *limonata* at a table on the pavement when I caught a glimpse through the red roofs of the jagged peaks of the snow mountains thirty miles away, their tops painted crimson and gold by the late-afternoon sun. Beyond them, I guessed, must be Salzburg, the home of Mozart.

My reverie was interrupted by the squeeze of Giulio's hand on my shoulder. It was time to go.

The Great Lakes

My friendship with Giulio had to end in late July when he was promoted to a more responsible position in a hospital overlooking Lake Garda. One day before taking up his new post he had to visit the hospital for a meeting and he asked if I would like to come too. It happened to be one of my off-duty days.

We were in the small open-topped Fiat truck and there's no better vehicle for sight-seeing. Fiat evidently believed in speed first, safety second and comfort last, but I enjoyed every minute. The first part of the journey took us through two of the cities I had known but not really seen in the days of my depression, – Vicenza and Verona. How different they looked bathed in sunshine under the bluest of summer skies!

I would have liked to revisit San Martino, not only to see what the village looked like without its mantle of snow but to enter once again the church which had been the scene of my confession and 'conversion'. But it would have involved a detour and Giulio's appointment was important. I knew he would not want to arrive late.

Twenty minutes driving westward from Verona brought us to Peschiera, a small town situated at the south-east corner of Lake Garda. Here we left the main road and took a by-way which followed the eastern shore of the lake.

Giulio drove through fairy-tale villages with harbours so tiny they looked more like toys than the real thing, past trees with lemons hanging from their branches, under spire-like cypress tress as tall as churches, alongside dense masses of large shrubs smothered with red and white blooms. Occasionally the lakes would be obscured for a moment by huge weeping willows arching over the water and dipping the tips of their branches below its surface. And always there was the glowing sapphire blue of the lake water, like a vast mirror.

We lurched around the projecting base of a large promontory which gave the most breathtaking views in every direction and then, braking so hard that I was nearly ejected from my seat, Giulio pulled up in the *piazzetta* (tiny square) of a miniature village. It was a hamlet called San Vigilio.

We jumped down and walked to the waterfront. There were railings to lean on and tubs full of bright red flowers I'd never seen before. With a gesture of outspread arms and raised eyebrows which undoubtedly meant 'Now what do you think of this?' Giulio asked me whether I would like to be left here until he returned from his interview, a matter of perhaps two hours. The only Italian word I could think of was '*Bellisima!*'

There was a tiny *caffè* with one table outside it. I ordered a fizzy *limonata* and while I sipped it through a straw I let my eyes drink in some of the beauty of my surroundings. After a brief conversation with the very friendly, very large lady of that very small *caffè*, I went off to explore.

At Cavella, under St. Peter's Peak, I had thought I was blessed with one of the most marvellous views nature could provide. Here at San Vigilio, I saw what the Val d'Astico lacked, – the placid tinted mirror of a lake in its foreground. I saw how an expanse of sky-blue water can transform superb beauty into sheer magic.

Of course I, a born lover of all natural beauty, could not but be captivated. Writers of immeasurably greater skill have extolled the praises of the Italian Lakes, attempted to describe the intensity of colour which is such a unique part of their beauty, and tried to analyse the secrets of their universal appeal and enchantment. It is quite impossible, for one cannot describe the indescribable. If you have <u>seen</u> Garda, and Como, Lugarno and Maggiore you will know what I mean. I hope that one day you will.

While Giulio was away I remember doing three things.

First, I made my way to the little church standing on the knoll, almost hidden by tall cypresses. I went inside, knelt and expressed gratitude that my sight had been spared so that I could see all the beauty around me.

Second, I climbed a couple of hundred feet up the steep vine-clad hillside until I reached an eminence where I could see the whole thirty-mile expanse of the lake spread before me, hardly able to believe that such beauty could exist in such abundance.

The third thing I did was to go back to the church in the cypress grove. Once more I knelt, and this time I was selfish enough to ask a favour for myself, – that the Almighty would work just one more miracle and allow me to come back here with Ella on our honeymoon.

I fished out the least grubby of the fifty-lire notes I had in my wallet and pushed it into the church's Poor Box. I don't mind admitting that I politely requested the Madonna near the altar to put in a word for me.

A day or two later I went to Fontanella to say farewell to Giulio. We never met again. I continued to visit the Post at intervals and on one occasion learnt that Giulio had won the highest possible award for bravery under fire at Caporetto, but would never wear the decoration, nor talk about how he had won it. I felt very humble after hearing that.

As for my special request, I did come through the war almost unharmed and Ella and I were married in the church we had both known from childhood. And after the wedding we did go off to the Italian Lakeland. Not to Garda, but to the equally beautiful lakes of Lugarno, Como and Maggiore. We drank *arancia* and *limonata* and ate *gelati* on wisteria-hung balconies overhanging their cobalt-blue waters. We sailed over miles and miles of their unruffled surface, intoxicated with the beauty we saw in every direction. We saw the vineyards, the olive groves and the mulberry orchards on the steep mountainsides of Lake Como; we visited the factory where the caterpillars' silk is made into cloth; we saw the Borromean Islands magically floating on the blue waters of Maggiore, and went ashore on two of them to make sure they were real; we saw the largest palms in Europe as well as the whitest peacocks; we took the funicular to the summit of the Mount of Our Saviour and saw 2,000 square miles of Switzerland and Italy in one sweeping glance; we watched an aeroplane fly below us; we took coffee under the lemon trees and breathed in air heavy with the scent of lime-flowers and oleanders; we sat on the Casino terrace at Campione d'Italia and watched the fountains of Lugarno across the lake changing colour every few seconds. Then we ordered a bottle of sparkling Asti and drank a toast to ourselves, each wishing the other everlasting happiness.

We climbed, by funicular railway, to the pilgrim church of the Madonna of the Rock, and gave thanks in it for all the pleasures we were enjoying. I photographed Ella sitting on the balustrade of the church porch with Lake Maggiore a thousand feet below.

We ate a supper of lake trout at our candle-lit hotel table, serenaded on his violin by the same Italian who in the morning had driven our taxi. We sat on our bedroom balcony, watching the myriad lights, and their reflections in the velvet-black water. They seemed to be suspended in the sky, but we knew they were shining from villas perched on the slopes of the invisible mountains all around. Never could we remember having been happier.

I hope I shan't be accused of blasphemy if I suggest that God has a sense of humour. Perhaps he was sufficiently interested in my puny affairs to play a little joke on me, by giving me a sort of rap on the knuckles for my presumption that summer day in 1918.

I told you the truth when I said that Ella and I went off to Italy after our wedding. But not the whole truth. Because the interval between our wedding and <u>that</u> honeymoon was over thirty-six years. We took off from London Airport on a June morning in 1961, forty-four years and eleven months after our first meeting.

I <u>was</u> able to provide the necessary funds from my own efforts. Not out of what I earned as a teacher, of course, but from the Retirement Gratuity a grateful nation awards you after a lifetime of scholastic servitude!

Yes, I'm inclined to believe that it was one of God's little jokes. Ella and I think that after all He was right to make us wait. We are thankful that we were given the patience, the health and the strength to appreciate it to the full when at last the happy day came.

Postscript (Yes, another one!)

Our real honeymoon, – the one that starts a few hours after the marriage ceremony, – was rather less glamorous and romantic. It began on the evening of our wedding day, 29 December 1924, and lasted well into the following year; to be precise until lunchtime on 1 January.

The weather was atrocious. More than half of that honeymoon was taken up working like Trojans to get our newly acquired flat ready for living in. We stripped, papered and painted walls and woodwork. Then we downed tools, shed our work-clothes, spruced up, donned our 'best', took the Tube to Picadilly Circus and walked through the entrance doors of the Regent Palace Hotel. Here we dined in style, went out to a show (– pit seats of course, although we thought of them as orchestra stalls –), took supper at the Coventry Street Corner House where Campoli was playing his violin, returned to the luxury of the hotel, opened the door of Room 404 and . . . well, as Samuel Pepys would have put it . . . and So To Bed.

The Thiene Service Men's Club. (Note Censor's effort.)
I sent this view-card to Ella in the summer of 1918.
The 'X' wasn't on it then. Had it been, someone
would have suspected a hidden message and the
card would have been confiscated.

CHAPTER SIX

Before the Battle

The Church of the Madonna of the Castle.

I resume my story in June 1918, a week before one of the fiercest battles of the Italian campaign: the Battle of the Asiago Plateau. At that time, my duties were divided between observing at Cavella and clerical work in the Battery Office on the plain. (I was also still acting as temporary Quartermaster Sergeant.)

At last the battery's move into new positions had been completed. We now had two guns and two Command Posts, one in the mountains, near to the Gun Sites, and the original Post down in Piovene. The men had been taken off road construction for good. Alf Sparrow was happy, – he was instructing them in the art of driving thirty-hundredweight trucks <u>round</u> hairpin corners instead of over their edges. His Thornies had arrived, eventually. Two of them! The first boiled dry and blew up before it got to the top. The second's brakes burnt out and it came back on its own initiative stern first. We jumped clear just in time. It knocked over the stone bollards on the outer edge of the hairpin and quietly and smoothly disappeared. Alf and I ran to see where it had finished its maiden voyage. It looked fairly comfortable sitting on its roof 250 feet below us, its brakeless wheels still turning. After that Alf resigned himself to the Fiats.

The arrival of reinforcements on 8 June brought us almost up to strength. Among the new men were two who will figure prominently in my next chapter. The first was a Sergeant called Weller, a dour, leathery-faced character twice my age with an 'Old Bill' moustache and close-cropped gunmetal hair. He was a Gun Layer, an old sweat brought home from garrison service in Gibraltar. I found it difficult to communicate with him. He was a morose, silent chap by nature and I was very young and only an amateur soldier. He probably thought me a bit of an upstart.

The other newcomer was a Bombardier T—, a rather colourless, insignificant-looking fellow, also years older than I. He was the newly qualified B.C.A. that Mr. Salisbury had mentioned, and he took an instant dislike to me. I was jolly pleased to discover they hadn't given him corporal's rank after all, as it meant that I was _his_ senior on account of my service 'in the field'. So I remained the battery's sole Observer (plus Anything-Else-Required), based at Cavella, while he became B.C.A., working from Bella Vista and the mountain Command Post.

I may have given the impression that no fighting took place along the mountain front. There _was_ intermittent fighting at many points along the eighty-mile confrontation between the Alps and the Adriatic coast, but a stalemate position had been reached in which neither side had the strength necessary to launch a successful attack. In our particular stretch of territory all <u>was</u> quiet; it had been so throughout the whole of the preceding winter and continued to be so, apart from sporadic long-range artillery firing, until the middle of June.

The winter of 1917/18 had been the most severe for a decade, paralysing all army movement and bringing fighting in the mountains to a standstill. With the approach of early summer the snow and ice melted, the roads became passable again and intermittent fighting was resumed. But if any major offensive were to be organized by either of the opposing forces it would have to be made around the Austrian-held town of Asiago, or down one of the river gorges leading to the plains, or across the River Piave north of Venice. The one part of the mountain war-zone where an attack by either side was completely impossible was the sector of the front into which <u>we</u> had been sent, – for the reason I explained earlier, viz. the presence of a 3,000-foot gorge.

Well, an offensive <u>did</u> come, not from the Allies but from the Austrians (now reinforced by German troops from Russia). The attack opened in the early hours of 15 June 1918. I was alone at Cavella when it started.

The official history of the Italian campaign specifically praises the 'magnificent contribution' made by the officers and men of 239 Siege Battery, R.G.A. But the official account of my battery's action is completely false, – in fact, a tissue of lies. Only a handful of men knew the truth of the matter in 1918 and they all kept it to themselves. Perhaps I am the only one left alive to-day who knows what 239 Battery <u>really</u> did on 15 June 1918.

A week before the battle Alf drove me to Vicenza to meet a supply train and collect some new equipment and stores. Back at our Piovene H.Q. I checked them over. Of course there were tons of stuff we could do without and an appalling shortage of what we needed most urgently, – medical supplies and tele-phone apparatus. I found two field telephones and a dozen coils of wire. Over and over again I had indented for <u>miles</u> of cable and all I got were <u>yards</u>.

I had a vested interest in the telephone cable situation, for until a line could be laid to the Command Post, Cavella was cut off from the outside world, – and I was working at Cavella most days and nights.

The next day I got permission to ask Alf Sparrow to drive one of the Fiat trucks from Piovene with stuff I needed at the moun-tain O.P. and the rest of my personal belongings. After Alf had left I rigged up one of the receivers on the table, connected it to the power supply (accumulator) and ran the cable along the fire-step of the disused trench in the direction of the Command Post, but half way the wire ran out. 'Oh hell!' I thought. Talk about Fred Karno's Army. A battery unable to communicate to its O.P. is blind and deaf, – and without ammo (as we were) it's darned well dumb too.

After lighting a log fire I brewed up some tea. The Austrians across the gorge didn't seem to worry about my fire-making, which must have been in full view of their Observers on the high peak opposite. I used to see smoke from <u>their</u> fires most days. Once I watched a group playing cards on the grass. 'Live and let live' is a most inappropriate motto for warmongers, but my opposite numbers, like me, must have considered it a fine philosophy. I don't suppose <u>they</u>, any more than I, had any per-sonal interest in the war, except to <u>survive</u> it.

My job at Cavella was to observe; that's what I'd been detailed to do. But one needs more than a good pair of eyes to do that effectively. Properly equipped observation posts have a kind of spy-glass-telescope mounted on a swivel, – rather like a surveyor's theodolite, – but this O.P. had nothing, not even a pair of field glasses.

I was now on a twenty-four-hour continuous spell of duty followed by a twenty-four-hour stretch 'off'. Normally, when there were relays of three doing the job, we would have six hours 'on' and twelve hours 'off', but at that time I was the only qualified Observer in the battery.

During my duty hours I wasn't expected to be spying continuously, only at reasonable intervals. At the end of each tour of duty I would report any significant developments. Most days I handed in a 'Nil Return'. During my free hours Cavella was unmanned, unless a junior officer was sent by the commander for a specific purpose, and that hardly ever happened. Sometimes, of my own choice, I would remain there, sleeping in the dug-out rather than making the tedious journey down to the Piovene base, eight or ten miles away.

I never felt lonely, nor did I ever feel nervous. I was happy in my own company. At Cavella there were no rats and no spiders; the only species of animal life were small green and brown rock lizards that liked the dry-stone walls of the trench system.

I made no friends among the new arrivals but often visited Giulio and his team at the Mountain Rescue Post (this was before he left for the Lake Garda hospital) and, whenever the mood took me, I found means of getting to Thiene and seeking out new (and old) friends at the club. I could also always have a decent bath there, and exchange an old shirt and vest for new ones!

One day, I was clambering down the mountainside to join the road to Piovene when I had a narrow escape from falling. I had become fairly expert in solo climbing and could get from Cavella down to the riverside in a little under an hour by goat track (climbing up took more than double that time).

The near-accident brought home to me the fact that I hadn't prepared myself adequately. The first thing I did when I got to Piovene was to track down a good roll of crêpe bandaging, some iodine and a spool of plaster, – all of which I stuffed into my haversack.

I also had the luck to unearth some binoculars, which I found packed with spare 'office' supplies. How they got there I have no idea, especially as they didn't appear to be Government 'issue'. They were English-made Ross glasses. There was no official marking; no indication of ownership on the leather case or carrying strap. I took them outside and put them to the test. Quite good, I decided, but too heavy to hold completely still. However, they were a lot better than nothing.

One of my tasks was to plot the positions of the two guns we now possessed on my O.P. map. Until this was done no pre-shoot calculations could be made.

Whoever had selected their positions had made some extraordinary choices. No. 2's site was away to the right of our new mountain Command Post and No. 1 a long way to the left; they were two miles apart. (In Flanders they were seldom more than a hundred yards distant from each other.) 'Oh well!' I thought. 'I'm not O.C. I suppose he knows what he's doing.'

I only hoped he had looked closely at No. 1 Gun Site. To me it looked jolly dangerous; not to the enemy but to its own crew.

It's wise to choose a site in which the gun flashes are screened from enemy eyes, as they can give away your position. Ordinarily, you either build a camouflage network around the sides and over the top of the gun or you place the weapon so that it has higher ground in front of it. Now this particular gun pit, levelled after hours of back-aching pick-and-shovel work, had a steep bluff rising high in front and very steep rocky crags on either side.

It certainly <u>looked</u> cosy, but suppose the gun was fired at a low elevation during the hours of darkness? However, the fellows presumably knew their job and who was I to go and tell them how to do it? I was an Observer, not a Gunner.

If events took their usual course, before the new howitzers were passed A.I. there would be practice shoots on what artillerymen call registration targets, for the purposes of discovering inaccuracies and defects. The gunnery officer would select an easily identifiable medium-range target and there would be a sort of rehearsal bombardment. (This was useful for chaps like myself too; – if for some reason we had miscalculated the range the results would be equally unsatisfactory.)

I imagined I were a bright young subaltern deputed to select a registration target. What object would I choose? From Bella Vista I'd most certainly opt for the partially destroyed railway bridge for my practice shoot. But from Cavella . . .

I gazed intently from my look-out over to the Austrian-held territory across the gorge. Trees, roads, ruined farmhouses, mountain crags? No, all useless for the purpose. But on the lower flank of San Paolo mountain almost directly opposite our O.P. stood a stone cross, silhouetted sharply against its background of distant hazy mountain shapes. I consulted my map. It was about 6,000 yards from the gun site. A perfect choice.

However, if my gunnery expert observed from Castello, the O.P. on the south side of my mountain, which could only be approached through the sixty-yard tunnel from Cavella, there was absolutely no doubt what he'd choose: the little church on the hill. It had every attribute a gunnery maniac could ask for: isolation, range, altitude, availability, – the lot. And if he wasn't disturbed by such nuisances as religious scruples, it would be precisely what the doctor ordered. A sitting duck! And wouldn't it be bloody good sport watching the absurd little building blown to Kingdom Come? A dozen rounds would raze it to the ground.

10 *June 1918*

I have been on duty since 6 a.m. at Cavella. The reels of cable still haven't come so I can't get the line completed. The only means of communication between me and the Command Post are my own two legs. Nobody ever sends a runner here.

I've been testing the Ross binoculars. They have good magnification but are too weighty to hold steady without elbow support. I've seen enough to make me feel very uneasy.

The Austrians have been putting up camouflage screens across their roads at night. They suspend them crosswise like banners so that one overlaps the other. You can't see any of the actual roadway but I've seen white dust rising. I am certain two new heavy batteries have taken up positions in clearings in the pine woods.

There's another new one whose position I have already plotted. One of its guns is dead in line with the part of our trench system which runs north–south. If ever they wanted to shatter our trench communications, that's the bit they'd blow to hell. They couldn't miss. But would they be massing artillery unless they're going to use it?

What's that?

An unaccustomed sound made me sit up with a start: the roar of an approaching aeroplane, a sound I hadn't heard before in Italy. I leapt up intending to run for cover but it had screamed out of sight before I could reach my dug-out entrance. The plane had swooped in from nowhere and had skimmed just above tree-top height over the trench-line leading to Bella Vista.

I scrambled as high up the slope as I could and caught sight of it again. It was wheeling over where I judged No. 2 Gun to be sited, over the Command Post, over No. 1 Gun, – and now heading straight back to me!

I flung myself flat and buried my face in the pebbles, expecting every moment to hear the rat-rat-tat of machine-gun fire. But none came. The plane zoomed over the tree tops and vanished into the blue. The whole incident began and ended inside three minutes.

There could only be one reason for a pilot to undertake a flight like that. He was on 'recce', shooting not with bullets but with cameras; and unless I was much mistaken he'd got some jolly good pictures of all the things we didn't want the enemy to know about: where our gun emplacements were, how many we had, the lay-out of the tracks that serviced them, – the lot!

I thought about the possible consequences of that enemy recce. I guessed our O.C. would want the new guns registered soon; perhaps to-day. I came to a decision: there was action I could take now which would prove that the oath I had taken in San Martino's church five months earlier was honestly meant. It might not <u>save</u> lives but it certainly wouldn't take any, – and it might, if I succeeded, prevent the destruction of a beautiful building and a house of God.

For a couple of hours I worked like one possessed, fetching and carrying stones, rocks and boulders into my cave. When at last, with hands bruised and bleeding, I had completed my attempt at dry-stone walling you would have needed very sharp eyes and a powerful torchlight to detect that there had once been a tunnel entrance leading into the mountain's heart.

What you would have noticed was a shallow recess hollowed out of the rear wall to form a niche, accommodating a shrine. A very rude shrine indeed, merely a flat-topped cairn of stones upon which stood a crude wooden cross. (Two pieces of pine branch held together by wire.) To its left you would have seen a candlestick, really a Chianti bottle with a candle in it, and on the opposite side a jar of mountain flowers. The inscription above – a board fastened to the wall – would have told you its purpose: SANTUARIO DI SAN PIETRO. A hermit's cell, evidently.

As for me, I was well satisfied with the result of my endeavours. Crude and primitive the shrine may have appeared, but as camouflage to disguise a tunnel entrance it was an expert piece of work. I was confident that nobody would ever suspect that behind that primitive façade was the blocked-up entrance to a second Observation Post. I had made doubly sure by destroying the only map which showed its existence.

I completed my task by screening off the rear corner of the cave, stringing a wire from the wall to a supporting post and suspending a spare blanket from it. I put my camp bed behind it and stacked some of the empty ammo boxes one upon another to form a bedside table between me and the shrine.

As for the other possible target, the stone cross, we could blow that to blazes and nobody would be any worse off. It could be re-erected in a day if anybody wanted it replaced. The nearest enemy hutments were a hundred yards away and I should arrange for my preliminary mis-calculations to ensure that the first shells we fired gave the Aussies adequate warning. After all they'd been jolly considerate to me; it was the least I could do, – and it was a part of the bargain I'd made with God. (I'm sorry if that sounds presumptuous.)

Every time I took part in an action, from then till the war ended, I did the same, – so that we never once hit an inhabited target, intentionally anyway, first time. Our first rounds always fell wide or short. I got great comfort from all this, feeling a sense of power that nothing else ever gave me. There was something quite unprincipled about it, of course, but as no one knew (apart from me and the Almighty, who I was confident looked the other way) I felt no sense of guilt whatever.

I knew that what I'd done was too insignificant to warrant swelling up with pride, but it was a personal achievement, and for a humble soldier to find the opportunity to act as an individual, using his own brain and his own pair of hands independent of all authority, was as exceptional as it was satisfying.

But if this achievement gave me pleasure, disturbing thoughts which persisted in coming into my mind did not.

Suppose trouble blew up suddenly. Suppose the enemy accomplished what we regarded as impossible, – and did get to our side of the gorge, for example by breaking through elsewhere and then outflanking our positions. They could then attack from our rear.

Suppose my mountain were an objective. It commanded three valley routes and would be a real strategic prize. There was no one else to defend it; its only denizen was me.

With no line to the battery I had no means of contacting my superiors. What would I do? I had no weapon, – and even if I had possessed a rifle I would have had neither the know-how nor the desire to use it.

I would be alone. It wasn't comforting to remember that attacks were invariably launched under cover of darkness. The only lighting equipment I possessed were candles. I'd got plenty of them, it's true. But in the open what use would a candle stuck in a bottle be, – except to give away my position? And if the enemy didn't get me the mountains would. One false step in the dark and I would be at the bottom of a precipice with a broken neck.

(You may think it strange that a fighting unit on the front line didn't possess a single electric torch. Some of the men had acquired flashlights privately but none had been issued.

Presumably the supplies of batteries had been exhausted.)

For the first time since I had taken up duties at Cavella, I felt nervous. I lit three candles that night and prayed for a quiet, <u>safe</u> night's sleep. It was granted, – but not before I'd made a resolution. After 0600 hours the next morning I would be 'off' for twenty-four. By fair means or foul, before darkness fell the next day I would find myself a lamp.

11 June

I've planned a shopping expedition for to-day. About seven miles to the north-west is a town called Schio which I believe is larger than Thiene and might be better provided with shops. In my haversack I have the Ross binoculars to trade.

I'm enjoying a morning coffee at Mario's Bar. I haven't made up my mind yet how I'm going to get to Schio but am waiting for something or somebody to turn up. Mario's is a good place to wait for things to happen; everybody coming into or leaving Piovene turns up there sooner or later.

Five minutes after writing the above I was joined by Alberto, one of Giulio's colleagues from the Mountain Post. Our conversation was 25-per-cent speech and 75-per-cent gesture but I had no difficulty in making him understand that I was paying for his refreshment; these chaps always wanted to treat me.

With a toot on its three-tone horn the Post Coach drew up across the square. The village Post Office was opposite Mario's and I watched the driver disappear into it. When he reappeared there was a shout of 'Lu-i-gi' from Alberto which brought him – 'post-haste' – across the piazza to our table. A quick-fire dialogue ensued between the two Italians, the consequence of which was that Luigi invited me to travel to Schio with him.

I was pleasantly surprised to discover that the postman's English was very good. As a young man he had worked as a waiter in an English-owned Riviera hotel whose patrons were mainly British. He was now around forty-five to fifty and a bronzed, short, broad-shouldered balding man with a face like tanned leather.

I was the only passenger that morning so I sat beside Luigi as he drove off. He described Schio to me as a clean, 'pretty' town built just before the war started. There were mills, he said, where silken and woollen cloths were made, and neat houses for the factory workers; there was a splendid *duomo* (cathedral), a college and a hospital for soldiers with 'hurt heads'.

We travelled northwards at first along the western side of the Astico river. He took a bumpy road forking off to the left which climbed in steep zig-zags to a less steep stretch of hillside. There I saw my first Italian cows, – they were of a colour I had never seen in England: greyish fawn, more the colour of deer than cattle.

Luigi told me we were nearing our first port of call, an isolated farmstead called Casetta de Roccia (Cottage by the Rock). We wouldn't actually see it as it was hidden by a clump of trees. Tall, pinkish-grey crags overhung it.

He stopped the bus at a point where a pebbly track led from the lane across a hundred yards or so of grass before being lost in the trees. He sounded his horn and waited.

A girl and a boy came running towards the coach, calling in high-pitched voices, 'Luigi, Loo-ee-gee!' They stopped short in their tracks when they saw me. Recovering from their surprise, they sped round to the driver's side, where the girl handed Luigi a letter for which he gave her a receipt. By his gestures I could tell he was saying he had nothing to deliver . . . this time.

The postman addressed the boy as Dino and his sister as

Vanna. 'Vanna! Dino!' I called out. The boy was round to my side of the vehicle in a second; the girl followed more slowly. They watched curiously as I rummaged into the depths of my haversack and abstracted a package. I paused, watching the children's faces, Luigi looking on amused. When I held up the treasure – a large block of Peter's Swiss chocolate – Dino's eyes almost came out of his head.

'Vanna!' I called, and beckoned. She moved close enough to hold up her hand and take the gift.

'*Mezzo per lei . . . e mezzo per Dino*,' I said, hoping it meant 'half each'.

The beginnings of a smile lit up the girl's face as she accepted my offering. Luigi said something in the local dialect, which caused her to reply, after a little bob of a curtsey, '*Grazie, Signore Tom-mee, Grazie.*' Dino echoed her words and then with more *grazie*'s and *ciao*'s we parted. Luigi started up the motor and we were on our way.

I thought what delightful kids they were and how nice it was to make the acquaintance of youngsters after living for over twelve months in a world where children no longer existed. I thought of my own sisters, and of my very young brother; and when I heard from Luigi a little of their tragic story (the children had been orphaned) I felt sad indeed.

Schio was just as Luigi had described it: a bright, clean, industrial town. He dropped me outside the Post Office, having told me where to find a shop which could supply my needs. He would take no payment but I did persuade him into accepting a packet of cigarettes. (I never met an Italian who could resist 'issue' cigarettes. With Argentine bully, English 'smokes' and Swiss chocolate, one had all the currency required for everyday use.)

The shop towards which Luigi had directed me proved to be what the Italians call a *Monte di Pieta*, which literally translated means 'Mount of Pity' but in actual fact is a pawnshop! I allayed the proprietor's suspicions by producing my Army Paybook as proof of my identity, – he had <u>good</u> reason for being suspicious; I was wearing my off-duty mufti and could have been a P.O.W. on the run. I explained as best I could that I wanted to do an exchange, trading in the Ross binoculars for something smaller and lighter in weight. I convinced him that they were my private property and by mime and words proved they had no Government markings on them. Soon I was trying out his stock, focusing on the mountains visible from his shop doorway. I eventually settled for a Zeiss pair, exactly the size I wanted, with excellent definition and magnification.

Near-by I found a sports outfitters and cycle shop. In a window display of climbers' equipment I spotted something I guessed would be very useful to me, – a wide canvas belt with two roomy pouches attached and several spring clips. I went inside and bought it. Looking at one of the bicycles it occurred to me how much more suitable for my purpose a cycle lamp would be than a pocket flashlight. It would have a carrying handle which I could visualize hanging from one of the belt clips, leaving both my hands free. So it was a cycle lamp that I came out with.

My shopping completed, I made my way to a square, three sides of which had shady shopping arcades while the fourth was open. It faced a small paved court with flower-beds and led to a wide stone flight of steps going up to the cathedral's main entrance. It was an imposing site and its mountain background showed up the building's white stone to splendid advantage.

A strange feeling crept over me as I sat there, looking across the piazza at the white, round-domed cathedral, the cypress trees and the high dark mountain range beyond. I was disturbed by an inexplicable feeling that I had seen it all before.

Normally I would never miss entering a church to whisper a prayer of gratitude for my deliverance from so many dangers, but that day something prevented me from doing so. I began to feel dizzy, and the whole scene in front of me took on an appearance of unreality, as though it were unsubstantial, a creation of my imagination. I was scared. It was a very disagreeable sensation.

I rose, crossed unsteadily to the nearby arcaded sidewalk and strolled slowly in its shade. The dizziness went off and my sight returned to normal. I struggled hard to shrug off the unpleasant sensations.

All the while an inner voice kept saying, 'You have been here before. Go and look inside the cathedral and you may remember.' But I said to myself, 'I won't! I don't want to. I have never been here before in my life.'

I wasn't enjoying this inner conflict and the longer it continued the more worried I became. The heat was terribly oppressive, even in the shade. I remember eventually saying to myself, 'Look! Be rational. Back in the winter you had a mental illness. You lost your memory. In the unlikely event of you ever having been here it must have been then.'

I don't know how far I had wandered before I became aware of a fine group of white buildings set back from the roadside. They stretched for a good quarter of a mile and in the spaces between were bright beds of flowers, tall pointed cypresses and flowering shrubs. Between what appeared to be residential blocks I saw two churches, each with a tall square campanile. I thought this might be the college Luigi had told me about. But I could see no students or staff walking about the grounds.

Just as I drew level with the wide entrance gates a Red Cross ambulance van turned off the road and drove in front of me into the college grounds. For a moment I thought I recognized its driver as Raymond, the young fellow who had taken me to the Vicenza hospital five months before. At that recollection a shudder of horror ran through me. But, had it been Raymond, I thought, he would have recognized me instantly; I was the only English soldier in Schio that day. Then, looking down at myself, I realized I was not in Tommy's uniform at all.

I went on, feeling even more disturbed now. That nagging inner voice was saying, 'You were there too. Can't you remember?'

'Rubbish!' I told myself. 'It's the heat. I should have had more sense than to sit in the sun so long.' But what had Luigi said about a hospital? There was a hospital for soldiers with hurt heads. Perhaps this wasn't the college, but the hospital he'd referred to. And when he said 'hurt heads' did he mean physically hurt, or mentally?

I stopped and looked hard through the railings, but nothing 'registered'. And all the time the beastly voice repeated, 'Can't you remember? You're not trying hard enough.'

'Hurt heads'. Yes, he must have meant brain disorders, or nervous diseases or, what did they call it . . . neurasthenia? There was no sign by the hospital entrance to indicate what its patients were being treated for. But after my shell shock I had had a mental breakdown. I knew that, even if I couldn't remember having it.

I said earlier that I was scared. I was more than scared; I was terrified. I remember asking myself, 'Did I have a hallucination an hour ago? Was that cathedral real?' If I'd had a mental illness once, – and there was no doubt that I had, – might it recur? Do people who've gone mad know that they have done so?

Oh! it sounds ridiculous now. All imagination. But that

summer's day over fifty years ago, I saw and felt nothing ridiculous or imaginary. The sensations were far too real.

I don't remember the conclusion of my day trip to Schio. It's about seven miles from Piovene by the direct route. I expect I hitched a lift.

13 June

I've come up to the mountain positions to see if any new supplies have arrived. No; nothing – so I'm still unable to complete the line between Cavella and the Command Post. I've been trespassing, taking another look at Bella Vista, where T— will operate from when he's not at the C.P. My panoramic drawing is still in position. T— should find it helpful. At least my leaving it will show I've no ill feelings.

I was inquisitive enough to see what they'd been up to. Calculations on the map table indicated they've trained No. 2 Gun on to the poor old railway bridge. I guess they'll do their registrations on that.

I have come to look at No. 2 Gun's position. None of the chaps are here as they're all searching for dug-outs. I notice no ammo has been brought up yet, so they can't do their registration shoot to-day.

Now I'm at No. 1 Gun Site; it's a hell of a hike. Sergeant Waller's a difficult chap to get through to; doesn't want me to forget that he has two more stripes. Once or twice I've been on the point of asking him about the safety of that gun's position but haven't had the pluck. After all, he's the Gun Layer and presumably the expert.

I've clambered up to the top of the rocky height in front of the gun and am sitting on a boulder with my map spread open. I want to know if there's a shorter way from here over to Cavella than the one I've been using, – viz. the front-line trenches. They zig-zag about such a lot.

It <u>looks</u> like a direct route would measure little more than half the distance, but if the contour lines are anything to go by the terrain could prove pretty rough.

I've decided to try it. You never know, it mightn't be too bad.

But it was! Much worse than I could have anticipated. All ups and downs. There were several dense patches of pine and fir trees and two lofty ridges with very steep treacherous ravine-lets between. Luckily, the streams, which would have been torrents after heavy rain, had shrunk to mere trickles and could be crossed without difficulty.

By the time I'd scrambled to the top of the second ridge I had to take a breather. I couldn't see them from there but I guess I was 200 to 250 feet above the level of the trenches I usually used. Well, my usual route might be longer but it was a darned sight easier.

When I'd got my breath back I went on. It was tough going <u>down</u> to the foot of the second ravine but much tougher coming up the further side. The whole slope was one mass of grey scree, – pebbles the size of ostrich eggs, all ready to slither downwards the moment you walked upon them. At my first attempt I managed to get just over half way before the whole lot slid down like an avalanche of stone. I finished up almost in the brook, with holes in the elbows of my shirt and a horizontal tear across the seat of my trousers. By judicious zig-zagging and picking out large boulders which didn't look easily movable I eventually reached the top. By the time I'd got to my destination I reckoned I'd travelled twice as far as I would have done the other way.

Having arrived safely in one piece, I brewed up some tea,

after which I made the necessary repairs to my torn clothing. Then I prepared a meal. I opened a can of cooked rice, gathered a mess-tin full of raspberries and strawberries and sprinkled Ideal tinned milk over the fruit. Result: raspberry risotto à la Cavella.

14 June

I was tired after last night's exertions and slept like a log. Just before dark I climbed high up towards the summit of my mountain and saw a glorious spectacle: the distant Dolomite peaks ablaze with all the colours of the rainbow as the sun went down.

I have put myself on laundry fatigue this a.m. Have washed out my socks and mended shirt and spread them on warm rocks to dry in the sun. I slept here at Cavella last night and came off duty (officially) at six this morning. If there's any transport going Thiene way I'll go and look up the boys at the club, or call on Giulio.

Clothes dry, I get myself dressed and tramp over to the Command Post, where the cookhouse is located, draw my day's rations and take them back. Plenty of exercise nowadays. I seem always to be coming or going!

I'll just clamber up to the peak and have one more look at the goings-on over the way. These Zeiss glasses are fine. Yes, the Austrian guns are installed in new emplacements. From up here I can look almost into the gun-barrels in spite of the camouflage. I'll check their positions in the O.P. and then mark them on my map.

There was a first-class shock awaiting me when I got back: two figures in officer's uniform standing in front of my cave entrance, surveying enemy territory through binoculars. One of them was the new O.C., Captain Hemming-Wale. He was a tall-ish, sandy-haired chap of about thirty-five who sported a gingery hairline moustache. I didn't know the Second Lieutenant with him.

I startled them as I jumped down into the trench and saluted. The Captain eyed me with an expression of near disgust, obviously strongly disapproving of my appearance.

'Who are you?' he asked.

I told him.

'You are improperly dressed.'

'Yes, sir. Excuse me while I get my tunic.'

'Stay where you are. Why are you going about dressed in that outlandish fashion?'

'It's more . . . practical, sir. For easy movement. For climbing, sir.'

'I don't like it. Go and get yourself dressed in regulation uniform.'

'Very good, sir.'

I went inside, grabbed my tunic and pulled it on. (I was still wearing shorts though.) The two officers followed me. I watched the Captain as he looked over my O.P. There was no candle burning behind my blanket-screen to attract his attention in that direction. Anyway, he didn't seem interested.

He seated himself at the Observer's table, looking closely at the drawing I had made and then examining the map below and the annotations and additions I had marked on it.

He pointed to my 'panorama'. 'Who did that?' he asked.

I told him. His reply was 'Um,' which I suppose you might describe as non-committal.

He proceeded to compare the drawing with the map and the real mountain panorama outside, seen through the look-out opening.

'Yes. I see the idea. Plumbley,' (– so that was the subaltern's name –) 'this may prove useful to you.'

('So Plumbley's going to conduct the first shoot,' I thought. 'Good luck to him!')

'I think it will, sir,' he said.

'Come outside. You as well, Bombardier.'

From the trench fire-step the O.C. scanned the landscape once more with his glasses. His gaze rested on one prominent object. He turned to me, pointed to it and asked, 'What's that cross thing, Bombardier?'

'I'm not sure, sir. It wasn't marked on the map, but I've plotted its position. Memorial of some kind, perhaps.'

'Go inside and find its range and altitude.'

'Very good, sir.'

Of course I had done all that long before his arrival. I fetched my list of suggested targets with the data I'd worked out entered beside each, and handed it to the Captain.

'Who instructed you to do this?' he enquired.

'Nobody, sir. I did it as a sort of pastime.'

Still looking at my paper he said, 'This is good. You evidently know your job.'

'Thank you, sir.'

The O.C. turned to his subaltern. 'Plumbley,' he said, 'we'll do our registration on that stone cross.'

'Hooray!' I thought. My prediction had proved to be right.

The Captain re-entered the O.P., followed by Plumbley. He was a rather undistinguished little fellow, apart from the way he shone. His buttons, boots, Sam Browne belt and cap badge positively glowed. His face, in the sunlight, was a shining pink. He was trying to grow a moustache but the few fair bristles on his upper lip weren't easy to see except in close-up. Oh! he was very new, very new indeed.

The Captain's voice rang out from inside. I stepped smartly in. His finger was on the phone buzzer, the receiver against his ear. He was pressing the buzzer repeatedly, – but of course nothing happened.

'Bombardier, what's the matter with this line? I want to speak to the C.O.'

'It's not complete yet, sir. I laid it myself but it only goes half way.'

'Why the blazes didn't you finish the job?'

I told him. (I noticed he referred to the Battery Commander as the C.O. We had been accustomed to saying O.C. Not that it mattered. Except surely he was the O.C., or C.O.)

Captain Hemming-Wale was addressing me. 'Is there anything fresh to report, Bombardier?'

I told him what I had just seen, explaining that the newly arrived Austrian batteries could only be seen from a higher altitude.

'Get going on the figures we shall need for silencing them.'

'Yes, sir.'

'And get the line to the Command Post laid before dark.'

'I can't, sir. We haven't any cable.'

'Good God, man. Use your head. Indent for some from the Q.M.S.'

'I can't do that either, sir. He's away sick. I am the acting Q.M.'

'Why haven't you contacted H.Q. stores?'

'I've been begging for wire ever since I was sent here, sir. I've asked the Duty Officer every day to—'

'I'll look into this.'

The Captain picked up his document case and turned to leave, saying as he did so, 'Bombardier, I like to see my men dressed as British soldiers. Especially when on important duties. Understand?'

'Yes, sir. I understand, sir. But I'm <u>off</u> duty now, sir.'

'What do you mean, – off duty?'

'I came off at 0600 hours, sir.'

'Then where's your relief?'

'I haven't one, sir.'

'Why the hell not?'

'I'm the only Observer, sir.'

He looked at me a little less disapprovingly.

'If you were off duty, why were you working here?'

'I like to, sir. I like the mountains.'

'Why aren't you with the men at the battery?'

'I haven't many friends there.'

'Then make some.'

'Yes, sir. But I have friends at the Italian First Aid Post. And at the Thiene Club.'

A pause.

'Am I right in thinking you served in Flanders?'

'Yes sir. Messines . . . Ypres . . . Passchendaele.'

'What happened?'

'I got knocked out. Shell shock, sir.'

'So I've heard.'

(I wondered how <u>much</u> he knew.)

'You're an unusual fellow.'

'Yes, sir.'

'Right! Complete preparations for that shoot. Then take the rest of the day off . . . And, don't let me <u>see</u> you improperly dressed again.'

(I noticed the emphasis placed on 'see'.)

'No sir, I won't . . . Will that be all, sir?'

He didn't reply, but stalked off along the steep track to where his driver was waiting.

*

I was still worried about No. 1 Gun's position and decided to go and talk to T— about it. I had found Sergeant Waller unapproachable, although he would be the man most closely concerned. I couldn't discuss such a problem with any of the officers; it would be seen as exceeding my authority. As B.C.A., T— would have to make all the calculations for the shoot, so after the Gun Layer he was the most responsible.

I had barely begun explaining what I thought was the possible danger to the gun crew when he interrupted me with a display of choice language.

'F— off, clever Dick,' he shouted. 'Have you forgotten who's B.C.A. these days?'

'No. But I think I have some information—'

He didn't allow me to finish.

'Are you telling me how to do my effing job?'

'No. I just want to prevent an accident.'

'Who the hell do you think you are, Bighead? Shut your gob and get back to the O.P. where you belong.'

After that unpleasant little encounter I was glad to find a stores lorry just off to the plains. I jumped aboard and at Piovene had the luck to run into Luigi the postman. He was bound for Thiene and gave me a lift. I don't remember exactly how I spent the afternoon apart from two minor events. One was that making my way to Carlo's I passed the music shop where the young *nipotina* had enchanted me with her piano-playing, and found it closed – for good. The other was that I was kissed affectionately by Mrs Carlo in return for a gift of bully-beef, and was able to get two whole slabs of Suchard's chocolate from her husband. I'm pretty sure I spent the rest of my free afternoon at the club, joining in another cosmopolitan sing-song. I believe that was the day when the Italian troops were first introduced to American jazz, when 'Alexander's Rag Time Band' and 'You Called Me Baby Doll a Year Ago' were added to the repertoire.

I hitched a lift back on the ammunition wagon, which was taking forty-eight rounds of ammo to the battery. Forty-eight! That was two dozen for each of our guns. (In one of the heavy bombardments at Ypres we had fired 300 shells an hour throughout the day!) But forty-eight was all H.Q. Stores could spare us. It was a damned good job the Austrians didn't know or they would have asked for an armistice forthwith. Yet, as a confirmed pacifist now, I was secretly glad; howitzers with little ammo are – almost – harmless.

Near the Command Post I ran into Alf, wearing a very new Bombardier's stripe on his sleeve.

'Good Lord, Alf!' I exclaimed in surprise. 'What did you get that for? Reckless driving?'

'Naa then. No bleedin' cheek from the likes of you! I'm one of the nobs now, Bombie.'

'I can see that, Alf. Congratulations!' I grabbed his hand and shook it. I was genuinely pleased.

'Ta very much.'

I touched the newly sewn-on stripe. 'Seriously . . . how come, Alf?'

'Cos I've been appointed chawfer to the Captain. Yus. Lord 'Emming-Wale himself. I've just dropped 'im at the C.P. and I'm waiting to drive him down to Povey. It's no use you 'anging about . . . No lifts for common people, only nobs! Sorry.'

Good old Alf! I had grown really fond of him. He had been the only chap in the battery I could think of as a pal.

I was just walking away when he called after me.

'Oh! I nearly forgot. Your ole pal's come back, Ron. The bleeder you asked me about . . . Snowy. Major Bleedin' Snow . . . So long, Ron boy!'

And that gave me one <u>more</u> thing to worry about.

The Hospital for Neurasthenics in Schio.

CHAPTER SEVEN

My Five Hours' War

This sketch may help you to visualize the setting.
I found it impossible to suggest the breadth and depth
of the gorge separating the opposing forces' positions.

14 June 1918

What a glorious evening! All around Cavella is a veritable Garden of Eden, Alpine variety. You'd never guess there was a war on. Here I gather it's because both Austria–Hungary and Italy claim ownership of the South Tyrol. It shouldn't belong to either; an area as beautiful as this should belong to the whole human race.

I think I'll sleep outside to-night; it's awfully black in my cave after sundown, even on moonlit nights. There's no moon this week, though.

I've placed my bed-head in a cleft in the rocks where it will be shielded from the wind. Not that there's any now. It's very still. After sunset the temperature drops quickly but I've an ample supply of blankets so I shan't be cold. As I make my bed I think back to the only summer night I slept al fresco in Flanders. It was some time in July; on the edge of a newly harvested cornfield near Ypres. I only had a groundsheet to lie on and gosh! wasn't the stubble prickly? And the poppies! The next field to us hadn't been reaped and it was a mass of red blooms. I've got poppies growing all around me here, – mostly yellow.

Night of 14/15 June

You think of all sorts of things when you lie awake under the stars alone. I thought, 'I'll have to teach myself a bit of astronomy after I'm demobbed.' About the only constellations I can name are the Plough, the big W of Cassiopoea and the cluster of little stars they call the Pleiades or Seven Sisters. That brightest one of all must be a planet, – either Jupiter or Venus.

There's no moon, so the stars look like fragments of diamonds blinking out of a vast umbrella of black velvet. When I was very young I used to wonder which star God lived in. In a way I still do.

I wonder if they're having as lovely a summer in England. It's fifteen months since I saw my sweetheart and my family. The longer I'm away the more I wonder whether the Ella of my thoughts is a reality or a dream-girl. Will she be disappointed in me when at last we do meet? Shall I be disappointed in her? That is something I refuse to think about . . . I'll just go on believing that we shall continue to love each other and that our love can be something different from the kind the older men talk about.

So many of my illusions have been shattered, I must hold on to this one. Nearly all the married fellows talk of their wives as nagging women whose only virtue is that their bodies can be used to gratify their desires. I can't believe that marriage is only that. If that is what marriage turns love into, I'll do without it.

Oh hell! what's the use of rambling on like this about love and marriage? I don't know anything about either – and anyway I've got to get through the war first . . . Let's get some sleep.

I woke up with a start and found myself shivering with cold, in spite of an extra blanket on my bed. I looked at my watch. Its luminous dial said 2.40. I pulled the cycle lamp from under my straw pillow and shone it around.

I was enveloped in dense white mist. It was the first time I had ever been inside a cloud and Gosh, was it cold!

I pulled the top blanket up, wrapped it around me and swung out of bed. (I slept in a vest and shorts during the Italian summer, not fully dressed as I had in Flanders.) I made for my dug-out entrance but it was difficult to locate because the lamp's rays only intensified the fog. The distance couldn't have been more than forty yards but I made several misses before hitting the target. I had left a candle burning inside.

I made my way back and carried the bed inside in order to resume my interrupted sleep. I was still shivering. I'd been foolish bedding down in the open. But it wasn't only the cold that was causing me to shiver; it was fear.

It's strange, but I'd slept alone more nights than I can remember without ever experiencing undue nervousness. But now a troubled feeling had come over me rather like the sensation I had experienced in Schio. There it had been the fear of something unknown and uncomprehended which was now past; here to-night it was a foreboding, a state of mind familiar to me from nights on the Flanders battlefields, a feeling of things to come that I had no power to prevent. The fear was increased by my total isolation. In Belgium I had always had comrades close by. Here I was completely alone.

I couldn't think of anything better for company than a blazing fire. At least in this fog it couldn't possibly be seen by the enemy. I soon had a roaring blaze going in the old brazier just outside my cave entrance and a minute later the kettle was boiling cheerfully upon it. I fetched the tin of cocoa and made myself a steaming mug. I'd much rather have a cup of hot cocoa than a single, double or treble of rum. I remember whispering a prayer as I sipped it: 'Please God, help me not to be a coward.'

I was just swallowing the last mouthful, sitting on the edge of the bed, when it happened.

At first I believed it to be a thunderclap, very close. But when the clap was repeated and then swelled into a roar of staccato crashes I knew it was no thunderstorm. There's only one thing that produces such a terrifying noise as I heard then, – an artillery bombardment. I rushed to my doorway. The dense fog had turned an uncanny colour, though the gun flashes and shell bursts couldn't be seen.

The Battle of the Asiago Plateau had begun. I didn't know it at 03 ack emma of course, – but it had.

I hurriedly pulled on my uniform and went out into the

trench. The upper layers of mist must have dispersed because I could now see the higher Alpine skyline lit by the flashes from guns and mortars. The noises reverberated and re-echoed from one mountain to another. I had been 'blooded' in artillery bombardments more concentrated than this but never one so alarmingly, astoundingly noisy.

The shells falling nearest were coming from an easterly direction, i.e. to my right. On my left all remained quiet.

What the blazes were the Austrians up to? This was no orthodox barrage, preparing the way for an infantry assault. Nobody could cross the Astico Gorge, unless they could fly. Either the bombardment was diversionary, an attempt to fool us into the belief that an attack was imminent, or its purpose was to prevent our guns being moved to a part of the front where they could be more usefully employed. If the second objective was their reason, they obviously weren't aware that we'd only got two guns and forty-eight rounds of ammunition to fight with.

Now that the uneasy silence was over, I felt less nervous. I made myself some more cocoa. I felt I had to do something: I couldn't sit on my backside idle and useless waiting for something to happen. There was that voice inside me, that part of myself which often became a nuisance, telling the other part of me what I ought to do. At first I refused to listen.

My mountain, St. Peter's Peak, was escaping the bombardment, which if anything had increased in intensity. I was expert enough by then to judge the direction of approaching shells by their sounds. I was certain the north–south bit of our trench defences was getting a murderous strafing. It was an obvious artillery target and by far the easiest one in the whole of our front line. But that was my only communication route with my unit, – with the rest of the British Army in fact.

Cavella was shell-proof and impregnable. If I wanted to remain safe and sound the intelligent thing to do was to stay where I was.

It was no use. 'You must get over to No. 1 Gun Site,' the voice repeated. 'You've got to get there before someone orders them to open fire.'

'It's not my business,' I said. 'T— accused me of telling people how to do their job; he called me "Bighead". Why should I think I'm the only one aware of the danger to the crew if they aim the gun low? T—'s a trained B.C.A. Surely he would have taken a look at the emplacements before now. He would have noted the danger and reported it.'

'But suppose he <u>didn't</u> inspect the gun sites. Suppose Waller <u>hasn't</u> had the chance to check safe elevations yet. They haven't done a practice shoot, you know. And it won't be daylight for an hour or more.'

For the first time in Italy I wound on my puttees. I buckled on my new belt, with compass and jack-knife already attached, and hung the cycle lamp on the spare clip. I had stopped arguing with my conscience. I knew what I had to do and how to do it.

As I have said, the enemy shelling of the trench line was so intense that it was useless to attempt to reach the mountain Command Post, where I assumed T— would be. I had no telephone communication, so there was only one other way to go: directly to No. 1 Gun Site.

I took the candle to the map table and laid the compass upon it. The reading to the gun position was easy enough to remember, – exactly 100°. (That's 100 degrees clockwise from magnetic north.) Then I studied the map to memorize every detail it showed, photographing in my mind the sequence of the hazards.

I checked over my equipment: compass, cycle lamp, water bottle, first aid pack, half a bar of chocolate, packet of cigarettes

. . . Anything else? Good Heavens yes: tin hat! (I'd nearly forgotten my shrapnel helmet. I hadn't had to wear it since I came to Italy.)

The din of the bombardment was incredible. The light from the gun flashes should have helped visibility but the fog was too dense for that. All it did was to become illuminated, which made the confusion worse.

On my map, the straight-line distance was about 2,000 metres; but that took no account of the two deep ravines and three ridges I knew I would have to cross. With ups and downs included it would be more than two miles of the toughest going I had ever encountered.

My watch read 3.20 as I set off. Once more I offered up a prayer for guidance and strength (physical and moral) and begged that the gun wouldn't be ordered to fire before I reached it.

I won't describe every detail of that nightmare journey, for nightmare it was. In spite of all my precautions, there were unforeseen circumstances no one could prepare for.

I had unexpected good luck with my first real hazard, the slippery slope which had given me trouble on my daylight trip. I did slip and I did finish in the brooklet at its foot, but no harm resulted.

I didn't expect so much difficulty with the second hollow, but I was over-optimistic, – it made amends for the first.

Have you ever strolled on a steeply shelving stretch of shingle beach? (We have a few at Bexhill after the spring tides have been to work.) If you have, and have tried to walk down the pebbly slope, you'll know what happens. You lose your foothold and are carried down helplessly on a mini-landslide. This was in essence what happened to me. Only my descent was perhaps 300 feet. I

completely lost my balance and cascaded downwards on a disin-
tegrating carpet of rocks and stones, accelerating in speed the
further it went. Just before my pebbly avalanche hit the bottom
I somehow scrabbled into an all-fours position, – and crashed
head-on into a boulder. The impact of the collision almost
stunned me. Had I not been wearing the helmet I had almost
neglected to bring, my mission and possibly my life would have
ended on the spot.

I dragged myself up; my compass was undamaged and my
torchlight still functioning. But now I was directly under the
path of shells screaming towards our gun positions. I don't
know which scared me most now: the shells, the dark, the fog or
the fear of an accidental fall. The shells, I think, – suppose one
fell short!

By lamplight I could see that I was now among a grove of
stunted oaks. I had taken notice of them the previous day and
knew that I was nearing my journey's end. Beyond them would
be one more steep climb, a hundred yards or so of thick pine
woods, and then at the summit of the next rise I would look
down straight into No. 1 Gun Site.

I was thankful that in the midst of the din of battle one sound
was absent: the roaring thud that your own gun makes when it
is fired close by.

I was among the pines when I heard the warning whine and
crescendoing roar of an enemy shell that was not going over. I
flung myself flat on to the carpet of leaves, buried my face in the
pine needles and held my breath. The shell screamed down very
close behind me, buried itself deep before it exploded, and made
the ground on which I lay heave as though it were alive. It had
been fitted with a delayed-action fuse, thank God.

Tree trunks and branches crashed down around me, followed
by a storm of earth and rocks. Something fell across my back

and pieces of stone pinged on my helmet. I held my breath again, waiting for the second, third and fourth shells to follow number one, but they didn't come.

At last I was able to collect my wits together. I managed to lift myself up sufficiently to pull my lamp out from under me. The bulb had, mercifully, survived a second near-catastrophe. I twisted round and saw in its beam that a large fir tree had fallen crosswise over me. Its lower boughs, resting on the ground, had prevented its weight from crushing me and the dense matting of twigs and leaves had acted as a cushion, protecting me from the hail of lethal rock debris. Another near-catastrophe had become another near-miracle.

But my troubles were far from over.

I cannot recall how far it was to the crest of the very last ridge, – 200 yards perhaps, – but I can remember with extreme vividness what happened just a dozen paces from the top.

There was a blinding flash, – even in the dense fog it was dazzling, – followed almost instantaneously by another; then a head-splitting double report. The second of the two explosions was I think the loudest noise I ever heard. The blast lifted me off my feet.

I don't think I was actually stunned but everything suddenly went quiet. I felt a sharp stab of pain between the ears . . . then, apart from a continuous buzzing sound, silence. No more roaring of shells, no din of the distant bombardment, no noise at all . . . just silence all around.

Yet again I pulled myself to my feet and felt all over. I was still in one piece. I staggered onwards and upwards, almost uncomprehendingly.

I was still holding my lamp, although by now its light was less bright. My compass had gone. It didn't matter now. As I clambered up that last steep slope I heard no noise from my feet nor any of the din of battle. By the time I reached the crest I was breathless, ready to drop with fatigue. I shone the rays of my lamp downwards, hardly understanding why.

I was on the very edge of a cliff and thirty feet below me, in the midst of a cloud of swirling white fumes, was a howitzer. A howitzer . . . My brain cleared. This was our No. 1. This was the place I had to get to!

The pungent white fumes filling the gun pit weren't mountain mist. They were the gases from a cordite charge and the explosion of a missile filled with lyddite. (Austrian shells used to burst with black smoke, ours with white – unless we were using T.N.T.)

I stood for some seconds, motionless, waiting for my brain to take in what I could see.

Slowly a realization came to me. The thing I had hoped and prayed would not happen, – the thing it had been the object of my mission to prevent, – had happened, and I had arrived three minutes too late, – three minutes too late to save the men who had fired that gun from death and injury. My eyes filled with tears, – of disgust, frustration and disappointment.

I had heard a double blast: first the report of the firing of the shell, then (a split second later) the explosion of the shell itself as it hit the rock face.

A cloud of acrid white smoke floated up to where I stood, and started me off on a coughing spasm. Almost immediately there was a plop in my ears, followed by the noise of shells screaming overhead and bursting uncomfortably near-by below, the continuous roar of a distant artillery bombardment, – and the dreadful noise of men groaning, men below me buried by falling rock.

I could hear again! And I could think clearly again too. I slithered down to the emplacement level on a cascade of loose rock debris. By the fading light of my torch I saw heaps of rubble, –

rubble brought down from the cliff in front and the near-vertical bluffs at either side of the excavated pit. There was no visible sign of the crew – only those horrible groaning noises coming from the piled rocks.

I shone my lamp-beam around and it dimly illuminated the shape of a man ten or twelve yards distant. At first I thought he had been blown there into a sitting position, then I saw he was swaying back and forth, his face covered by his hands, screaming what sounded like 'You bloody fools . . . you bloody lot of fools.' I rushed over to him. It was T—.

I gripped him by the shoulder and yelled at him to run back to the Command Post to fetch help. He took no notice, continuing to rock to and fro. 'They were bloody fools . . . all the lot of them . . . bloody fools.'

'Why were they bloody fools?' I asked, but he wouldn't answer. I cried, 'For God's sake, man, pull yourself together. There are men buried. We want help.'

He just sat there deaf to my pleading. I could get no sense out of him. He showed no signs of physical injury yet he was acting as though he was demented. I couldn't tell whether he was shell-shocked, play-acting or in the worst stages of blue funk. Whatever it was, he wouldn't budge.

Some yards away I could distinguish figures climbing out of a near-by trench. They ran towards my lamplight and together we hurried back to the gun pit. We had only my miserable light to work by, – and our bare hands, – but we struggled like demons dragging away the fallen rocks to free the buried men. One of the rescuers went off to find some crowbars.

We were working on a fellow whose legs were underneath a boulder larger than an upright piano. It was he who had been groaning, though he was quiet now. We had to give up: we couldn't lift the rock.

We got out two other men, both unconscious but alive, using shovels we found near the gun-trail. I hadn't yet seen the Sergeant, although, being the Gun Layer, he would certainly have been there when the gun was fired.

As I searched, I wondered what crazed idiot had given the order for an untested, unregistered, new-from-the-factory howitzer to be fired on an unknown target in total darkness. Whoever he was, I considered him a murderer.

At last, on the further side of the gun-limber I saw Waller, just as two more men stumbled towards us in the blackness to help. There was nothing we could do for him until the chaps returned with the crowbars. They arrived carrying candle-lanterns and levered up the rock so that we could pull him free. His face had been so badly battered it was almost unrecognizable. I was glad our lights were so feeble. He was unconscious, but still alive.

I shouted to the nearest man, 'Go and get some more help.' He disappeared into the darkness.

An enemy shell came roaring down and pitched twenty or thirty paces away, showering us with stone fragments. Apart from temporary 'wind-up' we were all O.K. Once again I ran to T—, still cowering against a hollow in a cliff-face. He was the only man who could find the way from here to the Command Post. I shook him, shouted at him, and begged him to go and report the accident and send instructions. But it was useless. He wasn't a man – just a lump of quivering jelly.

I knew the battery had no M.O. on its strength. It seems absurd now but it is absolutely true. The extent of the medical supplies available for eighty or a hundred men was one small Red Cross box, which I had dumped at Bella Vista O.P., over three miles away. We were totally unprepared for an attack. But we had been at war for <u>nearly four years</u>, – and well-planned attacks always came when and where you weren't ready for them!

I've described myself more than once as a very amateur soldier. I was young in years too. But I was the only N.C.O. on the spot and somebody had to do something. It wasn't the time to stand around waiting for a superior in rank to turn up and take control. As I couldn't contact my superiors I would have to act on my own initiative, – and take the consequences. I would go to the First Aid men at Fontanella and enlist their help.

I called to the gunner who was trying to make Waller comfortable, 'Watch out for any officer or N.C.O. who turns up. Tell him Bombardier Skirth has gone to fetch an ambulance. I might be half an hour.'

I raced off along the dirt-track and down on to our supply road. It wasn't till then that I noticed the fog had gone. I was thankful to see the first glimmerings of daylight in the eastern sky. All along the mountain massifs the bombardment was continuing at the same peak of intensity.

It was a race against time. Sergeant Waller and the other injured men required skilled attention immediately. I had failed them once; I wouldn't fail them again.

I gambled and took the goat-path down. It was risky, but if I avoided an accident it would take only half as long. I prayed that Giulio would be at the post and that I would get there safely. Both my prayers were answered. I was yelling 'Giulio, Giulio' at the top of my voice as I came out on to the road one hairpin above his depot. Three figures appeared in the dawn gloom running to meet me, Giulio leading. I clasped his arm and, breathless, did my best to explain what had happened as we hurried down to the post.

I made myself understood well enough for Giulio to take charge. '*Accidente, accidente . . . Presto!*' he cried to his comrades. He detailed one of them to telephone a hospital and then he, Alberto and I jumped into the ambulance wagon.

He drove like one possessed, – with headlights blazing. In the cities of the plain, forty or fifty miles away, anyone awake must have wondered what had happened to the black-out regulations up in the mountains as we swung round the hairpins.

I was able to guide Giulio almost into our gun pit and he manoeuvred the vehicle so that its headlamps floodlit the site. A voice roared, 'Put out those bloody lights!' but we took no notice. If an enemy pilot were crazy enough to fly his plane over right now, – well that would be just too bad!

During my absence extra helpers had arrived, though there still wasn't an officer, or even a senior N.C.O., among them. The rescuers had extricated seven men and it seemed that all the gun crew were now accounted for.

Alberto and I acted as stretcher-bearers. The man with the crushed legs was groaning pitifully again, but the one in the worst shape was Waller. I had thought that what I had seen at Messines, Ypres and Passchendaele had hardened me to the horrors of war injuries, but I found my mouth filled with saliva, as it does just before you're sick.

I couldn't tell whether the Sergeant's injuries had been caused by the rocks which had rolled upon him or the blast from the bursting shell, or both. I won't attempt to describe them: I'll just say that I was firmly convinced that if he ever were to recover, which I thought impossible, no one would be able to recognize him.

I did my best to fight off my nausea and obey Giulio's instructions. He had given me a huge roll of cotton wadding to help staunch Waller's bleeding, having demonstrated on his own face what I had to do.

With the injured men all aboard Giulio leapt into the driving seat and we raced away.

I was beside Dick Waller. I was glad that inside the ambulance it was dim, though it was getting lighter outside. My task was to lay pads of wadding across his battered face to soak up the blood. Before we had completed half our journey I had used up the roll. I dragged my personal supply out of my haversack and used that, wrapping its ends around the back of my patient's head. I was glad he was unconscious.

My supplies of wadding were exhausted very quickly. What should I do? Alberto hadn't any: he was busy with splints and bandages, straightening out the legs of the man who had been groaning. (He was unconscious as well now.) I had an idea. I unwound one of my puttees and used that as a bandage to secure the last dressing of cotton wool, blood-saturated as it was. I wound it twice around his head to keep the part where his eyes should have been covered. After that I hoped I wouldn't have to touch him any more.

Three of the other men were able to take the cigarettes I offered them. One kept coughing blood but he went on smoking just the same. I'd seen a man do that at Messines: he was bare to the waist and there was a little square hole almost in the middle of his back. I was walking behind him ready to help him to the Dressing Station. Suddenly he slumped on the ground, dead, with the cigarette still between his lips.

Half way down the mountain we ran into trouble, – a part of the road which was under enemy shell-fire. Several shells fell pretty close, before the frightening scream of one made Giulio brake hard. The vehicle skidded to a stop and we flattened ourselves on to the floor. The shell must have narrowly missed the ambulance roof before it pitched on to the next lower section of road, thirty or forty feet below us. When we raised ourselves up to look we saw the crater it had made exactly in the middle of the highway.

Giulio drove on, creeping carefully round the sharp hairpin

and stopping a few feet from the crater. He jumped down to inspect it. It was impossible to drive either side. There was only one thing to do: fill the hole.

I don't suppose you have ever had to fill a pit eight feet across and five feet deep with rubble you have collected with your bare hands. Believe me, it's a job you don't want to do more than once in a lifetime. But we three did it. I've no idea how long it took but our hands were sore and bleeding long before we had finished. Then, to add insult to injury, just as we were finishing the Austrians sent over a shrapnel shell, which burst in the air just away to our left. We dived underneath the ambulance, listening to the lethal bits of hot metal sing downwards. I heard Giulio exclaim, 'Santa Maria!' I couldn't see him properly from my hiding place but I called out to ask if he was O.K. 'Yes, O.K., O.K.,' he replied. We waited a minute more and then crawled out and got back into the vehicle. There was daylight coming in through several new holes in the canvas roof.

The hospital was on the outskirts of Vicenza. We found the casualty staff standing by. Medical auxiliaries ran forward to take our stretcher cases into the building. As Waller was lifted down I saw he was past all human help. I thanked God He had let him die painlessly.

Doctors and nuns had taken charge now. There seemed to be nothing more for me to do, – except the one thing I didn't want to do there, and that was be sick. I felt completely humiliated, unworthy and disgusted. But if nature says, 'Be sick,' you are, whether you're in a hospital, a church or your own home, and there's nothing you can do about it. I remember how sympathetic the staff were. '*Pazienza*,' an orderly whispered. 'Don't worry; it doesn't matter.' But it did, – to me.

I was led into a small anteroom and someone brought me a large beaker of coffee. Soon Giulio reappeared, with a sheet of paper bearing the names of our seven casualties. (The details would have been taken from their identity discs; we all wore them.)

I was instructed by the Hospital M.O. to report to my Commanding Officer immediately upon my return and request him to telephone the hospital as soon as practicable. The poor fellow with the crushed legs had died, not from his injuries at the gun site, but from a piece of shrapnel from the overhead shell-burst; the splinter had come through the ambulance roof and penetrated his chest. The one with the cough had a 50/50 chance of pulling through.

Giulio was in the room adjoining, washing away the blood from his hands and forearm. Alberto stood by with a bandage, which he wound over a dressing he had applied just above Giulio's left wrist. I looked at my hands. The blood on them was the Sergeant's. As I washed them clean my eyes filled with tears.

I asked Giulio how he had hurt his arm. '*E niente*,' (It is nothing) he said and laughed.

I told him as best I could about my climb in the fog and dark from my O.P. 'Giulio, if I had been five minutes earlier at the gun pit I would have saved them.'

'You did your best,' he said. 'No man does more than the best. You were . . . how you say? *Coraggioso*.'

'Courageous? No, Giulio, I failed.' This time I did weep; I could hold back the tears no longer.

'No! No! You did well, Rinaldo. Because you did not fail, five men live. Without you, all five die. Is it not so? *E vero* (It's true).'

I didn't know whether it was true or not.

Just as we were about to leave, a nun wearing a wide white starched hat came running into the hallway to hand me the puttee I had used as an emergency bandage. It had been machine-washed and dried. I thanked her as gracefully as I knew how. As I replaced it, it came to me that I must have presented a rather comical appearance with only one leg puttee-clad. I managed a smile through my tears and we set off.

'*Andiamo, Alberto,*' Giulio called to his young comrade. I climbed into the seat beside him. Before we left, Giulio put his hand on my arm and said, '*Rinaldo, amico. E Guerra* (It's war). One does not worry . . . The war is this . . . There are two men . . . One man must die, one man must live. *Il Dio decide* (God decides). You not decide, me not decide. So I say . . . always . . . *che sarà sarà.* How you say in English?'

'What is to be, will be.'

'*Si.* Oo-at ees to be oo-il be. *E vero.*'

My mind went back to that dreadful November day in the quagmire of Passchendaele. I thought of Jock and me . . . It was true. God had decided then, – one man lived, and one man died.

Giulio started the engine and we set off along the Piovene road. There was no fog now; the sun shone brightly from the eastern sky. It was going to be another lovely day.

As we approached the village I observed that Giulio had only one hand on the steering wheel. The other was hanging limply by his side.

'*E niente,*' he repeated when I asked him about it. 'Piece of *bomba* make little hole in arm.' He applied the brakes and pulled to a stop on the right-hand verge. 'Little piece.' He moved his arm and rested it upon the wheel, pointing to his forearm and the bandage. 'He go in here . . . He come out here . . . *Finito!*'

'But Giulio, you drove us all the way from the shell crater to the hospital! You should have stopped to have attention.'

While I had been feeling sorry for myself in the hospital, my friend had avoided doctors and nurses, concealed his injury and sought out an orderly to give him an anti-tetanus injection, rather than make himself a nuisance.

'Giulio,' I said shamefacedly, 'you called _me_ brave, while all the time—'

He interrupted: 'You were brave boy, _si._'

'While all the time you did nothing! And I did nothing too!' Giulio was smiling. I began to feel better. 'Do you know, Giulio, in England we call people who are no good "good-for-nothings"?'

'_Buon per niente?_ Good-for-nothings?'

'Yes. I reckon we are two good-for-nothings. Giulio and Rinaldo!'

'I like that! You. Me. Two good-for-nothings.' We laughed.

So Giulio added one more expression to his English vocab.

He was just going to restart the motor when he put his fingers to his lips, and then to an ear. '_Ascolta!_ (Listen!) . . . _Ascolta._'

We both held our breath and listened. And what did we hear? Nothing. No rumbling of guns, no distant shell-bursts, no noise of battle whatever. The mountains were as silent as the plains.

I wondered what the time was and looked at my wrist watch. Its glass had splintered. The dial had a minute spider-web pattern of cracks making it impossible to see its hands or figures. I held it to my right ear but could hear nothing.

'My watch is broken,' I said. I wondered which of my morning's tumbles had been the cause.

'No,' Giulio replied. He lifted my wrist and put his ear close. 'It goes. I hear it.'

I put the watch to my left ear and heard the steady ticking. Yes, it _was_ going.

(This little incident brought home to me for the first time that my hearing had been permanently affected. I didn't know it then, but slowly and surely for the next forty years it would continue to deteriorate.)

'*Silenzio!* All is quiet,' exclaimed Giulio. '*La Guerra e finita! Evviva la pace!*'

We laughed together again. All might be quiet now, but we knew the war hadn't finished.

Giulio sat me down in the *piazzetta* in Piovene. We shook hands as though we were parting for good, although we both knew we were not. Was it because that morning we had faced death together?

Giulio had joked that the war was over. Well in a sense it was, – for me anyway. My 'Five Hours' War' had ended.

After the Battle

I found the Piovene Command Post unoccupied. I had hoped to see Mr. Salisbury there. He, alone of my superiors, was the one I could talk to about the morning's events.

I knew I should have to give satisfactory reasons for absenting myself from the battery without leave. Technically I had been on duty since 6 a.m., – so I should have remained by the telephone at Cavella. (The fact that the phone wasn't connected was of no military significance.)

I tore off a sheet from the message block on the table and wrote as follows.

Premature	shell-burst	No. 1 Gun	0600 hours
approx.	Caused	seven	casualties
in gun pit.	Two men	died of	wounds
five men	injured.	Only I	knew
position	of Italian	Mountain	Rescue Post.
Receiving	no instructions	to the	contrary
I went	and asked	assistance.	Willingly
given.	Casualties	transported	to Hospital
Vicenza.	Details on	form	given by
Hospital	M.O.		

I addressed the message to Officer Commanding 239 Battery
R.G.A. and at the foot added my regimental signature and rank.
I clipped the hospital's report form to it and hoped that would
cover me. Whatever I was going to be charged with to-day it
couldn't be desertion in the face of the enemy or dereliction of
duty.

Tired as I was, I hurried over to the cookhouse and told the
fellows there of my adventures. It was still only early morning
but I had recovered from my nausea and I was feeling famished.
I'd had only two mugs of cocoa and a beaker of coffee in the last
fifteen hours.

The two cooks fixed me up with an appetizing repast of bacon
and fried bread plus canteen tea. I discovered from them that
the firing had ceased at 8 o'clock. No doubt both Allies and
Austrians were digging in; it wouldn't be long, I thought, before
there was a counter-attack to regain lost ground.

Leaving the cookhouse, I saw Mr. Salisbury coming out of the
Command Post. I asked him if we might have a few words in
private.

Listening to my account of the events of that morning and the
action I had taken, he seemed sympathetic. But he made no

comment other than 'You'd better report to the C.O. immediately.' Wherever he had intended going he changed his mind and preceded me into the post.

Sitting side by side at the table were Captain Hemming-Wale and Major Snow.

Why hadn't Salisbury warned me? Perhaps he thought it better this way.

So this was it! After seven months we were face to face again. This, of all days, was the one fate had decreed that I should meet him: the very time when I least expected it and was least prepared.

My God! how he had changed. Come to that, so had I. Had I not changed I would never have dared to act and speak as I did. I saluted correctly; then, incorrectly, I spoke first, without asking permission as military procedure demanded.

'Bombardier Skirth reporting for duty, sir. In place of Bombardier T—, who is sick.'

I placed my papers in front of him, then stepped back and awaited his reaction. Captain Hemming-Wale lowered his gaze and busied himself with some documents on the table. I saw Mr. S. standing beside him, waiting for something to happen.

I observed the trembling fingers of the Major's hand as he picked up the two forms to examine them. I didn't feel in the least afraid. I once again had that strange sensation of watching and listening to someone who wasn't really me. As he read my abbreviated report I studied his face. He looked quite twenty years older, very tired, haggard, emaciated; like a skeleton that had been thrust inside a shrivelled skin too small to hold it comfortably.

The papers quivered as he held them before his colourless eyes. It seemed that only slowly was he grasping their significance.

At last he laid them side by side, tapping his fingertips on the table beside him.

He picked up the hospital sheet and passed it to the Captain. Then, slowly, he took my report between a shaking finger and thumb and looked up at me for the first time. His glance sent a cold shudder through me, not so much of fear as of loathing. From my face his eyes moved to Mr. Salisbury.

'Adjutant,' he said in a dry, parched sort of voice, 'do you know this man?'

'Yes, sir. He is our Observer, sir.'

His tired eyes came back to me. He looked very hard, as a man does whose sight is defective but who refuses to wear glasses. It was a look of bewilderment. Gradually in the next few seconds the truth seeped into my brain. He didn't recognize me! He didn't know who I was. To him I was a complete stranger.

When he spoke again it was as though each word was being forced out of him. Still holding my report, he pointed it at me and said, 'This – is – a – lot – of – bloody – nonsense . . . There – was – no – premature – shell-burst . . . The casualties – were – caused – by – enemy – action.'

I remained silent, for the very good reason that I couldn't think of anything to say. I was the bewildered one now.

The Major was repeating, 'All – bloody – nonsense. Casualties – caused – by – enemy action. Enemy action . . . Understand?'

I was beginning to. I watched him as he lifted a box of Swan Vestas from the top of his Abdulla packet and took out a match. He struck it and applied the quivery flame to the bottom corner of my report. I watched the flame curling upwards towards his finger and thumb. I recalled seeing something like this once in a cinema; I had never thought to see it enacted in real life.

After the ashes had floated down to the dug-out floor, he rapped out, 'Who gave you permission to leave your post? Who gave you authority to call on the bloody Italians?'

I had anticipated that these two questions would be asked at some point, but I had no militarily convincing answer to either.

'I did, sir.' As I was hesitating, racking my brains, the quiet voice of Mr. Salisbury saved the day for me. I hoped the brief glance I gave him expressed my gratitude.

'Then forget you ever did so, Adjutant,' Snow commanded. 'And as for you,' he turned to me again, 'I do not need you to replace Bombardier T—. He is as fit as you are.'

He pointed to the ashes of my report form on the floor. 'You will forget all about that. You never made out any report. If you did, I never received it. You will forget all about it. That is an order . . . Understand? Now, get out.'

I did so. I understood perfectly, – understood that if in war the truth is an embarrassment, you tell a lie. You suppress inconvenient truths when expedient and order your subordinates to keep their mouths shut. As a soldier I was required to obey, not to think. That had been impressed on me frequently. Now in addition I was required to forget, because my commander ordered me to do so.

So that is the story of my reunion with the only person in the world for whom I ever felt real hatred; the one human being of whom I was for many months desperately afraid; the man who in a mad rage would have shot me dead on the battlefield at Passchendaele.

It is a cliché that truth can be stranger than fiction. That meeting, on the day of the Battle of the Asiago Plateau, was in some respects the most extraordinary of the many unusual events which befell me during my service as a British soldier. There I stood, facing an officer who, but for a disorder of his brain, would have had me placed under instant arrest and charged with two of the gravest offences it is possible for a soldier to commit: insubordination and desertion, either or both of which could incur a heavy prison sentence, or even death by firing squad. But he, because of the malfunctioning of his brain, remembered nothing of what had happened.

I clambered twenty or thirty paces up the steep mountainside and sat at the foot of a pine tree. I wanted some time to think; my mind, like my body, was becoming fatigued. It had been an exhausting day already, – and it was only half over.

Ten minutes had elapsed when Snow, the Captain and Mr. S. emerged from the Command Post. I watched them making their way, as I guessed, towards Bella Vista O.P. If that was their destination they would be out of my way for the best part of an hour.

I scrambled down and re-entered the Command Post. There was something lying on the map table which contained very important information.

There it was: the firing orders for the early morning, entered on the appropriate form and signed 'R. T—, Bdr'.

That small sheet of paper told me all I wanted to know: map reference, range, altitude, and deflection and elevation calculations. The target No. 1 Gun had been trained on was the new battery I had reported to the Captain. Whoever had been in charge that morning – Snow probably – had ordered an untested, unregistered gun to fire at an elevation of only 30°, which had made certain that the first shell would hit the rock-face.

I left the Command Post unobserved and tramped over to the scene of the tragedy. The gun site was deserted. A fir tree was hanging at a drunken angle over the cliff from which the rocks had fallen, one third of its roots clawing out into empty air. The gun had slewed round and was off its mounting.

I was able to examine the gun-sights, which had escaped

damage. Sure enough, the elevation had been set at 30°. I went back to the ammunition store and counted the shells: twenty-three. The charges: twenty-three. The fuses: twenty-four delayed-action and twenty-three No. 106 (instantaneous-exploding). So one of the latter had been fitted.

There could be no possible doubt about it. It <u>was</u> one of our shells which had caused the casualties, either from blast, shrapnel splinters or rock falls, – or all combined.

After a prolonged search I found one of the gun crew who had escaped injury. He had been temporarily stunned by the blast but had recovered sufficiently to give me further information.

Enemy shells had been directed against our two gun positions, although neither had been hit, and there had been no casualties as a result. One shell had cut a telephone line between No. 1 Gun and the Officer Commanding. 'We hadn't got a signaller to go out and repair it so we got no orders through,' the Gunner told me. 'Then along came Bombardier T— with a candle lantern. It was dark and foggy. There was some sort of argument between him and the Sarge.' (That was Waller.) 'T— lost his temper and I heard him shout, "Those are the Major's orders. You're to fire at once." Sarge kept looking at the paper he'd brought. I was humping a shell along to the loaders when we heard a "Jerry one" coming. We thought the b——r would drop straight in the gun pit. We all ducked. Anyway, it pitched short. On the top up in front.' (I wondered if that was the shell that had brought the tree down behind me.) 'I saw T— run off. He squeezed himself in a crack between the rocks. He was windy as hell. I watched the blokes load the shell and then went off to fetch another one. That's when the gun went off. Don't know <u>who</u> fired it. Didn't hear any order from the Sarge. The blast knocked me for six.'

'Gun blasts don't knock you out,' I said.

'Not that blast – the bloody shell hitting the cliff.'

'Are you sure that's what happened?'

'Course I'm sure.'

'Who fitted the shell fuse?'

'I did. No. 106.'

'Thanks, chum,' I said. I didn't need to hear any more.

As I was going he said, 'That sod T——. He's the windiest b——r I've seen. When that shell was coming you'd a thought it was going straight up his backside.' (He used an army synonym for the last word.)

I set off to find T——'s dug-out. The last time we'd met he'd refused to let me have my say. This time he was going to listen.

Now don't think I was condemning a man for being scared when under fire for the first time. When shells fall close everybody is scared, every time. We all have the wind up then. But if there's a sudden crisis and your mates' lives are in peril and they are unable to help themselves, you have to hurry to their assistance. You don't have time to think whether you're afraid or not, – not until it's all over. The one thing you don't do is scuttle away to comparative safety and skulk unseen until the danger is past. That is an unforgivable sin in war-time and that is what made T——'s behaviour despicable to me.

When I eventually found him he displayed precious few signs of genuine shell shock. If anybody could recognize the real thing I could.

It isn't easy to get a message through to an angry individual whose only responses to your remarks are 'Shut your bloody gob' and 'B——r off', but I persevered.

'Through negligence you helped to kill two of our chaps and wounded five more,' I began. 'Shut up and listen! You helped to kill Sergeant Waller and his mate. You worked out a gun eleva-tion that made a shell hit the cliff.'

I stopped. He was livid with anger and was coming towards me. His narrow dark eyes were blazing. He was, I suppose, a good ten years older than I was, but I was taller and quite a half-stone heavier. He stopped just out of range of my boot, which would have contacted a very sensitive part of his anatomy had he taken another step. I noticed for the first time that he was cultivating a Kitchener-style black moustache; no doubt to add a little distinction to his otherwise characterless face.

'Stay where you are, T—. I'm not a fighting man but I'm not a coward either. You're not the first rat I've come across. SHUT UP! Don't kid yourself that you're a fighter. You wouldn't lift a finger to help rescue those fellows you'd helped to bury. Stop swearing. I've said what I wanted to . . . I just hope I never see you again, – and if I do, I shan't know you.'

He didn't move an inch as I stepped to the dug-out entrance and pulled the gas blanket aside. As I left, I called back, 'I bet they'll give you a medal for your bravery this morning.' He was shouting more obscenities at me as I went out into the trench.

My last remark was sarcastic of course. But my sarcasm was wasted – because they did!

So far as I can recall, I never did see T— again.

I believe it was still only a little after noonday when I wearily plodded my way back to Cavella. I still had seventeen hours of my twenty-four-hour duty spell to complete but I was so dog-tired I just didn't care. If anyone wanted me they could jolly well come and get me.

I had just reached the O.P. entrance when the silence was abruptly broken. For five hours at least everything had been quiet. Now the sudden rumbling roar of distant artillery fire away to my right told me the battle had been reopened. Somehow I overcame my fatigue and found enough energy to climb the steep slope of the peak to my pet viewing point up above. The Allied forces on our far right were putting down a heavy barrage on the plateau eight or nine miles away. That meant the '48 Div' were going to launch a counter-attack to recapture the ground lost in the enemy's early offensive.

'Oh well!' I thought as I clambered and slithered back down, 'Battles around Asiago don't concern me. They're out of range of our guns anyway. And if Cavan or one of his minions thinks up some bright way of getting 239 involved in the scrap, they can jolly well get on without yours truly. I'm going to get some sleep.'

I slung my trappings on to the floor beside my bed and threw myself upon it. I'd barely had time to finish a brief prayer of gratitude before I was dead to the world.

A unique incident occurred that afternoon of which I was completely unaware at the time. I was honoured by a visit from no less a personage than our revered Commander-in-Chief, the Earl of Cavan himself. He came in person to inspect my observation post and gaze at my handiwork.

He and his accompanying Brass Hats had entered my retreat while I was sleeping off my exhausting morning. Presumably nobody realized that technically I was still on duty and should therefore have been at my table, for I was never put 'on the carpet' for neglect of duty that afternoon. Had anyone bothered to pry behind the curtain they would have seen the bogus shrine of St. Peter and the recumbent figure of the Observer sound asleep in front of it! But obviously nobody did. So there I was peacefully slumbering, – evidently not snoring, – only a few yards from the Big White Chief himself, blissfully ignorant of the honour bestowed upon me.

*

When I awoke, the distant bombardment had died down to per-functory shelling; I supposed the counter-attack had finished. I got up and made myself a kettle of tea.

I took off my tunic to give it a brushing over. One of my shoulder tabs was missing and the metal R.G.A. had gone with it. Then I noticed the holes. There were three or four about three quarters of an inch across and they were not tears; they could only have been made by shell splinters or rock fragments. Two of them were just below my breast pocket, – indicating that something had gone in and come out again parallel with my ribs. That was a near miss and no mistake! There was a similar pair of holes just below the shoulder.

(After my demobilization I brought that tunic home. I never mended the holes as I was slightly superstitious. Ella saw it herself, as well as my forage cap, with the top, sides and peak riddled with smaller shrapnel holes.)

When I examined my helmet I had more reason than ever to be grateful. I knew what the big dent in the top of the crown was a memento of: my head-on collision with the boulder, but what about the two new holes in the side of the brim? Not dents, holes, – talk about a charmed life!

All the same, my feelings of gratitude were mixed with sadness. I knew I had done my best, but five of our men wouldn't be in hospital now, and two would be alive and well, if only my best had been just that little bit better.

The 'Official' Report

One quality I had never given Major Snow credit for possessing was imagination. I was fully aware that I had been given more than a fair share of it, but our battery commander . . . Well, as it turned out, I was wrong.

I have told you how, on the afternoon of the day of battle, our Commander-in-Chief paid our battery a visit and inspected my O.P. while I was asleep. I have very good reason for believing that he and Snow spent a profitable hour that afternoon putting their hoary heads together in order to concoct a report on that battle, and in particular on 239 Battery's share in it.

One morning, perhaps a fortnight later, I was doing a spell of duty at the Mountain Command Post. Lieutenant Salisbury entered, asked the usual question: 'Anything to report?' Got the usual answer: 'Nothing, sir,' and then handed me an important-looking foolscap envelope.

'Read this,' he said. 'Remember it's confidential. Apart from me and the C.O. no one has seen it. Strictly speaking you shouldn't see it either. But . . .' He hesitated. At the door he said, 'I'll be back in twenty minutes to collect it,' and strode away.

There were nine or ten sheets of what appeared to be stencil copies of a report on the part played by British troops in the Battle of the Asiago Plateau, 15 and 16 June 1918.

I glossed over the first seven or eight pages, which contained matters of only passing interest to me, – details of the Austro-German offensive against our 48th Division mainly. Apparently they had regained all the lost territory on the second day. But when I came to the last two sheets I sat up and took notice. They contained what purported to be an account of the activities of 239 Siege Battery on the morning of 15 June. I read them with what I can only describe as uncomprehending astonishment.

In the early hours of 15 June, Austro-German forces made a surprise attack against the British positions on the southern crest of the Val d'Astico. These positions were unmanned by our Infantry. Behind them were the howitzers of 239 Siege Battery, R.G.A. To counter this attack the Commanding Officer, Major Snow DSO, ordered the heaviest possible barrage to be put down ahead of our front-line trenches. Leaving only skeleton crews to serve the guns, the remainder of the personnel rushed forward to man the unoccupied trenches in readiness to repel the enemy attackers. Because of the accuracy of the battery's shelling, the enemy infantry sustained heavy losses and only a small number succeeded in crossing the river valley and scaling the heights on which our trench-system had been constructed. Bitter hand-to-hand fighting ensued and although our artillerymen were untrained in trench warfare they improvised weapons with which they held the invaders at bay. Finally in spite of severe casualties they were able to repulse the attacks. The few enemy survivors withdrew.

What I had read turned my stomach over. I began to feel sick, – literally. I had to go outside and fill my lungs with some fresh mountain air.

It was a tissue of lies. The only thing missing from the account was the Truth.

The concluding paragraph expressed Lord Cavan's personal opinion of the operation, – that, had it not been for the valour displayed by our men, there would have been a catastrophic enemy break-through. In short, 239 Siege Battery had saved Italy from complete and utter defeat.

Who, I asked myself, is going to believe that? I thought hard . . . Everybody, – except those who knew the truth. And who knew the truth? Snow? As far as I knew, he'd never been near the front line. Jordan? Yes! He and Salisbury, like me, knew that a crossing of the Astico Gorge ahead of our positions was impossible. (The Italian authorities had known it too, which is why they had evacuated the sector.) But Captain Jordan had gone, so that left only Mr. S. and myself. None of the lower ranks would ever know about the document I had been privileged to read. So it boiled down to this: only two people knew for certain that <u>no</u> attack of any kind whatsoever had been made against our pos-itions that fateful morning, and those two were the Lieutenant and me.

The truth was this: 239 Battery had only two howitzers, both untested. We did not possess a single rifle, bayonet, machine-gun or hand-grenade. We had exactly forty-eight 100-pounder shells plus their fuse-caps and charges. Our No. 1 Gun fired one shell, which hit a rock-face and burst prematurely, killing two of our own men and wounding five, and putting the gun out of action. Our No. 2 Gun fired its twenty-four shells against a rail-way bridge which had already been destroyed. Several of our men received slight injuries during the enemy shelling but none required hospital treatment. <u>Not one enemy soldier crossed the Astico Gorge.</u> There was no assault to repel. As a fighting unit, 239 Battery contributed nothing whatever to the Allied victory at Asiago, – if there was any such victory. <u>That</u> is the truth.

I had just refolded the typed sheets and returned them to their envelope when Mr. Salisbury reappeared.

'Well, Bombardier,' he said, 'what do you think of that?'

'Sir,' I replied pleasantly, 'as a soldier, I have been told I'm not paid to think.'

A half-smile appeared on his face.

'Really?' he said.

'Yes sir, but . . .' I hesitated.

'Go on,' he said encouragingly.

'Who wrote it, sir?' I handed him the envelope.

'It bears Lord Cavan's signature,' he said.

'Oh! I hadn't noticed.'

'And you an Observer! I'm surprised, Bombardier.'

'But . . . was it supposed to be true? I thought, sir, if you'll forgive me saying so, I thought it was a piece of fiction . . . something written by H.G. Wells or . . .' Again I hesitated.

'Or Swift? *Gulliver's Travels*, you know,' he suggested.

'Or Lewis Carroll,' I added.

The Lieutenant pulled a wry face.

'Time to stop thinking, Bombardier,' he said as he walked off.

My story will have shown that there was a somewhat unusual relationship between Lieutenant Salisbury and Bombardier Me. Had it not been for the two pips on his cuff and shoulder we should probably have been friends. But the officer/other ranks gap was unbridgeable. In the Infantry regiments, officers led their men 'over the top'. Their lives often depended as much on the loyalty and affection of the men they commanded as those men's lives depended on their officers' skill and leadership. In action, they were all comrades and caste was forgotten.

In the Artillery, not so. The officers rarely had any direct contact with the lower orders. Only when their duties required the assistance and cooperation of an Observer, a B.C.A. or a translator-clerk were people like me in their company – and then, with the very rarest of exceptions, they treated all other ranks with contempt and/or condescension. Friendship between a commissioned officer and a lowly Bombardier would be considered prejudicial to military discipline. But Salisbury was a decent chap. I liked him and I think that he liked me. A few days earlier I had thanked him for coming to my rescue during that sticky interview with Snow, but he had brushed the matter aside. Our relationship, even if the unbridgeable gap forbade a friendship, was a tacit mutual understanding – which is <u>nearly</u> the same thing.

Since the battle I had taken odd spells of duty at Snow's Command Post in between turns of observing at Cavella. I was convinced that he had no recollection whatever of our previous association. The result of all this was that I had a strong advantage: I knew much of which he was completely ignorant. Perhaps that is why I was no longer afraid of him. I judged him to be a sick man, but could feel no compassion towards him; memories of the mental torture he had inflicted upon me were still too keen. Neither could I help despising him. The last example of the depths to which he would sink in the pursuit of his ambition only added to a detestation which I already found it difficult to conceal.

Fortunately, throughout the rest of that year Snow was more often absent from the battery than in command of it. Where he went and why I neither knew nor cared.

One morning in early July I was on duty with Snow at his Command Post. The C.O. had just completed putting his signature to some official documents. Having placed them in their respective envelopes he pushed the lot across the table to me. As was his custom he didn't speak; there was no need to. I knew what was required of me, – viz. to take charge of them until the Dispatch Rider arrived and then hand them to him.

As I recall, it had been a pretty boring morning. I had finished writing out our revised Nominal Roll, – something like a school register, listing the names of all the men now on the strength of the battery, their service dates, home addresses and so forth. From this a remarkable fact had emerged – that owing to war casualties, sickness, transfers, promotions, etc., only <u>two</u>

of the 130 men who had sailed from Southampton on 31 March 1917 were still with the battery: the man on the other side of the table and me.

Snow cleared off and I was left alone to await the D.R.'s arrival. Idly I toyed with the correspondence, laying the letters side by side, then one on top of the other. I saw a flap projecting from the end of one envelope. Evidently it hadn't been sealed. Closer examination showed that none of the flaps had been stuck down.

I was curious, – and quite unprincipled, I admit. I went to the doorway to make sure no one was approaching. Then I did what you might have been tempted to do. It was, at least, a small relief from boredom.

Or was it? The contents of those envelopes were about as boring as you can imagine: 'returns' re this, 'requisitions' for that, 'receipts' for the other, etc., – all tremendously uninteresting to me, yet no doubt of extreme importance to some tin-pot official.

And then I came to the last one. It was addressed in Snow's handwriting to the Commander-in-Chief, Italian Expeditionary Force, G.H.Q, Italy, the Right Honourable the Earl of Cavan, – and in the top left-hand corner it was marked 'Personal'.

I wonder what you would have done. Said, perhaps, that opening other people's letters isn't the done thing? Well, this was already open. That reading other people's letters is unethical? Perhaps. But remember they opened almost every letter I wrote, – 'personal' or not.

I stood on guard in the doorway as I read its contents, which went something like this:

My lord,

I have great pleasure in accepting your award of Bar to my Distinguished Service Order and promotion to the rank of

*Lieutenant Colonel, in recognition of my leadership in the
course of the 15 June Battle. It would be in accordance with
the contribution my battery made to that victory if one
Military Cross, one Distinguished Conduct Medal and one
Military Medal were made available for distribution among
the remaining personnel. I suggest these three awards would
be adequate in the circumstances.*

My grateful thanks, etc. etc.

R.A. Snow, Major, R.G.A.

Now I understood the purpose of the fictitious report. Snow and
his Commander-in-Chief had devised it as a means towards
their own self-glorification. Cavan had thought up the original
futile scheme (– sending us to defend positions that needed no
defending –) and wanted to justify it to his superiors back in
Blighty. So together they had concocted a string of falsehoods
which would be accepted as gospel truth in Whitehall. Their
'report' implied that Cavan, with a military genius far superior
to any Italian general's, had put his finger on the one vulnerable spot in the Alpine defence-line, and by 'holding' a surprise
attack made against it had prevented a major disaster. Snow,
being the perfect yes man in a situation such as this, had col-
laborated.

I doubt whether after fifteen months of service in the field I
had many ideals left. But if I retained any belief in the decency,
honesty, and integrity of our officer hierarchy this letter killed it
stone dead.

Our unit commander and his chief had together drawn up
a 'report' which was false in every particular, and presented it
to their superiors as historical fact. Not content with inventing
an enemy attack, they had fabricated a battle (– only a little one,
it's true, but you can't invent big ones –) ending in a glorious

victory. <u>Now</u> they were going to invent some heroes by whose valour the victory had been won. And Snow had already received his share of the spoils!

Now I had heard tales of medals 'coming up with the rations' and had dismissed them as 'old sweats' yarns'. But here in front of me was written proof, – decorations parcelled out like packets of cigarettes to be distributed to whichever Tom, Dick or Harry took the C.O.'s fancy.

Of course, many men must have earned the medals they wore; of course thousands who deserved awards never got decorated, but how many received honours because a number had been 'sent up with the rations'? And what were those decorations worth?

A couple of days later I was summoned to the Command Post. I found the C.O., Captain Hemming-Wale and Mr. Salisbury there. I stepped to the table, clicked heels and saluted, waiting to hear why I was 'on the carpet'.

Major Snow spoke. 'Bombardier, you are to receive a Military Medal for your part in the battle on 15 June.'

I was appalled and dumbfounded. Me? <u>Snow</u> couldn't have selected <u>me</u>. I didn't know what to say. It was something I was totally unprepared for. At last I managed to stammer out, 'But . . . sir . . . I didn't take part in any fighting that day . . . I was—'

The Major interrupted: 'I am recommending you for a decoration. You will receive the Military Medal. That will be all.'

I was gradually recovering my composure. 'No, sir,' I thought, 'that will <u>not</u> be all, not by a long chalk!' Somehow I had got to decline it and damn the consequences. I couldn't live with my conscience if I accepted.

Snow must have been studying my face and have observed my lack of concentration. I heard him repeating the words 'You will receive a Military Medal in due course.'

I had to say something. 'I feel . . . honoured, sir . . . but I could not accept a decoration for carrying out everyday duties. I did nothing to deserve it, sir.'

I couldn't believe Snow knew anything of my solo effort to prevent No. 1 Gun from firing. All he knew was that I had gone for assistance. What I'd done in the early hours of that day no one knew but me, and I didn't want a medal for that.

An incredulous look spread over the Major's face. He turned to his two subordinates.

'What is the matter with this man?' he asked. 'Has he been behaving . . . normally lately?'

'Yes, quite normally, sir,' Mr. Salisbury replied. Captain H-W nodded his agreement.

Snow turned his glance on me and the vile scowl which used to terrify me reappeared.

'Bombardier,' he growled, 'if I instruct you to receive a decoration, you receive a decoration. Understand?'

'Yes, sir. I understand, sir. But . . . I beg you not to give that order, sir.' I could see he was livid with anger, but I went on: 'It isn't easy to explain, sir. It's to do with my religion . . . My beliefs won't allow me to accept rewards for helping to . . . to kill people. For a long time I have had a conscientious objection to taking part in killing. But I have always done my duty . . .'

I couldn't think of anything else to say. A good thing, probably; I'd said too much already.

Snow's face showed signs of colour for the first time. The pale parchment skin began to change its hue, – patches of purple appeared upon it. I thought he might have a seizure. He was almost choking as he snapped, 'A bloody conchie! You little rat! Get out of my sight. And don't come near me again.'

I saluted smartly. My cheeks were burning as I said, 'No, sir. I won't, sir. Thank you, sir.'

And as I left I didn't dare look across at the other two. I would have hated to see disapproval on <u>their</u> faces.

In one way at least fortune was kind to me, because it decreed that I shouldn't see Snow again until the late autumn. Circumstances, unknown to me, took him elsewhere.

I was uneasy for a time, wondering what unpleasant consequences might ensue from my confession. They wouldn't block my promotion I knew (– I had already declined it –) but they might reduce me to Gunner's rank. Well, they didn't, but they managed to do one disagreeable thing, – a thing I suppose I ought to have foreseen. I was due to go on Blighty leave two weeks after the interview. A day or two later I was summoned to the B.S.M.'s office and informed that my leave had been indefinitely postponed, on instructions from my Commanding Officer.

Back home in Bexhill, Ella, – and, of course, my family, – went on wondering why I never came home. They saw that other Tommies rarely had to wait six months, whereas in my case more than sixteen had gone by. I never wrote to tell them the reason; how those unfortunate 'principles' of mine were proving my undoing. In fact even Ella never knew the reason, – till now.

After my interview with Snow I removed my two blue service chevrons and gold wound stripe. I didn't feel it consistent to continue wearing <u>them</u>. In any case, their main function was to impress people at home; they never impressed <u>anybody</u> in the firing line!

Over the course of the war, hundreds of men, mainly of the younger generations, refused decorations, – although I didn't know that at the time I declined mine. The most eminent, I suppose, was the poet Siegfried Sassoon, who was certified insane as a result.

*

Around mid-July, an important-looking sheet appeared on our battery's notice board:

Awards have been made to the following officers and other ranks, for their participation in the Battle of Asiago Plateau, 15 June 1918.

1. To the Commanding Officer, Major R.A. Snow: –
   The award of a Bar to his Distinguished Service Order and promotion to the rank of Lieutenant Colonel.
2. To the Deputy Commanding Officer, Captain A. Hemming-Wale: –
   The Military Cross.
3. To Sergeant R. Waller, killed in action: –
   The posthumous award of the Distinguished Conduct Medal.
   Because of his heroism and devotion to duty under heavy enemy shell-fire which cost him his life.
4. To Bombardier T—: –
   The Military Medal.
   For meritorious service to his Battery Commander throughout the operation.

Signed
Cavan, Field Marshal
Commander-in-Chief, B.E.F. in Italy

I was glad about No. 3 on that list: the award of the D.C.M. might bring consolation to Waller's relatives. As for the other three, I would rather not comment, though I need not tell you that the selection of T— gave me a shock.

*

In April 1919, after my demobilization, I received two letters, both unexpected.

The first was enclosed in a very official-looking Artillery-crested envelope. It consisted of one hand-written sheet of paper and a glossy photographic print. The writer proved to be no less than my former chief, now Colonel R.A. Snow, D.S.O., etc., etc.

The letter expressed his appreciation of my loyal service, both to him personally and to the battery under his command. He was glad to inform me that as a consequence of my 'untiring devotion to duty' I had been mentioned in dispatches. (This was considered the next best thing to winning a medal.)

The original of the print he had enclosed had been taken by an R.F.C. pilot who 'observed' a shoot during which I worked unaided for two nights and a day. It pictured the damage to roads and railway at a place called Conegliano. The damage done had been severe enough to seriously interfere with the movement of enemy forces in that area and the excellence of the gunnery had been largely down to my calculations.

I suppose the fact that the Colonel had acknowledged my existence, let alone written appreciatively, should have given me a glow of pleasure, but it didn't. I destroyed both the letter and the photo forthwith.

Only a few days later the second letter came. This one surprised me even more than the first – and that's saying something.

Dear Old Comrade,

I thought I must write to tell you I think you were a real sport to cover up the way you did concerning a certain unfortunate incident out in Italy. It was real decent of you to keep your word and not split on me.

I hope you're getting on alright.

Your old comrade and pal
Sergeant R. T—, M.M.

Incredible as it may seem, he signed his letter like <u>that</u>, – with a reminder that his gallantry had won him a Military Medal, and promotion! I don't know whether he was aware that he'd got it second-hand after I'd refused it, but he did know that <u>I</u> knew that of all the things he deserved for his conduct in the early hours of 15 June 1918, a medal for bravery wasn't one of them.

This letter was another souvenir I didn't trouble to keep.

'The proper study of mankind is man,' wrote Pope. Well, I had plenty of time and opportunity to study men throughout the war, – and I have enjoyed over a half-century of further study since, – yet there are some members of the genus that I still can't understand. High up on the list is Sergeant R. T—, M.M.

Old bridge over River Piave. This was done in pencil on the spot and transformed into an Indian-ink pen drawing while at college in 1920.

CHAPTER EIGHT

Filling in the Blanks

Terme di Montegrotto. 'Marvellous recoveries from radioactive hot-mud baths. Spa water for arthritis, etc. Recuperative treatment following injuries, wounds, nervous breakdowns, etc.'

Very few happenings of that summer have remained in my memory. We were in action in several of the battles for Monte Grappa and for a while were billeted in the badly strafed hill-town of Bessano, which must have been a very picturesque place before the war. Later we were moved to a village called Spresiano, another twenty miles east on the Venetian plain. A mile north of the village was the River Piave, the No Man's Land between the opposing forces. It flows, in summer-time, in numerous shallow channels with dry shingly banks between them, and is nearly a mile wide. Some of the bitterest fighting of the war took place on its banks, – and in its waters.

I was at Spresiano throughout the months of August, September and October 1918. Unknown to either of us at the time, Ella's brother Ernest was also there for six weeks of the time I was. (We discovered this after the war! – although I ran into quite a number of his regiment, the Gloucesters, I never saw him all the time we were both there.)

I have one more story to tell, not entirely a war story although it could hardly have happened in peace-time. My first attempt at relating it, – an unsuccessful one, – made me search again among my picture post-cards and other war relics in hopes of filling in some of the big gaps in my memory. This second investigation (June 1971) bore fruit: it unearthed clues which my earlier searches had missed.

These clues were contained in a small coded crossword puzzle made in faint pencil on the back of a folded pocket map which I carried all the time I was in Italy. Underneath was written, 'Ella holds the key.' I have no recollection of compiling it and did not know of its existence until last week. As the original is almost illegible I have made a copy.

A	B	C	D	E	F	G	H	X	8
K	F	T	U	S	O	M	O	■	I
I	N	J	K	O	R	X	X	T	I
O	H	M	U	B	V	Q	W	■	Q
O	X	U	P	I	S	U	P	■	L
X	Z	L	S	P	P	S	■	■	V
K	S	P	I	N	W	L	G	W	K
M	S	Q	J	P	M	B	X	W	3
S	U	P	Q	R	R	S	D	D	9
L	M	P	X	K	Q	T	T	F	I

At first I thought it must be something quite trivial, a means of passing away a few moments of boredom. But something made me take it seriously enough to attempt to solve it.

I assumed I had used the standard military code; I must therefore discover the code word. The clue to it was 'Ella holds the key.' I tried the first three solutions that entered my head: her address, her second Christian name and her surname.

Her road's name was Windsor. That was a failure. So was her second name: Mildred. Everything now depended on Christian. And Christian it was.

I decoded the message using the letter-arrangement below (it was obvious that the top line could be ignored): –

C	H	R	I	S	T	A	N	B	D	E	F	G
J	K	L	M	O	P	Q	U	V	W	X	Y	Z

									I
H	Y	P	N	O	S	I	S		9
M	U	C	H	S	L	E	E	P	3
S	K	I	N	V	B	A	D		M
S	E	N	T	M	O	N	T		A
E	G	R	O	T	T	O			R
H	O	T	M	U	D	R	A	D	C
I	O	A	C	T	I	V	E	D	H
O	N	T	A	L	L	O	W	W	I
R	I	T	E	H	A	P	P	Y	8

The right-hand upright gives the date with the year number reversed: 3 March 1918. (Ella's birthday). The remainder of the message reads as follows:

> Hypnosis. Much Sleep. Skin v. bad. Sent Montegrotto.
> Hot mud radioactive. Don't allow write. Happy

So, after a lapse of more than fifty years, the solution to a little crossword puzzle has filled in <u>some</u> of the gaps in my memory. It has told me that I received some form of hypnosis therapy in hospital and spa treatment in the radioactive mud of Montegrotto. On p. 243 you can see a card which I must have obtained during my stay there.

This discovery induced me to write to the Italian State Tourist Office. I received invaluable help from them, including an illustrated brochure of the Montegrotto Spa. Treatment there is fabulously expensive, yet people come from the world over to receive it.

Apparently the hot-mud springs at Montegrotto were known and used by the ancient Romans. During the war the whole complex was requisitioned by the Italian Government for experimental health work on war casualties. I believe I was one of their 'guinea pigs' and may have been one of the first ever patients to receive radioactive mud treatment; when my memory partially returned, although I recalled nothing of my stay, my skin ailment had been completely cured and my 'gas-cough' had disappeared too. (My mental restoration was I believe the result of the hypnosis/sleep therapy I was given, presumably at the hospital in Schio.)

Raymond and Hem

August 1918

One day I was detailed to take two G.S. Wagons to Mestre to collect supplies and stores. We were based twenty-five miles north at that time, near the village of Spresiano.

Mestre is one of the industrial suburbs of Venice, situated on the mainland. During the war it was an important depot and railhead. The road and railway run on a viaduct over the swamps and across the lagoon into the city centre.

There was a British Army R.T.O. at the station and it was to him I had to report. I was informed that the supply train had been delayed and wasn't expected until the next day. By now I was so accustomed to hearing this kind of news that if a train had arrived on time I should have suffered from shock.

As it wasn't possible to telephone my C.O. at Spresiano, I persuaded the R.T.O. to give me a 'chit' of explanation – otherwise I would be considered to have taken French leave. The R.T.O.

also helped me to billet the four men I had brought with me for driving and loading. I left them to their own devices until the morrow and strolled across the station piazza into the shopping street adjoining.

In those days, Mestre wasn't exactly a place to write home about. All the same I did, – I bought some view-cards and wrote messages on them while taking a demi-litre of *vino rosso* at a pavement *caffè*.

I heard the clop-clopping of military boot-heels as a smart young fellow wearing the grey uniform of the International Red Cross Brigade approached. He stopped, leaned towards me staring hard and exclaimed, 'Holy Moses! If it isn't young Spotty!'

I recognized him instantly as Raymond Raggett, the chap who had taken me from San Martino to the Vicenza hospital several times the previous January.

He joined me for a drink and I explained why I was at a loose end in Mestre for the next twenty-four hours. Luckily Raymond had just begun a two-day leave spell. In a minute or two he had fixed me up with board and lodging at the Red Cross Headquarters nearby.

We sat for a good hour talking. The great advantage of an Italian pavement *caffè* is that you can sit and chat almost indefinitely without being harassed into buying more than you want. Before long we had exchanged many confidences. I felt like I had known Raymond for months instead of minutes.

We had a great deal in common. To begin with there was an unusual physical resemblance between us. (Twice we were taken for brothers.) He was a little older than I, but in height and build we were very much the same. I rather envied the way his hair swept across his brow; mine stood up like wire unless it was soaking wet or greased.

Like me, he was a lover of the arts, – particularly painting and music. Like me he was meticulous about his personal appearance. Many of our dislikes and prejudices were the same. As soon as we got to talking about the stupidity of wars, especially the present one, I found I had at last met someone with similar opinions to my own. He was the only fellow I came across the whole of the time I was a soldier who dared to express the feelings I had come to hold.

He was a bright, cheerful companion with a distinctive sense of humour. Because his ambulance driving took him everywhere, he knew everybody and, I gathered, everyone seemed to like him. He was a chatterbox, but never a bore, – at least to me, – because the things he talked about interested me too.

Ray was a cosmopolitan chap with an Italian-speaking Swiss-born mother and an English father. From his mother he had acquired a good knowledge of the Italian language, which was why he was often the only Liaison Officer available to bridge administrative difficulties. His rank was equivalent to Warrant Officer in the Regular Army – that is, intermediate between the highest-ranking N.C.O.s and the commissioned subalterns. But rank was a superfluity where Raymond was concerned.

We walked to the Red Cross building and had a nice meal in the canteen. There I discovered that one of the amenities provided was a hot bath. Such a luxury couldn't be refused!

I rejoined Raymond in the Club Room. He looked me up and down. 'Very nice,' he said. 'All clean, pink and shining. Now you'll want a girl.'

'What makes you think that?'

'Everybody does. Bath first; girl next. Casa Rossa is the best place. Two blocks away. Strictly for officers only, but with you being English they won't know the difference. Ask for Francesca. She's choosy, but you're her style.'

'Are you recommending her from personal experience?'

'Holy smoke, no! But plenty of other guys would.'

'Sorry, I don't happen to fancy it just now.'

'Why the heck not?'

'I'm windy. Scared of catching a dose. Besides, I've got a girl back home; it wouldn't be playing fair.'

'There's not many think that way.'

'Well I do.'

'O.K. Don't get shirty. Tell me about the girl.'

I did; and I showed him the photograph Ella had sent me in the spring.

'Gosh! She's pretty . . . Sorry about Francesca. No offence intended. Hope you have better luck with your girl than I had with mine.'

There was a cynical tone in that last remark. Later on I got the full story out of him. I think he was glad to have someone to tell it to.

At the very time when I had found myself falling in love with Ella, i.e. the summer of 1916, Raymond became engaged to his girl-friend Brenda. They were both just gone twenty-one. He told me quite unashamedly that he was deeply in love with her; she was the only girl he ever felt any affection for.

That was the year conscription was introduced. Ray had strong religious convictions which, he said, would not permit him to serve in any branch of the fighting services. Accordingly he told Brenda that he intended to volunteer for the Red Cross Brigade, where he could do non-combatant work, – not in order to dodge the war, but to assist the victims of it. His mother, though not altogether approving, had contacts in Geneva, where the Red Cross H.Q. was, and had agreed to help him.

But Brenda was horrified. She came from a long line of

Regular Army officers so, to her, <u>fighting</u> wars was not only right and honourable, but the <u>only</u> thing a healthy twenty-one-year-old lad should be doing in 1916. Her father was a belligerent Staff Colonel, winning battle honours while seated at a desk in the War Office in London. In his view all conscientious objectors should be shot for cowardice.

Brenda must have had somewhat similar feelings because she flew into a rage when she found she couldn't persuade her fiancé to alter his decision. She broke off the engagement, called him chicken-hearted and a few days later sent him a white feather through the post to add to his humiliation. The week after, he packed his bags and went off to Switzerland, where he enlisted in the International Brigade of the Red Cross – who dispatched him to Italy because of his knowledge of the language.

I could only commiserate with him, but he didn't want any sympathy.

'I've got over it. I've finished with girls – they're all bitches . . . Sorry, Ron . . . yours excepted. As for Brenda – it was good riddance. Anyway, there are better things to do than mess about with dames.'

'Such as?' I asked.

'Nothing. Forget it.'

Then he went on to tell me the story of another encounter, this time with a 'dame' of a very different type.

Shortly after arriving in Italy, and still feeing down in the dumps, he decided to console himself with a visit to what he described as a 'cat-house'. (This was in Milan.) I'd never heard of a 'red lamp' establishment called by that name before, but in view of what happened there it seemed to be appropriate.

Far from bringing him pleasure and consolation, the visit proved to be a dismal failure, a complete fiasco. As soon as Ray found himself closeted alone with the 'pussycat' of his choice, his enthusiasm waned and his ardour cooled, – so much so that he was unable to meet the needs of the situation. The pussycat, like a famous British Queen, was not amused, – in fact she was highly incensed. Regarding his lack of passion as something of an insult, she ordered him off the premises, – and proved her 'felinity' by engraving some painful mementos of their meeting on his torso.

Ray told me this little tale with wry amusement. 'Do you know, that's the only time I ever planned going all the way with a dame and I never even got started! What about you?'

'Oh! I'm a proper Don Juan. Can't count the girls I've had.'

Ray laughed. 'Ses you.'

'Ses I! No, Ray, to be truthful I'm as innocent as a newborn babe. Kissing and cuddling is as far as I ever got. And I've only done that with one girl.'

This was true. But the story I'd been listening to was something of a coincidence because I'd had a very similar experience only a few weeks before. This seems a suitable time and place for me to tell of it, so here it is.

First, though, let me remind you that every young soldier on the continent had seen the queues of soldiers outside the licensed brothels, which were situated only a few miles behind the line. There were two 'grades': one for officers only, the other for other ranks. Official trips were run from the trenches at intervals.

Most of my acquaintances, especially the married men, patronized these houses and took delight in describing to me the delights they provided, telling me what fun I too could enjoy if only I'd stop being 'churchy'. But I didn't go – and I never felt I wanted to. I had two reasons, one high-minded, the other practical. Firstly, I thought I could only prove my loyalty to my sweetheart by staying away from temptations of that kind, and secondly I'd seen men with V.D. and I was scared of becoming one of them.

But time went on and by the summer of 1918 I was a year older and glowing with health, – and one June day I put my principles aside.

I had been 'detailed' to take a lorry to Padua to collect supplies from the railway station. Padua is a university city and has some fine bookshops, in addition to many splendid buildings. I bought a book about Italian painting and architecture while I was there. (Perhaps you'll remember that at school my ambition had been to train as an architect.)

Well, after a lunch of fresh eggs, chips and spaghetti, two of my companions, both married men, persuaded me to accompany them to one of the licensed brothels close by. The *caffè* proprietor had recommended this particular '*Casa dell' Amore*' as being top class.

It was an extremely hot day and thirst had induced me to take considerably more wine than I was accustomed to, so I suppose my moral resistance was at a low ebb. Anyway I was both curious and excited after all I had overheard. I managed to push my principles into the background and agree to take the plunge. One of the other fellows slapped me heartily on the back, saying that at last I would have the opportunity of proving I was a man.

I accompanied them into a large well-furnished reception-lounge. The air was thick with a mixture of cigarette smoke and sickly perfume.

I won't describe what I saw beyond the fact that there were seven or eight soldiers and about the same number of scantily dressed females. The client selected the lady of his choice and then disappeared up a long curving staircase at the further end of the room. Not one of the 'girls' was in my age group, – some, indeed, were old enough to have been my mother, – and all of them looked vulgar.

I was unable to take in much more, owing to the sudden onset of queasiness in my stomach. The combination of nausea and disgust at myself drowned my curiosity, which now turned into revulsion. I made for the double doors, pulled aside the heavy red velvet curtains, hurried along the dimly lit entrance hall, ignoring the stately Signora seated in her plushy alcove, and fled in utter panic into the street.

In retrospect all this seems highly diverting. But I assure you I found nothing amusing about it at the time.

I knew that within minutes I would need to be sick. I ran along the narrow street looking for a suitable place. Fortunately it was siesta time and the shops beneath the arcade arches were shut. No one was about. At the far end, bathed in bright sunshine, I spied an open space with trees, – a piazza or something. I reached this oasis just in time and hid myself in a clump of oleander bushes.

With that particular crisis over, I was able to absorb the fact that I had taken refuge in a small public garden or perhaps a churchyard, – for across the road I could see a large, almost windowless, domed building. The noonday heat was intense. I crossed the deserted street and sought shade and coolness in the church's interior. It didn't strike me then what a strange transition this was: from bordello to church in the space of a few minutes.

There was very little light inside. I sank into a chair just inside the doorway, feeling terrible, – ready to flee into the garden should the nausea return. At the far end of the building a woman was doing something with flowers and in front of a small side chapel a hooded mother was lighting a candle to the Virgin Mary. Apart from these two I was alone.

I shivered, although bathed in perspiration, and, after the women had gone, moved to a chair at the further end of the back row, close to the side wall. I didn't feel quite as sick now. I thought I ought to pray, but couldn't bring myself to do it. The sickly scent from the brothel seemed to have seeped into my clothing. Gradually the incense which pervaded the building took its place, and as my physical discomfort diminished I was able to think again.

I came to the conclusion that this last experience was yet another of the things that set me apart from my fellows, that made me the 'unusual' person I was said to be. Perhaps, as they had said, I was still only a boy, a prudish goody-goody who hadn't yet grown up. They had, presumably, and it was evidence of their adulthood that they could walk into a kind of shop, select a female body from the limited stock on display (one that a previous customer had just finished with), hire it for five minutes of sex-gratification and then return it to the management for the use of the next man in the queue.

I thought if that is the sort of conduct which distinguishes the men from the boys I'd prefer not to grow up. Of course I wanted to be 'intimate' with a girl. Not with any girl, but with my own girl, – the one I could approach with love and tenderness, unhurriedly. It had to happen in the right place and at the right time. Not like that. Not there.

Now all this while I had been sitting close to a wall which, had I known then what I know now, I would have examined with great interest. But the light, as I said, was very dim indeed. The windows had all been either boarded or bricked up on account of the threat of air raids.

More than fifty years later I saw what I had missed on our television screen at home. In one of his *Civilization* programmes I heard Kenneth Clark praising the frescoes on the wall of that chapel as possibly the finest paintings of their kind in the whole world. Over six centuries before I was born, the Italian master Giotto had covered that very wall with scenes from the life of Our Lord. They are, I believe, after Michelangelo's Sistine ceiling, the largest in Italy.

Now <u>that</u> was the story I <u>didn't</u> tell to Raymond. When I thought about it I felt very self-conscious. I'd sentimentalized the whole episode so heavily that he would have thought me soppy.

'If you don't fancy a girl,' he said, 'what the heck <u>do</u> you fancy?'

'A trip into Venice,' I replied.

'Imposs. Not a hope. It's out of bounds to all troops and that includes you.'

Then, gradually, a broad grin spread over his face.

'Ron,' he said, 'I've got an idea. No harm in trying.'

The street in which the Red Cross H.Q. was situated led into a road running alongside the canal. There were a number of fishing boats and other small craft (– no gondolas, though! –) moored to little jetties.

After some bargaining, a grizzled old Mestrian was persuaded to hire us his antiquated motorboat. We heaved out its mast and sail, which Ray regarded as unwanted ballast. The thing didn't look very seaworthy. Ray asked if I could swim, and having been assured that I could, he appointed himself captain, chief engineer and navigator. I was glad, as what I knew about motorboats wouldn't have got us away from the mooring post!

We hopped aboard, relieved to discover only a couple of inches of water inside, and set off. I think we both felt like a couple of truanting schoolboys making the most of our freedom while it lasted.

From Mestre the canal runs parallel with the long viaduct carrying the road and railway across the marshes and over the lagoon. No traffic was moving on either, as Venice had been declared an Open City by the Allies. This meant that all troops, artillery, war installations and equipment had been withdrawn and the place put out of bounds to military personnel of all nationalities. In return the Austrians and Germans refrained from attacking the city.

In twenty minutes or so we reached the mouth of the canal. In front of us were the broad waters of the Lagoon of Venice, looking like a sheet of lead-coloured glass under a grey sky. A couple of miles distant was the hazy outline of Europe's most beautiful city.

Raymond burst into song. He had been singing since the age of nine or ten. As the only child of parents who were more often apart than together, he had been a boarder in the Choir School at York Minster until his voice broke. Music was his principal hobby. He had an extensive, – and very catholic, – repertoire and would burst forth into operatic arias, oratorio solos and popular ditties of the period without warning, especially when driving. I remembered his flair for this kind of impromptu entertainment from my journeys in his ambulance to and from the Vicenza hospital the previous winter.

We were in mid-lagoon with Venice less than a mile away when a launch appeared, as if from nowhere. It sped across our bows, churning a crescent of white foam behind it. A uniformed official with a megaphone ordered us to halt.

This was where I had to act like a dumb idiot. (Ray had said my uniform would get me out of any fix; I just hoped he knew what he was talking about.)

The launch pulled alongside. It was the Italian Military Police, of course. Ray did the talking – and the listening. The chief Redcap gave him a stern lecture on the meaning of out of bounds and ordered him to follow them to their depot for questioning. But Ray possessed such charm that his apologies softened the hearts of authority; they relented and agreed to make no charge against us. However, they demanded that we follow them back to Mestre.

Ray said later that his Red Cross uniform, plus my baby-faced look of bewildered innocence, plus the fact that I was one of the few *Inglesi* they'd ever seen there, won the day for us.

So we returned to the mainland with a police escort, Venice unvisited. En route Raymond entertained them with some of his operatic repertoire, – whether they were able to hear much above the noise of their engine I don't know, – and he concluded, for good measure, with 'Ilkley Moor Baht At', with which I was able to join in. (The Yorkshire ballad had sad associations for me since it was poor old Windy Clark who had taught it to me only a day or two before he was gassed, but I didn't let that memory spoil the occasion.)

At the Mestre quayside, Ray invited the two policemen ashore to share a bottle of *vino*, but duty forced them to decline, – with obvious reluctance. So, having given us another mild ticking off and an admonition not to repeat the offence, they swung their craft round and sped away.

Thus ended my visit to the Pearl of the Adriatic! I hadn't seen any of its glorious waterfront: St. Mark's, the Doge's Palace and the rest, but I had caught a glimpse of its dingy back-end.

Back at the depot, Ray showed me the Assembly Hall. It was equipped with a stage and a grand piano. On the piano lay the score for a production the club's Operatic Society were preparing with the help of some of Mestre's civilian population.

The luridly coloured cover showed a flaxen-haired girl leaning on a saloon counter, but this proved to be no light musical. It was the conductor's annotated copy of a full-scale opera score, autographed by the composer with 'Wishing You Well, Giacomo Puccini'. Its title: *La Fanciulla del Ovest*, or *The Girl of the Golden West*.

I only knew Puccini's music from Palm Court Orchestra selections from *Bohème*, *Butterfly* and *Tosca*, but Raymond knew the man himself. He had come along specially to rehearse them only last week. It seemed out of character: Puccini + Cowboys. But Ray said it wasn't, – the composer loved Western movies, so why shouldn't he write an opera about the California Gold Rush?

Ray himself had a quite important part in the show. He turned the pages of the score until he found one he especially liked. I sat and played and was able to hear what his voice really was like – a baritone with almost the range of a tenor. Before we had finished there was a sizeable audience of Red Cross chaps and helpers listening.

That night we lay on the top bunks of two double-decker beds, talking until long past midnight. How long was it since I had enjoyed a conversation, since I had spoken with anyone whose interests went beyond gambling, booze and fornication? Why hadn't I had the good fortune to meet someone like Ray back in the dark days of last autumn and winter? Someone my own age who shared my interests, a friend I could have confided in. Perhaps I would not have reached the depths of depression that I had.

He asked me if I was a religious sort of chap. I said, 'Yes, sort of, but not sanctimonious, I hope. I've got my own beliefs, but really, Ray, I'd rather not talk about them.'

'O.K.,' he replied, and then went on, 'At home, Ron, in the room I called my bedroom (– though I wasn't in it for more than a few months each year –) there was a motto inside one of the criss-cross frames. You know the sort I mean?'

I nodded.

'It said "God Is Love. He Cares." After I'd been through hell at Caporetto and seen what war <u>did</u> to people, – women and kids as well as soldiers, – I asked, "Why does God allow this sort of thing to happen? <u>Does</u> he care?" As time went on I said, "That's all hooey. If God <u>really</u> cared he'd stop this bloody war, – send another Flood or an earthquake or something to swallow up all the bastards who want it to continue." It wasn't long before I started thinking, "<u>He's</u> not interested in our troubles so why should we be interested in <u>his</u>? Or in <u>him</u>?" So I just stopped believing in him, and in that bloody motto. "God is love. He cares." Does he hell?'

That was the only occasion I remember Ray swearing. I didn't argue with him about it. I suppose I was a bit shocked, certainly surprised. After all, Ray had been a cathedral chorister and a communion server. But then, I reminded myself, so had I, and there had come a time when I too had lost my faith in God, so I tried to understand.

Ray and I spoke about ourselves, our families, books, poetry, music, singing, movies, our local cricket teams, and Heaven knows what else. Not much about girls as far as I can remember.

The most appealing character he spoke about was his special 'buddy' (he'd acquired a number of Americanisms), whom he referred to as Hem or Hemmie.

Hem was one of the ambulance men who gathered at the Mestre Depot. To my surprise, – and pleasure, – it turned out that he was no other than the reporter whose articles about wartime in Italy I had read in the American newspapers at Cittadella.

Ray told me how Hem had packed in his job on the Kansas paper, scrounged some money to come to Europe and enlisted in the Italian Army so that he could see war 'from the inside'.

The Italians wouldn't have him in a fighting unit because of his foreign nationality but accepted him for their Medical Corps, giving him Lieutenant's rank. He was soon in charge of a whole section of ambulance wagons and several Field Dressing Stations as well. He drove whenever other duties allowed him to.

Three weeks earlier there had been an enemy strafe on the Italian positions at a place called Fossalta. I knew the village well myself; it was on the Piave only a few miles below Spresiano. Hem was called upon to convey some of the casualties from the front-line trench to the Advanced Dressing Station. Because of man-power shortage he had to take on the job single-handed. One by one he carried half a dozen badly wounded men into his ambulance and brought them away. The road was under continuous shell-fire but his vehicle didn't get hit. He left the wounded men at the Dressing Station and set off for another part of the trenches where he had some Italian buddies. He'd promised to take them some cigarettes, chocolate and books.

'Just after he climbed out of his ambulance it was blown to pieces by a shell,' Ray told me. 'He made his way to the bay where his three pals were. He was just handing round the bars of chocolate when a minnie[15] came over. I expect you know them?'

I did indeed. 'You usually see them before you hear them,' I replied.

'Well,' Ray went on, 'they saw this one and flung themselves on to the trench floor, but the mortar bomb came down almost perpendicular, right on top of one of the Italians. The other two were knocked unconscious. Hem saw it all happen before he passed out.

'He was the first to come round. Nobody else had arrived

15 Minenwerfer – a mine-thrower or trench mortar.

on the scene. There were those two guys lying unconscious and bleeding badly. The third one was . . . napoo! . . . not a trace.'

I could hear from the thickening of his voice that Raymond was being affected by the story.

'Poor old Hemmie was badly hurt himself. But he's as strong as a carthorse, and somehow he heaved one of them onto his back and staggered with him all the way back to the Dressing Station. Must have been a quarter-mile at least. Then he set off back to fetch the other guy. He didn't get far before he collapsed himself.'

Raymond paused.

'How is he?' I asked.

'Oh. He's alive. Just! He's in a hospital in Milan.'

'Will he be O.K.?'

'We don't know. The day before yesterday I dodged duty, borrowed a truck and went to see him. I had to drive like hell, just on four hours each way. God! Ron, his leg is in a mess. Do you know they've dug out nearly a hundred bits of shrapnel from that blasted minnie? How'd he get the strength to carry a man that distance with all that lead in him? Oh! Bloody hell, Ron, why is it always the nice guys who get hit?'

I couldn't think of a suitable comment so I didn't attempt to make one. We went to sleep after that.

Before breakfast the next morning we were in the wash room, freshening up and nattering. Now shaving requires a certain amount of concentration and through lack of it I nicked myself with the razor just below the ear, exactly in the place where a similar careless razor cut had sparked off serious trouble earlier in the year. My thoughts raced back to that time: how rapidly the sores had spread, how scared of them everyone else had been, –

and the painful treatment I had received for them! I still wondered, eight months afterwards, how the ailment had been cured.

'Ray,' I said, 'when you took me from San Martino to hospital, what happened after I passed out?'

'They gave old Dr. Muller some brandy.'

'Dr. Muller? Who was he?'

'The guy you kicked on the shin.'

'Did they keep me there?'

'Don't you know?'

'No. I don't remember a thing.'

'Come off it.'

'Really, Ray. Did they keep me there?'

'No. They transferred you to a special place. A hospital for neurasthenics.' He tapped a finger around his temple.

'You mean a loony bin.'

'Sort of.'

'How do you know?'

'Because I took you.'

'Where was it?'

'Schio.'

(Schio! The town I'd visited to buy my lamp and binoculars. Where an inner voice kept telling me I had been before! It had told the truth then.)

'Do you know how long I stayed?'

'Several weeks, I reckon. I didn't go there for nearly a month. You'd gone by then.'

We'd both finished our ablutions and were putting on tunics.

Ray continued, 'When I saw you weren't there, I asked Hemmie. He was there that day.'

'How would he know me? We'd never even met.'

'Oh yes, you had. In the hospital. He had buddies there.

Everybody knew you. You were the only *Inglese* in the whole goddam joint. And the youngest. We didn't know your name so we called you Spotty. Don't mind, do you?'

'Not at all.'

We were both dressed and ready for our meal. Before we went, I caught Ray's arm.

'Ray, tell me. How were my spots when you last saw me?'

'Bloody awful! That's why they booted you out of Schio.'

He came over, spun me round and lifted up my tunic to yank my shirt up to my ears.

'By heck, that's marvellous. You should have seen your back. They sure made a good job of <u>that</u>. Smooth as a baby's bottom. Come on, dope, breakfast!'

Later that morning Ray walked with me to the station. The train was in, and I set the gunners to work loading the goods we had come to collect. I joined Ray at the table outside the station trattoria. Over a last cup of cappuccino I asked him what his plans were for after the war.

'Oh! Stay here in Italy, I guess. My father wants me to enter the Dip. Service – keep the blasted flag flying in some godforsaken hole.'

He dipped into his pocket, took out his wallet, abstracted a small card and wrote on it his name and address. He said I was to be sure to come and visit him after the war.

'What would be the use, – if you're not going back?'

He laughed that question off. 'Well, wait and see.'

The men were coming across the piazza, obviously to tell me the loading was finished. It was time to go. I patted Ray on the back and said, 'I hope your show's a success. *Au revoir*, – and thanks for everything.'

'*Arrivederci.*'

In both languages the expression means the same: 'Till we see each other again.' They were the last words we said to each other. But even then I knew they meant nothing. We <u>wouldn't</u> see each other again, that little voice whispered inside me as I walked to the first wagon. 'You know you won't. You won't even write.' And the voice was right: we didn't.

Funny how <u>close</u> you are to somebody for only a few hours. You feel you've been friends for years. Then you part, – and never see one another again.

The drive back to Spresiano gave me time to reflect on the last twenty-four hours. I wasn't feeling very happy. All the talk about Ray's broken love affair had revived doubts which I'd been harbouring in my mind for some while. I began asking myself how I could be certain about Ella. Of course I knew the circumstances were different, <u>his</u> girl having broken up their affair because of irreconcilable differences of opinion. But Ella and I had met when we were mere children and had parted when she was barely sixteen. Ours was a boy and girl romance, what older folk called puppy love, – a teenage infatuation which couldn't possibly last.

Time was passing – and time certainly wasn't on my side. Eighteen months since she had last seen me, and each of those months to <u>me</u> a year! How do you measure time when parted from loved ones? On a battlefield awaiting the opening of a bombardment, every <u>second</u> is a <u>minute</u>; and when hell has been let loose all around you, every <u>minute</u> is an <u>hour</u>. A week on leave, I thought, would see the days flash by, but a week under shell-fire seemed a lifetime. Time doesn't exist as such when each hour may be your last.

<u>Ordinary</u> time, – the passage of weeks, months and years, –

changes things – and people. Teenagers become adults; they alter their opinions and tastes; they grow up. The fact that I hadn't changed didn't mean anything. Ella wasn't me. And of course I had changed.

Suppose after all that my confession had passed the censor. (It was unlikely – but possible.) Ella would have read it and received a shock. So would her parents, and mine. They might all have said, 'That's not the Ronald we knew and loved.'

Folks at home had little time for people with opinions like mine. They called them conchies and regarded them as traitors to their country. That was why Brenda had jilted Raymond.

But would Ella still write in the vein she did if she had ceased to love me? Was she just keeping up a pretence of loyalty, fearing I might do something foolish if she were to tell me the truth? Once more I reminded myself of those wounded soldiers recuperating in Bexhill's convalescent homes, many doubtless young and good-looking. Suppose she met one whom she liked better than me! When would I find out?

'Oh! Shut up,' I told myself. 'Keep on hoping.' Well, what else could I do? So I kept on, hoping for the best.

Things had happened in Spresiano since I had left the day before. The previously damaged buildings had been further strafed – and shell holes in the road were being filled by fatigue parties. I handed over my stores and transport to Q.M.S. Thompson. (The original Quarterbloke, now recovered and as bad-tempered as ever.) The telling off he was ready to give me was cut short when I showed him the chit explaining my overnight stop in Mestre. I hurried off to find out what had happened in my absence.

From Paddy the cook I learnt that just before dawn there had been a surprise bombardment of our infantry's positions along-side the Piave.[16] The men thought it heralded an attack from across the river. H.Q. ordered our C.O. to silence one of the Austrian field batteries. Paddy thought we had done a 'good job' on them, but the flashes from our howitzers gave away their positions and the enemy's heavies retaliated. One of our guns had been knocked out, Paddy said. We'd lost men, but how many he didn't know. Some of the chaps' billets in the village had been hit. He didn't know the names of the casualties.

I hurried to the Command Post. For some reason it was unmanned: no officer, no N.C.O., no Signaller! On the O.C.'s table was a carbon copy of the casualty list. There were about fif-teen names on it, – and Bombardier Alfred Sparrow was one of them. My heart sank.

I knew where his billet was. Only a couple of days earlier he'd helped me build my bivvy against a wall of Spresiano's ruined church; for himself he'd chosen the small ground-floor room of a badly damaged villa.

From one of the villa's other occupants I learnt what had happened. A shell had burst in the room next to Alf's and he had received a piece of flying shrapnel in the shoulder, as well as suffering injuries from falling brickwork. One of his legs was suspected broken. He'd been sent to the Dressing Station.

I didn't wait to hear more. I suppose the D.S. was about a mile and a half away and I ran most of the way. There I was told that the hospital train had just left, – and Alf was on it.

I tracked down the R.A.M.C. man who had transferred the casualties on to the train. Yes, Alf was one of them all right. He remembered him because he'd been so bloody cheerful

---

16 After the war ended I learnt that Ella's brother was one of those on the receiving end of the enemy shelling.

throughout the operation! Kept them all in fits, he said.

They had set his leg – it was broken just above the ankle – and the shell splinter had made only a flesh wound above the collar bone. He'd be all right, the orderly said, – good as new in a month or two. He'd got just what he wanted (– what we'd all said we wanted now and again –): a nice Blighty wound – serious enough to require treatment at home, but not so bad that you wouldn't be A.1. by the time the war was over.

I can't tell you how relieved I was to hear that Alf's injuries weren't more serious. He'd been jolly good to me, – and jolly good _for_ me as well.

But it wasn't unalloyed happiness I was enjoying. I was going to miss Alf sorely; he was the only chap in the whole battery that I could have called a friend. It seemed that within the space of a few hours I had lost the only two pals I had, – not by death, thank Heaven, but by circumstances.

The war dragged on for three more weary months. They kept me in the Army for another six. I made no more friends. From that day on I was entirely alone.

There was no need to hurry back. The daylight was going now and a huge golden moon was rising above the distant silhouette of the Alps. No one but I was on that stretch of road. All around was silence.

On either side were unfenced vineyards, the vines growing over stunted little trees, neglected and untended. For two years nobody had cared for them. The fruit was beginning to show its purple colouring, but even when they were fully ripe I knew no one would come to harvest them.

As I walked I thought about the war. I remember this clearly because, strange as it may seem, the soldiers actually thought about it very little. I suppose we knew less about the war than anybody. We knew what was happening in the square mile of territory we occupied, but that was about all. As for strategy or the chances of victory, we never discussed such things.

At intervals 'Official' News Bulletins were displayed. We read them as disbelievingly as we read the newspapers sent out from Blighty. The stuff they printed sickened us. They wrote how high and unshakeable our morale was, when all the time the men were on the verge of mutiny (– they actually did mutiny just after I went on leave –); how vile and despicable the enemy were, knowing that they had no more desire to kill us than we had to kill them; and how honoured, respected and loved our commanders were, when most of them, we knew, would have received a bullet in the back had they dared to come near the front line when the troops' morale was near breaking point.

Every soldier I knew, every soldier I met, hated the war intensely, – but the German and Austrian fighters only incidentally. There was of course the hatred of revenge one saw in the heat of battle, – whipped up by deep emotion at the death of a comrade, – but it never lasted. It all ended, eventually, with the longing, common to friend and foe alike, to get out and go home. Neither victory nor defeat mattered a scrap to the individual soldier. All he yearned for was Peace – and the sooner it came, the better.

It was bright moonlight now, very calm and still. Would the Aussies open up again to-night? The only time for weeks that we'd been shelled was the night I was away in Mestre! My good fortune couldn't go on indefinitely.

I remembered Alf once saying, 'You were born lucky, Ron. Remember, there's two kinds of luck: good and bad. If you're having a run of good luck don't bleedin' well push it.'

At the battery, now that daylight had gone, there was great

activity. The three undamaged howitzers were being dug out and hauled away to fresh positions. (It would be suicidal to leave them where they were now that the enemy had them 'taped'.)

I ran into the B.S.M. 'Jump to it, man,' he ordered. 'Collect your effing kit and get aboard. We're off in five minutes.'

'Right, Sergeant Major!' I replied and hurried away. But I was an old soldier now. I'd say 'Yes, sir,' and do the opposite, if it suited me. I didn't collect my gear, but I did hop aboard one of the supply wagons. Just as I expected, – the new gun sites were less than half a mile away and the Command Post remained where it had been. There was no need to look for a fresh billet; 'Windsor Castle' was conveniently near both.

I had given it this distinguished name for two reasons. Windsor was the name of Ella's road in Bexhill, and the back of it looked like a castle (a very ruined one, it's true).

Spresiano church must have originally been a beautiful building, but now only half the walls remained. For my shelter I had chosen a site under the archway which had framed the vestry doors. All the movable church woodwork – the doors, the chairs, the choir-stalls, – had been burnt as firewood last winter.

None of the other fellows fancied a billet so close to a graveyard but I didn't mind. I expect my superstitious beliefs persuaded me that I would be closer to my spiritual allies if I built a bivvy against a consecrated building.

None of last night's shells had fallen near the church, but that didn't mean none would. I thought once again of Alf's advice – and rather than 'push my luck' I decided to reinforce my shelter. I couldn't protect myself against a direct hit, but I could strengthen my overhead and side-wall protection.

So bright was the moonlight that I had no difficulty in locating a store of sandbags. I would have to fill them with stone as no sand was available.

I went inside the roofless church. The marble flooring was covered with rubble. The moonlight glistened on the silvery fibres which had been woven into the golden altar-cloth. Only a quarter of the beautiful gilded material remained. I tore off a piece a few inches square and placed it in my cigarette case. Silly, isn't it? But I didn't think so then.

I filled the sacks with stone and plaster rubble. I piled them along the outside of the iron framework that Alf had helped me construct and stacked a double layer of sandbags on the roof. When I'd finished I had what looked like an Eskimo's igloo – minus the ice-blocks. I was satisfied I had as safe a bivvy as anyone.[17]

I arranged my bedding ready to settle down for the night. I had scrounged some supper at the cookhouse (– formerly a cow shed! –) but I still felt peckish. Then I remembered the slab of chocolate in my rucksack. I hadn't carried the bag since leaving our mountain positions. I tipped its contents on to the ground-sheet I'd spread on my bunk and examined them by the light of a candle.

A motley assortment I had. Books (*Golden Treasury, Italian Art and Architecture, The Path to Rome,* my Italian exercise book and four pages of saucy cartoons from a year-old *La Vie Parisienne*);[18] a pair of Wolsey undervests which I couldn't wear because I dislike wool next to my skin; the Zeiss binoculars; a compass; rope-soled climbers' sandals; a pocket note-book with a Flanders-mud stain on its black shiny cover and a bar of Peter's chocolate, wrapped in sheets of old newspaper.

17 My confidence was justified. When the big Allied 'push' started on 24 October the village was heavily strafed by artillery. Very little of the church remained standing, but the wall against which 'Windsor Castle' stood survived, as did the bivvy itself.

18 *Alice in Wonderland* had by now been lost – down some rabbit hole perhaps!

I turned over the note-book's pages as I munched on the chocolate. It contained long pencilled accounts of some of my doings the previous year, but the entries saddened me and I put it down only half read.

It reminded me of so many of the friends I had lost: Bill and Geordie, the Tyneside twins whose talk I could barely comprehend; Jock Shiels, blown to pieces as he took a cigarette from me; Windy Clark, suffocated by the poison gas he'd tried to cough out of his lungs; and Hans, the young German who should have been my enemy. Then there was Dick Waller, who wasn't a pal at all: two months ago I had tried to make his last hours comfortable and my hand had been lightly resting on his shattered, bandaged face when he died; you can't call a man you've been as close to as that just an acquaintance. And now I'd lost Alf, only an hour or two after parting from Raymond. Both gone, – not dead, it is true, but gone. I confess I wept at the memory of them all.

In those days we didn't throw old newspapers away; they were too hard to come by. I smoothed out the sheets in which the chocolate had been wrapped and picked them up from the floor. They were pages of the *Kansas City Star*, dated March 1918.

I was keenly interested now, since realizing that their one-time correspondent was none other than Raymond's chum Hem. On the last sheet I saw the headline STAR'S REPORTER ON ITALIAN FRONT: LATEST DISPATCH. It was Hem's work all right.

As I re-read it I felt I knew its author as well as I had got to know Raymond. (I suppose, according to Ray, we had been acquainted during my 'lost' months.) The article told how he had helped to evacuate casualties under shell-fire, but didn't emphasize that he'd been in grave danger himself. He included a description of the Red Cross Depot in Mestre and a humorous account of an establishment known as the Casa Rossa, or Red

House. This, of course, was the 'club' that Ray had recommended to me.

The whole thing was extremely well written, informative and amusing, – and if you think <u>that</u> remark somewhat patronizing, you're right, in view of what I learnt about Ray's friend much later. I had understood him to say that his buddy was called Hemming-Wale, no doubt because <u>that</u> name was almost daily in my thoughts. But the newspaper put me right: their correspondent's name was Hemingway, Ernest Hemingway.

The canal in Mestre. We hired the motorboat from a
fisherman who used the jetty under the tree on the left.

CHAPTER NINE

War and Peace (Not by Tolstoy)

*'High Speed Greetings from Padua. 17.11.18. Am on
my way home, but don't know whether I or this p.c. will
arrive first. Ti adoro. Your Own R.'*

Do you remember how my last interview with Major Snow
ended? His parting words to me were 'Get out of my sight. And
<u>don't</u> come near me again!' They were words I was only too
pleased to hear, yet in a sense he had to eat them – and I had to
go very near to him.

As I've said, where the Old Man, now Lieutenant-Colonel
Snow, spent the late summer months I have no idea, but he was
back in command of '239' just before the final big 'push' began
in October. The last battle opened with a tremendous Allied

attack all along – and across – the Piave River. On the night the preliminary bombardment began I found myself once again on B.C.A. duty. Snow's memory must have been in pretty poor shape for he didn't seem to realize that I was the 'bloody conchie' he'd ordered out of his presence a few months before.

The other ranks were billeted under canvas in a vineyard. The fruit was ripe but the grapes, purple ones, were small and tough-skinned. I ate only a few, spitting out the thick skins and pips, but many of the men gorged themselves. There followed an outbreak of dysentery. Some maintained that it was caused by polluted drinking water but I think the grapes had a share in it. Whatever the cause, I escaped with a mild 'tummy upset', but most of the men were seriously ill.

When the order for the bombardment came many hadn't fully recovered, but somehow the fit ones kept our guns firing for the three days and nights considered necessary. My part in the battle didn't trouble my conscience as our targets were roads and railway yards in Conegliano – a town long past evacuated by civilians and not even garrisoned by enemy troops. We were shooting at bricks and mortar, not men.

The shortage of fit men and the fact that I was the only N.C.O. in a reasonable state of health were the causes of my taking over the double duty of Battery Commander's Assistant and Observer. I suppose T— was either sick or skulking around somewhere safe; I didn't see him throughout the battle. The only officer I might have regarded as a friend, Mr. Salisbury, had recently been transferred elsewhere. The result of all this was that Snow and I had to put up with each other. I worked nearly sixty hours with him without relief, chasing continuously between his Command Post and my O.P., – and they were a good half-mile apart.

This Observation Post was, I believe, quite unique. It was a remarkable camouflaged construction built by the Italians and was called 'I Cipressi', which as you might guess means 'The Cypresses'.

Situated at the eastern end of the vast Venetian plain, it overlooked the Piave River. The Piave was No Man's Land and beyond it was Austrian territory: a few more miles of plain as level as a billiard table, then foothills covered with vineyards, then higher mountains rising in tiers until they were lost in the mists of Slovenia.

Two huge cypresses had grown so close together that their branches intermingled. About sixty feet above ground level was a sort of bird-watcher's hide, only larger, built inside the twin trees. It was reached by a triple ladder, nearly vertical, with two small platforms between ladders. This was 'Cipressi' O.P.: a sort of log cabin about nine feet square, fitted with all the paraphernalia an artillery Observer requires. The dense foliage had been cut away in front to provide a splendid panoramic view.

The King and I

On 4 November 1918, the day after the Austrians asked for an armistice, I had been up to the cabin to collect some of my possessions because orders had come through that we were to be moved to another part of the line.

I slung my bits and pieces into my knapsack, feeling on top of the world – literally and figuratively, full of optimism that soon I would be on my way home. Below me I could hear joyful singing and shouting in Italian. (Their infantry had some rest billets near the foot of my ladder.)

Either through lack of concentration, or because my filled knapsack swung me off my balance, my foot missed a rung. I slipped, – and fell awkwardly on to the lower platform, only saving myself from tumbling on to the heads of a group of fellows below by hastily grabbing at a tree branch. Luckily it was a strong one, or I would have fallen a good twenty-five feet.

When I had collected my wits together, I saw with surprise that the group below were V.I.P.s, – three brass-hatted, gold-epauletted Italian officers, together with a short man dressed rather like a cartoon French policeman, with peaked pill-box hat and wide green cape.

None of the group had raised their eyes; I was sure they hadn't heard the little drama just enacted above them, – another group a few yards off were throwing caps in the air and cheering *fortissimo*. I sat on my haunches – unobserved – until they had gone.

The Big-Wigs strode away and climbed aboard a limousine with an Italian tricolore flying from its bonnet. I clambered gingerly down and asked one of the infantrymen who the visitors were.

'*Visitatori!?*' he replied in astonishment, clearly indicating that you don't call people of that kind visitors. '*Visitatori? Troppo importanti! Il Generalissimo Diaz e il Re Vittorio Emmanuele! E due Generali!*'[19]

I'd jolly nearly fallen on top of the King of Italy, – and the chief of his armies! I thought a scraped shin and a bruised ankle a low price to pay for (near) admission to such distinguished company.

---

19 'Visitors? Much too important to describe as visitors! Supreme General Diaz and King Victor Emmanuel! <u>And</u> two other Generals!'

Peace at Last

The war in Italy ended a week earlier than in France, exactly twelve months after my miraculous escape at Passchendaele. A second winter was heralded by the return of overcast skies and flurries of snow, the type of weather which had so depressed me the previous year. But now I felt nothing could depress me for long, for at least the war was over.

The battery was on the move again, this time ten miles southward to Treviso, a minor provincial capital still partly inhabited.

The last official task I remember being given was to translate the Italian Commander-in-Chief's 'Victory Bulletin', – a bragging précis of the fruits of our last battle, its colossal haul of prisoners and war material. Its appearance was greeted with supreme indifference. Fine words, whether in Italian or English, mean little to war-weary men waiting for one thing only, – the time when they are allowed to go home.

In my secretarial capacity, – which was now my only military role, – I dealt with all official correspondence except that marked 'Confidential' or 'Top Secret'. As a result I frequently got to know of matters not intended for the eyes of humble beings like myself. One of these was of considerable personal interest to me: I read that a scheme was being introduced to allow selected officers to visit some of the 'Art Cities' of the country. The word 'officers' didn't deter me; straight away, without consulting anyone, I sent an application to the department concerned. I apologized for the fact that I held no commission, gave a brief résumé of my service in the field and hoped they would consider my application favourably on the following grounds: –

1. Before the war I had been 'studying' Architecture. (This had at least a vestige of truth in it.)
2. I should be entering university shortly after my release from the Army. (This was wishful thinking.)
3. I was extremely anxious, before leaving Italy, to see some of the treasures of Pisa, Florence and Rome (which was <u>completely</u> true).

My audacity paid off. Fools rushing in don't <u>always</u> come to grief. And my luck was 'in' for Snow was away. Hemming-Wale, now Major, showed me the letter replying to my application. It stated that provided I had my C.O.'s approval and could prove my means to pay the expenses incurred, 'cultural leave' would be granted.

Major H-W was a sport, – he didn't even tick me off for apply-ing without permission. He gave me his formal blessing, only raising his eyebrows slightly when he saw that I had sufficient money not only for the week's travelling and accommodation but for an extra week at a top hotel on the Riviera had that been available! (I'd been saving up for the best part of a year and there was a good sum of un-drawn Army pay owing to me as well.)

So at long last I was granted leave, – not to Blighty it was true, – but a whole week's freedom to roam where I liked. I'd head for Rome first, and hope they hadn't closed the Sistine Chapel – so that at last one of my boyhood dreams could come true and I could see the Michelangelo frescoes. I was too excited for words.

I needn't have been. As Robbie Burns said, 'The best laid schemes o' mice an' men / Gang aft agley' – and this was no exception.

The very next day a notice was pinned to the messroom board announcing that one N.C.O. and five other ranks were eligible for Blighty leave. The N.C.O.s decided that the fairest way to determine the lucky one was by drawing lots. I had worked out my penance and was no longer under suspension, so my name went into the hat with the others. I'll give you one guess as to whose name was drawn!

The home leave was to take effect from the following day, only a week before I had arranged to travel to Rome.

It never rains but it pours, they say. I had waited nearly two years for an offer of leave – and then two had come along at once. I had to make a choice; I wasn't allowed to have the 'cultural' trip deferred, so I chose to come home. Botticelli's *Primavera*, Pisa's Leaning Tower, Michelangelo's ceiling and St. Peter's Basilica had managed without me for quite a few centuries; they could afford to wait a bit longer. (They're still waiting, as it happens.) Not even that lot could prevent me from speeding home to see my girl!

On Leave

I stopped on the quay at Southampton in the early afternoon of 22 November, 597 days after boarding the paddle steamer (– now at the bottom of the Channel –) which had taken me to France.

It was a mild, murky, drizzly day. I had left Italy nearly a week before with the dazzling sun making the snow-covered Alpine slopes glitter like sugar. Here, everything was grey, – but who was I to complain about that? This was Blighty, England, my homeland.

It's funny but for the whole of that first day I felt like a foreigner, a traveller in a strange country, not a soldier happily going home on leave. As the troop train rolled slowly past Winchester I saw with amazement that the two 'mountains' I had loved climbing as a boy had vanished. In fact the whole of the Hampshire landscape seemed to have been ironed flat by some gigantic steam roller. There wasn't a hill to be seen.

Of course the little hills of Winchester were <u>there</u>. They hadn't grown smaller physically as I'd grown older. I had acquired a new sense of scale, and every foot of St. Giles Hill was a thousand in the Venetian Alps. I'd been living among giants for so long now that I couldn't see the dwarfs!

At Waterloo station I sent telegrams to Ella and my parents saying that I would arrive at Bexhill mid-morning the following day. That afternoon I had other things in mind, – first and foremost to get myself cleaned up. I resolved to stay overnight at the Union Jack Club, which is quite near the railway terminus.

A hundred yards from the station I was confronted by a female figure, highly perfumed and very . . . well, 'decorative' might be the appropriate adjective. She was wearing a low-cut blouse, a highly slit tight skirt and black silk stockings, – and probably a fussy hat on top of her blonde tresses (I can't remember). She said I was lonely, wasn't I? and called me dearie. I didn't know my way around London; perhaps she could show me the way, – but first why didn't we go along to her place and have something to eat. She knew what young soldiers like me fancied.

This form of welcome to the metropolis was a surprise to me. I hadn't realized till then that such ladies existed in England – which shows how naive I was! On the continent they were not met in the streets, and this was my first experience of the English approach. I didn't like it.

I said, 'Thank you very much, but I'm on my way to meet my fiancée', at which remark her mood instantly changed. Only a minute before I had been a lovely boy; now I was a lousy bastard with nothing better to do than waste her time!

It was strange she should have used the term 'lousy', though of course she hadn't meant it in the literal sense. When I said my first priority was to get cleaned up, that was exactly the thought in my mind. Since my discharge from hospital eight months before I had managed to keep myself louse-free, something which had been impossible in Flanders. But I had run across the odd louse occasionally and I didn't intend on going into either my parents' home or Ella's wearing clothes that might be harbouring vermin.

In the same street as the Union Jack building I came across an outfitter's shop, where I was able to buy three sets of decent underwear and three officer's khaki shirts. (These were made of softer material than those issued to the other ranks.)

I 'booked in' at the club, dumped my kitbag on my bed and went off to the bathroom carrying my new purchases with me. I remember how marvellous it felt to have a really hot bath with some Lifebuoy soap. (In Italy soap was practically unobtainable.) I must have used half a bar at least.

I wrapped my discarded clothing in paper and left it in the bedroom. I don't suppose it was the first such parcel they'd come across.

Feeling clean and wholesome again, I locked up my room and took the Tube to Charing Cross. This was about the only part of London with which I was familiar. It was nice to see lights coming on again after the long war-time black-out.

I went to the Strand Corner House and ordered the best meal I could think of. I'm sorry I haven't the faintest recollection of what it consisted of – but as I hadn't tasted fish for well over eighteen months I could make a shrewd guess.

It was evening now and I walked along the Strand – thronged with soldiers on leave and their girl-friends of the moment. At the end of the Strand stood the Gaiety Theatre (alas no longer there). I liked the look of the pictures in the foyer and bought an upper circle seat for the evening performance. It was a musical comedy called *Going Up* and the star of the show was a young actress called Evelyn Laye. I didn't enjoy it as much as I expected, and I realized why when I looked around me and found that the audience was comprised almost entirely of couples. I made a resolution there and then – that before my leave was over I'd go to a London show with <u>my</u> girl and buy the best seats in the theatre. Then I would be as happy as all the chaps around me.

I travelled down to Bexhill by the first train and went straight to my house. I found this 'coming home' to be most strange. Once again I felt like a stranger in an unfamiliar country, and the sensation persisted as I walked up to the house. Everything around me looked so different: the town, my road, the people I passed, even our own front door.

My parents were of course delighted to see me home safe and sound. I ought to have been equally happy, but I wasn't. Somehow I didn't seem to belong. Was that the effect long absences from loved ones and living so close to death had on people? That they found it difficult to adjust to <u>ordinary</u> situations? I just didn't know.

Mother had laid on a welcome-home meal in my honour. She kept plying me with questions about life at the front, how wicked I must have found the Germans, how heroic all we brave boys had been, – all the things I felt completely disinclined to talk about. I tried to make a brave show of agreement and enthusiasm but I doubt whether it was very convincing. Poor Father looked on, pretending to take it all in but utterly unable to do so. His deafness had worsened a lot since I had left home. I saw how proud of me both of them were, – as though I had upheld the honour of the family as well as that of my country, by volunteering to be a soldier and thus a hero. I didn't dare disclose my real feelings about wars, patriotism and the like.

Ivy Clare, the youngest of my two sisters, now thirteen, and Jim, my kid brother of nine, came home from school. Both had grown a lot, particularly Ivy, whose hair looked so different I hardly knew her. I remembered it falling below her neck and in front of her shoulders in ringlets like darkened rolls of barley sugar. Now it was tied behind the neck with a wide red bow. I thought she looked very pretty.

Both she and Jim were shy and distant. Perhaps my uniform disguised the fact that I was their big brother; perhaps my manner didn't help either. Then my elder sister came in, – and I saw that she had changed even more than the younger ones. Although only two years separated us she had always seemed so much younger than me. But not now. There was something very adult and mature about her. She had 'put up' her hair and the change had cancelled out the age gap between us. She seemed very formal – and unaffectionate.

I couldn't feel as happy as I ought at my homecoming. It was all so difficult to understand. Nobody was as I had expected. Nothing was quite as it should be.

Of course everything was as it should have been. All of them were right; it was I who was wrong.

Mid-afternoon had come before I could bring myself to head for Ella's house, though she lived less than fifteen minutes' walk away. I set off hesitatingly, finding myself unable to go there directly. Believe it or not, for nearly an hour I walked the streets, meeting not a soul I knew, gazing in windows of closing shops without seeing any of the wares on display, dawdling along the Promenade listening to the sound of the waves on the shingle, turning things over and over in my mind. If I had seen so great a change in my family, what change was I to see in my sweetheart?

Why did I continue to hesitate? – when almost every day for over a year and a half I had longed for this moment to come, the time when I would see her open her door and I would say, 'Here I am, darling! Better late than never'?

Of course the truth was that I was afraid. I feared further disillusion – and greater disappointment than I felt capable of bearing, the discovery that I had been in love with a dream-girl all the time.

The daylight had gone when I walked up to the door and gave a timid knock. The door was opened by Ella. The moment of truth had come.

We couldn't see well because the hall was only dimly lit. Unsure of ourselves for a moment or two we stood silent and still. Then stepping boldly forward I flung my arms round her and drew her close.

And what do you think were the first romantic words my beloved said to me after our long separation?

'Do you know I've been waiting for you all the afternoon? Where have you been?'

So matter-of-fact, so down-to-earth, – as though I'd gone out half an hour before to post a letter!

'I've been taking a walk . . . round the town.'

'Well!' she said. 'I like that!' But the tone of her voice told me she didn't like it one little bit.

Then she stepped back to switch on the light and turned once again towards me. We saw each other properly for the first time in over twenty months. I watched a smile light up her face and I saw that her eyes were shining. She had been teasing, playing at being angry. A wave of happiness swept over me as she came close, put her arms round my neck and reached up to kiss me. If that wasn't the happiest moment in my whole life, I can't remember what was.

She led me into the house. All my fears had vanished. I suffered no disenchantment, for here <u>was</u> my dream-girl and she was <u>real</u>! I had last seen her as a blue-eyed fair-haired flapper[20] – I saw her now as a beautiful young woman. She had grown up; she was all that I could have wished her to be and more than I had ever dared to hope.

My cheeks were burning and my heart was pounding as we entered the living room and I went to give Ella's mother a hug and a kiss. She was beaming with pleasure as though it were her own son returning from the wars. (To the end of her days I regarded her – and loved her – as a second mother.) Soon Ella's father entered and not long afterwards her sister Evelyn. They both greeted me affectionately.

Evelyn was a few months younger than me and a lovely girl. She and Ella were so unlike that you would never have taken them for sisters. Evelyn was a finely built girl with a much more rounded face and figure than her younger sister – in fact beside Ella she looked almost plump. Her colouring was very different. She had an apple-blossom pink-and-white complexion and hair which really was a 'crowning glory', – a kind of golden-auburn which hung in loose waves about her temples. It was the exact hue of a golden half-sovereign, – as her mother once proved to me by placing one against a lock of it. There's no gainsaying that she was as pretty as a picture and I thought what a lucky chap her boy-friend Horace was. They had become engaged a few months before.

---

20 Girls in their early teens who wore their hair long down their backs were known as flappers; when they felt grown up they put their hair up.

Why have I written so much about my sweetheart's sister? Was it because I was half in love with her myself? No! I liked her immensely, but I loved only Ella. Ella who with her oval face, wide blue eyes and slender body possessed a more delicate and refined, almost fragile, beauty. The more I saw of her the more I loved her.

The fragile beauty outlived the other. Not one of us there that evening, – or anyone else for that matter, – could possibly have guessed that the strong-looking one would not live to see her twenty-first birthday.

I walked home with my head in the clouds, hardly aware it was raining until I got indoors. The house seemed different now, and not because the family had all gone to bed, for they always retired early, – it had begun to feel as though I belonged in it. How lovely it was to slip between cool white sheets for eight hours of unbroken sleep.

It was an unforgettably happy fortnight. The war had only recently ended, Christmas was approaching and everywhere there was the spirit of goodwill. It was the first peace-time Christmas for four years.

We visited friends and relations, and if the weather was favourable walked down to the sea front in search of an unoccupied shelter. At our homes we were never left together unchaperoned. On the Promenade – especially after dark – we obtained the seclusion we needed, though there were certain things we both agreed could wait until we were married. We were quite certain now that we were made for each other.

Indoors we made music together. Did I say that it was Ella's singing voice I had originally fallen in love with? During my absence it had matured and become a silvery mezzo-soprano, – the result of the training she had been receiving. She had won a number of diplomas at area music festivals to add to those she had been awarded for her piano playing. She had never mentioned these new accomplishments in her letters and I loved her all the more for her modesty.

We played piano duets together, with her parents and sister for audience. Ella sang of course, I sang (very badly) and we all sang together. Looking back, we are convinced that they were indeed the Good Old Days.

I remember the first piece she sang. It was an operatic aria from Gluck's *Orfeo* in the original Italian. I was very happy to discover that she had acquired some knowledge of the language I myself was learning.

The words of the first lyric are '*Che faro senza Eurydice?*' in which Orpheus asks what he would do without <u>his</u> sweetheart. She sang it so beautifully that I was unable to read the accompaniment and nearly ruined the performance as a result. (It's a good thing this was a family occasion.) Nevertheless it was heartily applauded by the entire audience of four, which included Evelyn's Horace, – who <u>still</u> hadn't been called up because he was doing something somebody considered work of national importance. (He did get 'his papers' in the end, – that very week!)

We had lighter musical moments too. 'If you were the only girl (/boy) in the world' was one of the Top Ten in those days and we sang it together. And of course at my request the programme included the little ballad that had entranced me two and a half years before on the evening we met: 'Love, Here Is My Heart'. This time, though, the words were sung with a depth of feeling that had been lacking in the first performance.

On the two Sunday mornings we went to church. It was only right and proper that together we should offer thanks for my safe return in the building where we had worshipped since we were children. But oh! how austere, how <u>naked</u> St. Barnabas Church looked after the baroque glories of San Martino! And how solemn and unhappy the congregation seemed.

One memorable evening we sat in stall seats at Hastings Gaiety Theatre, where the Carl Rosa Opera Company were performing the double bill of 'Cav and Pag' (*Cavalleria Rusticana* and *Pagliacci*). For three delicious hours we shared the loves, hates and passions of those oh! so British Italian characters. Then, despite my temporary affluence, we travelled home the cheap way, – by tramcar instead of taxi-cab. I'll explain why: –

I suppose the coldest, most uncomfortable and least glamorous form of transport then known to man was on the top deck of an open Hastings tramcar; we had it entirely to ourselves. The vehicle was unlighted, unheated and had seats of wooden bars so hard they printed musical staves on your buttocks. The bitter wind whistled round our ears. We wrapped woolly scarves over our heads, cuddled up close to keep warm and enjoyed every minute of the world's least comfortable journey: a glorious end to a perfect lovers' outing!

On the last Wednesday I took Ella to London. It had to be a Wednesday because that was the only day of the week a so-called theatre train ran from Charing Cross to Hastings, leaving London about 11 p.m.

It was the first time either of us had visited the capital properly and we certainly got around! First we found our way to Kensington for a shopping spree. The stores were gaily lit and decorated. I haven't any recollection of what I bought, but I have a very clear memory of Ella's purchase. I can see her now standing before a long mirror, looking apprehensively at herself. (We had been turned away from the Ladies Clothes Salon as the store had nothing small enough to fit her, and we were now in the Juvenile department!)

The outfit was of a velour cloth trimmed with beaver fur, its colour a little deeper than the turquoise of her eyes. Wearing it they had become sapphire blue, and they were saying, if ever eyes said anything, 'It's much too expensive, much more than I can afford.' I stood there gazing in admiration: she looked, as they say to-day, a million dollars. On the impulse of the moment I snatched out my wallet and laid it on the counter. Ella protested, but I wasn't in any mood to take a refusal.

(I believe some 'white lies' had to be told to her mother on our return. In those days for a young man to buy a girl clothing was considered almost immoral in our provincial town – regarded as the first step to imminent seduction.)

It was some time before Ella's feeling of guilt wore off. I eventually managed to convince her that I was more than happy to spend money on her, that I had saved it up specifically for that purpose and that I hadn't finished yet, as I intended buying her a really personal present.

'Oh no!' she protested. 'You are not. You've been too extravagant already!'

'Oh yes, I am!' I replied. 'What they won't let me spend on myself in Rome I'm going to spend on you in London!'

She shook her head, but her eyes were positively glowing with happiness.

'But before that,' I said, 'there's a church I have to visit.'

We jumped on a bus and alighted at Trafalgar Square. I took Ella's hand and led her up the steps of St. Martin in the Fields.

'I've got a personal interest in St. Martin,' I told her. 'He did me a good turn once. I'll tell you the story one day.' (I didn't know she would wait fifty years before she heard it!)

We entered the church and both offered up a silent prayer. I don't know what Ella's was, but mine was of gratitude for having been spared to see this day. We walked around the building and in a dark corner I kissed her. 'You shouldn't do that in a church,' she whispered, but I'm sure she didn't mind and I'll bet neither St. Martin nor God objected either.

I was going to take her to the Trocadero, but it had an 'Officers Only' look about it (– I was in N.C.O.'s uniform of course –) so we settled for the Strand Corner House, which I had visited on my previous evening in London.

On the way out I enquired where the Ciro Pearls shop was. Over lunch I had asked what I could buy Ella for a personal present. Of course she had said, 'Nothing,' but I had wormed out of her that pearls were her favourite jewel and that the string I had sent her from Salisbury were very nice, but . . . That was all I wanted to know.

In Ciro's shop in Bond Street she saw the necklace of her choice, but said that it was much too expensive. 'Good!' I replied, and told the salesman that we would take it. He fastened it around her neck then and there. I never saw her look prettier.

We cannot recall how we filled in the time until our theatre visit. I had bought two second-row stalls seats for 12s 6d. Fantastically expensive! Again I was reproved for my extravagance, but once more I explained that I would have spent ten times that amount just on myself had I chosen the Italian holiday instead of coming home.

The play was a farce called *Nothing but the Truth*, performed by an all-star cast of whom we can't remember a single name! We enjoyed it immensely – I because I had my girl beside me, and Ella because it was her first-ever visit to a London theatre. It was the <u>only</u> time we ever sat in second-row stalls, – at the Savoy or anywhere else!

Good fortune smiled on us at the end of that wonderful day. We found an empty compartment for the two-and-a-half-hour journey home and no ticket collector disturbed us. It was I think the shortest 150-minute journey I ever made. And in spite of the privacy, in spite of the length of time, in spite of the intense cold, our love-making was as innocent (– almost –) as it would have been in Ella's drawing room with her mother and father looking on.

It wasn't too bad for us when my leave was over and parting time came. I don't know why but I cannot remember saying farewell. I'm sure that this time Ella came to the station to see me off but I'm certain she shed no tears. I would have remembered that.

I had plenty to think over during the six-day journey back. In spite of a perfectly foul Channel crossing to Cherbourg I wasn't sea-sick. And all the way the words of that little ballad were singing inside my head: 'And yet I love her till I die.'

During that fortnight we had both discovered that something which till then we had only hoped, had happened in reality. I think we had both feared that a near-two-year separation might have changed us so much that each would find the other a different person from the one he or she fell in love with. Paradoxically, we found that our separation had brought us closer together. Ella knew that I was the only boy for her as clearly as I knew that she was the only girl for me. She confessed, if that's not too strong a word, something to me later. You remember how worried I was that the longer our separation lasted the stronger the likelihood was that she might turn to someone else for consolation? Well, it so happened that before my leave she had become friendly with one of the wounded soldiers convalescing at Bexhill. Luckily for me it hadn't developed beyond the stage of preliminary friendship, though it had reached the point of Ella agreeing to 'go to the pictures' with him – on the very day I came home. The receipt of my telegram caused a hasty cancellation, so perhaps I returned in the nick of time.

I Celebrate my Twenty-First Birthday –
Unconventionally

Earlier I described in some detail my first journey across France, en route (unknowingly) to Italy. That had been a year ago – almost exactly. Now I was making the journey for a second time, and <u>this</u> journey merits a detailed description too, for in its way it was as unusual and memorable as the earlier one, – and not only because I celebrated my twenty-first birthday in a cattle truck! (I didn't <u>receive</u> any cards, but I sent quite a few!)

This time I had a map with me so I was able to follow the route taken by the train. On 11 December it pulled up at the spa resort of Aix-les-Bains in the centre of eastern France. Before the war it had been probably the most fashionable inland resort in the country.

The troop train, – a string of horse boxes, of course, HOMMES 40, CHEVAUX 8, – arrived there in mid-morning. It had been running in and out of tunnels excavated from the steep slopes skirting the shores of Lake Bourget. All around were lofty hills, covered with snow which sparkled in the yellow winter sun.

'No one is permitted to leave the train at any point of the journey.' That was the uncompromising order issued by the Train Officer. But as you will have gathered by now, I wasn't one to be bound by red tape, rules, regulations or Brass Hats' instructions.

In any case, <u>the war was over now</u>! Who cared about little Kaiser Train Officers and their stupid orders? It was my twenty-first birthday and I deserved a celebration. I left the train, unobserved.

Aix-les-Bains had numerous plushy-looking hotels and one of those ornamental continental casinos that look as though they were originally designed in sugar icing. But war-time neglect had removed much of the gilt. It seemed that nearly all the hotels were closed and the bright sunshine drew attention to their peeling stucco and fading paint. The lakeside promenade is very beautiful and you could imagine the peace-time patrons, – the idle rich and members of royal families, – driving past in style. But that day, 11 December 1918, Aix looked passé, almost dead, – scarcely the sort of place for a youngster of twenty-one.

I got back to the station to find that the train had departed without me. Not that I cared! As I bought refreshments at the Buffet, I explained that I had been careless enough to miss the troop train bound for Italy. 'Oh! what a pity!' everyone exclaimed. '*C'est la guerre,*' I replied, – and then corrected myself: '*Non, ce n'est pas la guerre. C'est la paix!*', which they all thought quite funny. Suddenly there was the sound of another train arriving. I called out '*Au revoir*' and rushed across to the opposite platform. The board indicated it was bound for Genève, Suisse. 'Now, that's more like it,' I thought as I clambered aboard.

According to my map Geneva was about fifty miles away. I was on a passenger train and remained standing in a corridor to have a good view of the scenery en route. In a little over an hour we halted at a small place called St. Jean. I saw the ominous notice board: '*Douane*' (Customs). Then I heard the cry from uniformed officials boarding the train: '*Passeports, s'il vous plaît. Passeports!*'

Of course they'd want passports before you entered Switzerland! Why hadn't I thought of that? I'd just have to act dumb and trust to my proverbial good luck.

Oh! what a silly mistake I've made, I told them. Getting on a Geneva train when I wanted to go to Italy!

Everyone was most sympathetic towards the poor lost English

soldier. I would have to go back to Aix-les-Bains on the next train, but in the meantime would I care to wait in the Customs Office and take a cup of coffee with them?

I think I acted my part pretty well. If I'd dared to tell them that to-day was my twenty-first birthday I believe they would have opened a bottle of wine in my honour!

They put me aboard a train which took me back to Aix. There I waited for the Grenoble express, which I was told called at Chambéry. From there it was about 120 kilometres to the Italian border.

There was snow falling when I reached Chambéry. It was surrounded by magnificent mountains which I could only just distinguish through the falling snow. I hadn't a greatcoat, – I'd left it on the troop train, which must by now have been a hundred miles ahead of me, – so I didn't venture far from the station. A grizzled old war veteran was in charge of refreshments there.

A couple of the old boy's cronies (– both wearing ancient blue berets –) drifted in, shook the snow off themselves and started up a conversation. They were all old soldiers and reminisced and cracked jokes which my schoolboy French (now rustier than ever) couldn't cope with, – but we laughed uproariously as I pretended to understand them. I learnt from the Buffet attendant that a Turin train was due in half an hour. I bought a bottle of *vin rouge* just before it arrived and gave it to them with my '*félicitations*'.

The Turin express steamed slowly in and, coatless and ticketless, I jumped aboard. I was living now from one hour to the next, letting things happen to me just as they wished and taking them as they came. I felt on top of the world, and I'd made up my mind to see as much of it as lay within my reach.

Suddenly, without warning the train drew to a stop. An

avalanche had blocked the line ahead, in front of the troop train I had 'deserted' from that morning. It was now mid-afternoon and the train I was in had caught up with the one I had left.

I slipped down onto the track and made my way cautiously along the line of horse boxes. Here was mine! I peeped inside to say hello to my truck-mates but they weren't there. My kit lay undisturbed in its corner. I clambered in, grabbed my greatcoat and put it on.

I soon saw why the truck was empty. The troops had been conscripted into snow-clearance work.

Well, if there's a more unwelcome, inappropriate way of cele-brating your birthday than by shovelling a hundred tons of snow and ice off a railway track, I've never heard of it! I calculated they had at least an hour's hard labour ahead of them. My best way of 'dodging the column' was to disappear into the surrounding scenery.

And what sensational scenery it was! Easily the most spec-tacular I had seen. It's true I'd been living in Alpine surround-ings for months, but that had been in the summer and only the distant Dolomite peaks had been permanently snow-covered. Here the slopes were snow-clad from summit to base and how much more impressive the high mountains look in their winter aspect!

It was not till I had crossed to the far side of the tracks that I saw the train had been stopped in the outskirts of a village. The horse trucks screened me as I tramped up a steep snowy slope into the main, or should I say only street. I soon found a little general store, where I was able to buy yet another view-card to send to Ella.

We emerged from the Mont Cenis tunnel at midnight, which meant that my twenty-first birthday ended just as I crossed the frontier. At Susa, which is the first town on the Italian side, we all detrained for an 'issue' breakfast.

We still had a full day's travelling ahead. We crept along through Torino (Italian spelling now!), Milano, Brescia, Verona, Cittadella, – and then we were in Treviso.

Treviso is a very ancient, very picturesque town and a minor provincial capital, about twenty miles north of Venice. Like that city it has a network of canals running alongside its streets. I had a very pleasant billet only a stone's throw from one of the canal basins. The Battery H.Q. was housed in an evacuated shop and my billet had originally been the storeroom on the floor above it. The shop windows were boarded up but you could still read the word '*Farmacia*' in fading print on the fascia board, and some of the chemist-shop odours lingered on.

One afternoon, off duty, I walked the several miles that separate Treviso from the nearer bank of the River Piave, where one of the bloodiest battles of the entire war had been fought. I had thought that by now the horrors of war could no longer shock me, but I was wrong. Three months after the fighting had ceased the mangled, putrefying bodies of men and beasts still lay awaiting burial.

I obliged the Army by staying in it for another two months before they decided to give me my 'ticket', in the last week of February 1919.

The day before my departure I spent an hour tidying up my work table in the battery office and collecting my belongings together. It was very cold and snowing heavily but my thoughts kept me warm: at long last I was going home to take up a life which had been interrupted more completely than I could ever have imagined twenty-nine months before.

But I was slightly grieved by one small loss. The horseshoe

mascot Ella's father had made for me, which I had carried with me everywhere, was missing. Lost, stolen or strayed, I didn't know. Perhaps, its mission accomplished now that I was safely through the war, it had used its mystic power to extinguish itself and vanish. Either way I never saw it again.

I had almost finished packing when I came across an Italian–English 'Digest' magazine I had found in Cittadella the previous spring. My attention was caught by a brief quotation at the foot of a page – some lines written by John Donne over 300 years ago. I remembered having come across them before, – in my 'Matric' English examination at school. We had been instructed to discuss their sentiments and make suitable comments of our own.

Well, I don't suppose I scored very high marks then as I was only vaguely able to grasp the meaning of the lines. But now I felt I knew what Donne meant.

No man is an island entire of itself; every man is a piece of the Continent, a part of the main . . . any man's death diminishes me, because I am involved in Mankind; and therefore never send to know for whom the bell tolls; it tolls for thee.

The truth of these sentences (oft-quoted and famous now, but not then) came home to me with tremendous impact, for with the deaths of Geordie and Bill, of Windy and Jock, of the German boy Hans (– I could never forget Hans –) something had died in me too. Their deaths had diminished me.

Looking back, a half century later, I can't help wondering if Hemingway first saw Donne's words in that same magazine. Twenty years later he used five of them as the title of his second war novel.

'It's a Funny Old World . . .'

There was something else on my mind that day. It was a topic which was barred from polite conversation a generation ago and couldn't be written about without much tut-tutting and eyebrow-raising. Just two weeks before my career as a soldier was to end, I had been confronted with a surprising proposition.

One of my battery's Signallers was a fellow called Ellwood, – 'Twister' Ellwood as he was known to the rank and file. He was a Yorkshireman of between forty and forty-five, a short, plump-ish, dark-haired, pale-faced chap who'd joined our outfit in the spring of 1918. He gave you the impression that the sun had never shone on him – and this, after six months' service through a real Italian summer! He had ice-blue eyes, and the expression-less look they bore reminded me of a large fish I once helped to drag out of a boat on Bexhill beach.

A day or so after his arrival he produced several packs of playing cards and a Crown and Anchor Board. To be accu-rate it was not a board, but a black cloth marked out in squares with the required symbols. Crown and Anchor is a gam-bling game played with dice, and was forbidden by the Army chiefs; the 'rollable' version can be rapidly concealed if danger threatens. Ellwood's dice were, I suspect, 'loaded' and his cards were no doubt trick packs, – although no one ever proved it.

Every available minute of his off-duty time he would collect a small school of gamblers around him. Nap and Pontoon were the commonest of the card games, but his favourite trick for parting fools from their money was Crown and Anchor. Over and over again I stood and watched men lose every penny of their fortnight's pay. Sometimes it took an hour, sometimes half that time. On several occasions I acted as moneylender to one or two of these unfortunates. (I wasn't exactly a Shylock as the only interest I charged on my loans was in kind – usually a bar of chocolate or something similar.)

I was one of the first fools referred to above, as I rose to Ellwood's bait early in our acquaintanceship. I and three other innocents played Pontoon with him for quite moderate stakes.

During my first few minutes of play I was unusually fortunate. 'Beginner's luck' it's called. I won frequently, but when my winnings approached three pounds (a great deal of money then) my fortunes mysteriously declined. Soon I had only a few coppers of my early winnings left, at which point, much to Ellwood's disgust, I withdrew. He called me a rotten sportsman, but I didn't care. I had learned my lesson: namely that those stupid enough to play with an 'expert' <u>always</u> lose.

In spite of his reputation, he prospered – because the supply of suckers never ran out. By the end of that year he had sent home enough of his ill-gotten gains to buy two houses, according to the rumour which went round the battery. This may have been an exaggeration, but it's certain he was making money faster than anyone for miles around.

Now all this is only incidental. The main point of my story is a proposition that Ellwood put to me only a few days before I left for home. And it wasn't connected with Crown and Anchor, Nap, Pontoon or any other of his gambling pursuits.

I had observed that for a while past his attitude towards me had changed. He had become quite affable, if not downright friendly. (The affability wasn't reciprocated; I found him impossible to like.) The change dated precisely from the time when my name first appeared on the roll of men selected for early demobilization.

One day, when he and I were alone together in the Command

Post (only manned to give us something to do), he came forward with his proposition. It caught me wholly unprepared. At first I thought he was having me on, but it proved to be offered in all seriousness.

It seems remarkable to me now that I didn't find his suggestion offensive and repellent. I can only assume that curiosity and disbelief overcame any feeling of disgust I might have had. Anyhow, I made no reply and waited for him to proceed and explain further.

He soon made it clear that he wasn't hoping to use my services for his exclusive personal pleasure. (That thought had been the first to cross my mind after I'd recovered from the initial shock.) He planned, if I would co-operate, to turn me into a profitable investment for the near future.

This was his idea. On my arrival in Blighty, after demob procedures had been concluded, I should go to his place in Bradford instead of to my parents' home. There I would meet his wife. Somehow, in correspondence which had foiled the censors, they had planned my immediate future. She would take me into their home, where I would live as one of the family. I would be a gentleman of leisure there until he came out of the Army in a couple of months.

He went on to outline the kind of career they would launch me into, – one which he told me few young chaps were suited for. He assured me that once I got going and 'played my cards' correctly, I would be well on the way to wealth in a couple of years.

It appeared that he and his 'lady-wife' owned a social club in Bradford, where drinking, gaming and other activities were available. Most of the patrons were wealthy businessmen who had somewhat unorthodox interests. Some were foreigners on business trips and visited the establishment because their particular tastes weren't adequately catered for elsewhere. They all had one thing in common, – an aversion to female company. They were very attracted towards good-looking lads like me, – Ellwood said I was exactly their type.

'With thy nice looks, lad, between us we would make a fortune. Them fellas is rolling in brass, tha knows, and would spend pounds at a time on a lad like thee. Thee could pocket more brass in a month in my club than thee'd earn in a year in thy school.'

Then, as a sort of final inducement, he added, 'I have a daughter same age as thee, lad, – a reet pretty lass. Thee'd find her champion company.'

Had I been anyone but the person I am, I expect my instinctive response would have been a 'What-do-you-take-me-for?' followed by a punch on the nose. But as you know I'm more of a peacemaker than a warmonger, so at this point I silently counted ten to restrain myself and began to work out how I should deal with this unexpected situation.

By the time Ellwood had finished speaking I had decided what I should do. I would pretend to 'play ball'; I would lead him up the garden path, see to what lengths he was prepared to go, and then, when it suited me, I'd tell him what I really thought of both him and his obscene plans. It would be a real showdown. I'd see to that.

At that moment in walked my relief, – much to my relief, if you'll forgive the pun. I didn't say anything to Ellwood on my way out. I didn't even look at him.

The 'showdown', as I presumed to call it, occurred the afternoon before I left for home. I went to see Ellwood at his billet and was lucky enough to find him alone. I had prepared what I thought to be an appropriate little speech. He was going to be taught a lesson.

He listened impassively to what I had come to say. His face bore a resigned half smile, but it showed no trace of anger or disappointment.

To the best of my recollection, this is the little 'speech' which I had prepared: –

'Thanks a lot, Twister, for inviting me to become a playmate in your brothel of a club. I've been thinking it over and as I'm off to Blighty to-morrow I've come along to tell you what I've decided.

'At first I thought, "What a bloody cheek! What do you take me for?" I reckoned you were a dirty beast, a bloke who when he isn't busy fleecing his pals runs a club where a set of apes come along and buy their special kind of fun.'

I hesitated a moment, expecting some kind of protest. None came, so I continued.

'I thought that what I'd have to do in that zoo of yours was revolting and I'd decided I'd turn it down flat. Then after a while I began to think I'd misjudged you, – that you weren't as black as I'd painted you, because you were generous enough to put something my way where I could make a lot of money. I believed you must have thought a great deal of me to do <u>that</u>, – to <u>give</u> money away to somebody instead of robbing them of what they'd got.'

Again I paused. Still he was as silent and unmoved as the Sphinx.

'Twister, I'm going to accept your offer,' I said. 'What made up my mind was you saying, first, that the "work" is easy and the money is good; and second that you've got a very friendly daughter my age. Well, <u>I</u> haven't got a daughter <u>any</u> age, but back in Blighty I <u>have</u> got a girl who I'm hoping to marry as soon as I can afford to. That means I'm not really interested in whether your lass is young, old, pretty or ugly. <u>My</u> girl's prettier than her, I bet. All the same, it was you mentioning your daughter that decided me. It gave me this idea, – that I'd go to Bradford as you said, introduce myself to your lady and see the accommodation you have to offer. On one condition: that I can bring my girl along too. Then, if your wife likes her, we'll get married and live at your place, – just like you said.'

His face was still expressionless. I began to realize that I'd lost the battle – if it is a battle when your opponent refuses to fight.

'Of course, before we go I shall explain in detail what sort of job I'm being offered, – to her and to her parents as well. I'll let them know how well off we'll be on my earnings and if my girl says, "O.K. I think we shall enjoy that sort of life," we'll go to Bradford together as soon as Mrs Ellwood can fix us up. Well, what do you say, Twister?'

He didn't turn a hair, didn't bat an eyelid. Nothing of what I'd said had made the slightest impression. He did show a flicker of disappointment when he replied, – as though he'd just offered me a half-share in a tin of bully-beef and I'd been ungrateful enough to refuse it.

'Sorry tha's taken it like this, lad . . . I was doing thee a good turn, thee knows. All the same, good luck . . . And in case thee iver changes tha mind, here's where thee'll find me.' He held out a piece of paper; I ignored it. 'Ah well . . . when thee gets to Bradford ask Stationmaster. He knows me. Pity . . . I shan't find another as good as thee. But, when tha does come, doan't bring t'lass wi' thee. Ah've nice jobs for good-looking lads like thee, but nowt for lasses.'

He was completely imperturbable. Ruefully I had to conclude that had I been half as clever as I thought, I could have saved myself both time and trouble by summarizing all I'd said in one brief sentence, such as, 'You're a rogue, Twister and it's no go; I don't happen to be your sort.'

Ellwood's last words to me were 'Good luck, lad. No hard feelings.' The hand he extended I pretended not to see. I didn't feel friendly enough to reply and silently walked away.

On my way back I did have <u>some</u> misgivings. Perhaps I should have taken his hand as a gesture of goodwill. I'd met worse men, – much worse; I'd only to look at our battery commander to see one supreme example. Twister Ellwood was a hypocrite. He was selfish, amoral. His religion, – his sole aim in life, – was the making of money. But his 'victims' were willing, – even eager, – to be preyed on. As he said to me once, 'I don't <u>ask</u> 'em to part wi' their brass, lad. They gamble because they enjoy it. Doan't thee be sorry for them.'

On another occasion, referring to his 'club', he'd said, 'It's a funny old world we live in . . . It takes all sorts. Some of 'em wouldn't get much fun out of it, if it wasn't for the likes of me.' I didn't deny it, for it was patently true.

You may think I have devoted far too much space to such an unwholesome character. An hour after the end of the 'interview' I had made myself forget him altogether. I allowed thoughts of <u>my</u> world to fill my mind. The world I could inhabit in imagination; a world of beauty, part of which I could see in reality from my roof-top.

It was mid-afternoon when I climbed the stone stairway leading up to the rest of the house. I pushed open the trap-door and clambered up to the walking space between the wall coping and the slanting part of the roof proper.

It had been snowing as I walked back from Ellwood's billet but now the weather was beginning to change. Breaks were appearing in the low overhanging clouds and the mists were clearing from the plains, which stretched flat as a table for miles. Away to the north, twelve or fifteen miles distant, were the mountains, – hidden in a persistent haze that restricted visibility to less than half that distance. Now that haze was melting into nothingness as pale sunlight began to colour the landscape. The giant shapes began to appear.

First came the mass the Italians called *Il Montello*, which we had nicknamed Mount Hippo because of its outline. It was an isolated hump of limestone, the nearest to Treviso of all the outliers of the Alps, and had been immensely important to both opposing armies, as a result of which 5,000 men had lost their lives attempting to gain possession of it. We, the British and Italians, were the final victors, – and the capture of *Il Montello* proved to be the turning point of the Italian campaign. Two weeks after it was won the Austrians asked for an armistice.

From my roof-top viewpoint I watched spellbound as the strengthening sunrays transformed the dull grey of *Il Montello*'s flanks to primrose yellow. Then, in minutes, the distant haze and the clouds above it thinned and dissolved to reveal the whole dramatic Alpine panorama, – as though a drop-curtain had been invisibly lifted.

My thoughts returned to *Il Montello*, and to the days when I was there. There the First World War had ended for 239 Siege Battery, R.G.A. Our guns had fired their last shells from emplacements excavated out of its stony slopes. Soon the Austrians had retreated beyond the range of our howitzers, leaving us with nothing to fire upon.

Ten days had elapsed before the battery came off 'Hippo' and into a so-called rest camp. By that time, unknown to us, the Great War had come to an end. Nobody told us until four days later that, on the morning of 11 November 1918, the morning we and all our trappings moved down to the plain, at precisely

11 o'clock, the fighting had ended, – not only for us, but for all the other war-weary survivors of that four-year conflict on <u>all</u> the battlefields throughout the world.

A little drama was being enacted in the street below. A horse-drawn covered cart had lumbered past and stopped outside a building a hundred yards on. I leaned over the coping to watch. An elderly couple clad in black climbed out of the vehicle. As the man came round to the near side, his wife, perhaps impatient at having to wait for him to help her alight, put her foot to the snow-covered cobbles, slipped, lost her balance and fell. The husband assisted her to her feet. No harm had been done, except to the woman's temper. She went off into the house while the man hung a nosebag under the horse's mouth before following her. I thought the poor creature looked half-starved; no doubt animal feed was in very short supply. The couple came and went, carrying pieces of furniture and bundles of their belongings from the wagon into the house. I wondered how many months, how many years, it was since they had been compelled to leave the home they were now returning to.

It made me wonder how many thousands of innocent people, young as well as old, had been forced to leave their homes because of the war. And, I asked myself, watching the old couple still trudging to and fro with armfuls of their household goods, what would many of those victims of war find when they <u>did</u> return? Heaps of rubble, most likely. And how many months, how many years would it be before all the shattered homes were made habitable again?

Arriverderci

I have now come to my last evening in north Italy. Having finished preparations for my departure, I was ready to carry out my last 'mission', a visit to church.

It was a Sunday, I remember, and snowing. Had this been a work of fiction I should have chosen a place of worship dedicated to St. Martin, but this is a true story and as far as I know there is no church of San Martino in Treviso. Instead I went to the Chiesa di San Nicolo. He of course is our old friend Santa Claus in disguise.

When I arrived the evening service had just come to an end. I recall very clearly a party of boys and girls who were the last to leave the building. They were in the charge of a short, plump nun whose wide starched hat barely cleared the door posts as she emerged at the end of the double column. Some of the children hesitated, staring in surprise at the khaki-clad foreign soldier waiting for them to pass, and received a mild scolding for their pains. But I waved my hand and smiled, saying '*Va bene, mi piace*' (It's quite all right, I'm not offended), and she in turn smiled back as she led her crocodile into the outer darkness.

Most of the lights had been extinguished by the time I entered the church, but the organist must have remained behind to practise some voluntaries, for glorious sounds were echoing splendidly round the empty building.

My so-called mission was a very simple one, – merely to spend a few minutes of my last evening in that foreign country in silent meditation and prayer. I could have done this equally well in my billet had I waited until the other men had gone out. But there something would be lacking: the consciousness of being close to a divine presence.

From a portrait high above, St. Nicholas looked down upon

me; Titian's *Madonna of the Flowers* hung to one side and a figure of the crucified Christ stood upon the altar. In spirit I believed St. Martin must have been there too. Only they, – and God, – know what was in my heart and what I wished to say.

Outside there was a beautiful soft light, not from the street lamps, which were still unlit, but from the half-moon's rays reflected by the fallen snow. I strolled slowly along the canal bank towards my billet, stopping at the basin to see if the ducks were still there. (They weren't.) I wondered where ducks go at night-time when it's bitterly cold. I had taken them some food scraps that morning and they had provided me with considerable amusement, sliding awkwardly over the ice in their endeavours to gobble up the pieces. Some fell into the water where the ice was too thin to carry their weight. Fancy remembering a little thing like that for more than fifty years!

That night I lay on my bunk glancing idly through my old war journal. I found myself skipping the parts which brought back unpleasant memories, – which was most of it, – and reliving in my imagination those I could recall with pleasure, – of which alas! there were very, very few. After that night I didn't look at it again for over fifty years! – until I decided to write these war stories. Without the little black book I couldn't have recalled half of what I have written.

I have it beside me now, its once glossy black cover limp and still bespattered with the dried stains of Flanders mud, acquired when it fell into a pool of slime in the autumn of 1917. Its final pages contained the story that follows, scribbled hurriedly in faint pencil, such that the writer himself had considerable difficulty in reading it. The date is interesting, because it shows that I undertook this excursion just seventy-two hours before the war in Italy came to an end.

31 October 1918

The pages of this book seem to be filled with violence, horror and bloodshed. It will make a change to write about what I did this afternoon.

I have been off duty ever since 6 a.m. yesterday. Last night I slept longer than I've done for weeks. No Austrian shelling now they've retreated towards the pre-war frontier. They are beyond our range now. It is almost uncannily quiet; just distant gunfire occasionally. Very distant now.

After scrounging some grub I slipped away from the battery unobserved. I took the Command Post map, my compass and binoculars and set off for a climb. It was as warm and sunny as if it were August instead of almost November.

I intended to get to the top of Hippo's hump. None of our chaps had been up there. (It had been No Man's Land until the enemy retreat began last month.) My aim was to reach the highest point of the ridge so that I could see down into the narrow valley on the northern side. I have had to study it on the map so frequently (– it contains many targets we've been ordered to fire on –) that I've made mental pictures of the scene.

Most of all, though, I was intrigued by the names of the villages which lie on either side of the stream which flows through the valley. The Italians have a knack of inventing place names that sound like characters in their operas: Cavaso and Corbanese, Capella and Crocetta, Cornuda and Casella.

An hour and a half of tough climbing brought me to a splendid vantage point from which I could look down into the entire eight-mile stretch of ravine. The map informed me that it was just on 300 metres; that's near enough 1,000 feet.

I seated myself on a flat-topped rock and spread out the map. The visibility was sharp enough to identify nearly every one of those places, which till then had been just names on a map. I was able to see in detail the damage our shelling had inflicted. (We'd had to shoot 'blind'; there were no O.P.'s on the north side of the mountain.)

I'd guess we made six misses for every hit. It was much less than I'd expected and I was glad. After all, if there was one person more responsible than any other for smashing up innocent people's homes it was me. I did the sums and the Gun Layers aimed their howitzers using my figures.

Away to my distant left was the village of Asolo. It was larger than the others, almost a small town. We'd had to strafe it on several occasions because on its outskirts there was a factory said to be turning out munitions for the enemy. The map told me that before the war it had been a 'Fàbbrica di Seta' (silk mill). There are groves of mulberry trees on the plains nearby which must provide grub for the silkworms.

I was able to see in detail the damage our shelling had done. The factory hadn't any windows left and not much roof. It was out of action all right. Some of the handsome villas which sprinkled the hillside above it had suffered severely too. All in all, we'd turned pretty little Asolo into a sorry mess. I was comforted to note that the church campanile stood apparently unharmed. We hadn't hit that.

What a glorious afternoon! Close beside me a brooklet was babbling its way downwards, dropping in miniature waterfalls from one level to another. I filled my water bottle from it. Spring water has bubbles in it and looks like sparkling white wine. It tastes even better than wine when you're really thirsty.

Well! I had seen and done what I had come for. It was time to go. As I pocketed my compass, stuffed the map back into my haversack and started on my descent, the fancy came to me that I had been gazing upon an actual corner of Heaven, a little portion which, at the end of Creation, God had had left over and placed in that tremendous mountain hollow for man's delight and enjoyment.

And what had _we_ done with it? Tried to turn a piece of Paradise into a corner of Hell. Well, we'd partially succeeded – only very, very fractionally though.

During my descent I was privileged to witness a splendid vision. I had chosen a different route to return by and had just emerged from the forested part of the mountain's southern flank when I came upon a goat track leading steeply down in the direction of the battery. The track took me round the foot of an almost vertical rock-face and brought me without warning on to a cliff ledge which commanded what must be one of the most astonishing views in all the Alpine foothills.

I stood 1,000 feet above sea level, looking down upon the vast plain of the Veneto. Below me, stretching from Il Montello's foot, the chess-board plain extended nearly forty miles till it reached a sheet of silver silk, which faded into nothingness where normally a horizon would be. Where the green of the mainland ended I saw a ribbon of pale blue water and beyond that, floating, – so it seemed, – was a city of silver and gold, glowing in the autumn sunshine. It looked unreal, a mirage. But it was no creation of my imagination, no phantom city. It was Venice, magically painted by a trick of the sunlight.

Then, turning my field glasses to the south-east, I picked out the unmistakable outline of the Euganean Hills, rising 2,000 feet in complete isolation from the apparently boundless plain.

From those very hill-tops a century earlier Shelley had witnessed a scene almost identical to the panorama spread before me. He wrote of how his soul and spirit reacted to the sight in a poem which is in my Golden Treasury: 'Lines Written Among the Euganean Hills, North Italy'.

The pages still have the notes I pencilled in their margins in an 'Eng. Lit' period at Rye. In my wildest dreams I could never have imagined then that in less than two years I would be seeing an almost exact duplicate of the scene which had so entranced Shelley.

Beneath is spread like a green sea
The waveless plain of Lombardy,
Bounded by the vaporous air,
Islanded by cities fair;
Underneath Day's azure eyes
Ocean's nursling, Venice lies,
A peopled labyrinth of walls,
Amphitrite's destined halls,
Which her hoary sire now paves
With his blue and beaming waves.

*I have only a quarter-page left. I'm stopping to re-read what I've
written . . .*

By now I was beginning to feel sleepy. I laid the journal aside,
pinched out the candle flame and pulled the blankets up to my
chin. It was going to freeze hard again before morning without
any doubt.

I fell asleep and slept like a log till just before daybreak.

Homeward Bound

It was barely daylight when I awoke on the happiest of all my
days as a soldier, – the day I should start my long-expected final
journey home.

I had no need to hurry. I got up and lit my candle, then lay
back pulling the blankets over myself again. There had been a
frost all right; my wash-basin water was ice-covered! Did I care?
Not a bit.

I was spared the trouble of discovering the correct military eti-
quette when the time comes for a very low-ranking 'amateur'

N.C.O. to present himself to a very high-ranking professional Big-Wig for the purpose of saying farewell, owing to the absence of the aforesaid Big-Wig. He, as the senior artillery officer of the British Forces in Italy, had been called to a conference of Allied Brass Hats which was taking place at Italian G.H.Q., some ninety miles away.

The further away from me Snow was, the more content I felt. Ninety miles, and no telephone communication, was just about right. Had I come face to face with Lieutenant Colonel Snow on the morning of my departure, the only words I could have said to him with true sincerity and feeling would have been 'Good bye, good riddance and I hope I never see you again!'

Before the arrival of the G.S. Wagon which was to transport the half-dozen lucky members of 239 Siege Battery to the leave train at Padua station, I had found time to deposit a sackful of useful clothing (including my unofficial summer wear) at the Red Cross Depot on the opposite side of the piazza. For travelling luggage our limit was a couple of kitbags and I was glad to be able to hand over things that I couldn't bring home.

Soon it was time for me to say, '*Addio, Treviso!*' – not '*Arrivederci*' for I was certain I would never see the place again.

At Padua station, the troop train was waiting, presumably bound for Cherbourg, the Channel port almost invariably used by our army in Italy, though they never <u>told</u> you your destination, not even with the war having ended three months before. The passengers, a cosmopolitan, polyglot collection of vari-uniformed men, French, American, British and others not easily identifiable, were awaiting instructions to go aboard.

I gave my ex-239 companions the slip for a very special reason. On my last trip home I had been caught by the R.T.O. and detailed to take charge of the Train Picket.[21] I wasn't going to let history repeat itself.

The first thing I did when the others had gone was to make a 'recce' of the train itself – and I was very pleased with what I saw. I had observed that the very last wagon had its sliding doors securely padlocked. Something made me examine the doors on its further side (near the station's side wall). They were padlocked too, but some careless individual, – bless his heart, – had slipped the padlock through the staple and left the key in it!

I had no means of telling whether it would be minutes or hours before the train started but I had to gamble if my plan were to succeed. I waited until I was unobserved, slipped round the rear of the train, climbed up and chucked my two kitbags onto the floor, – the old kettle I'd tied to one of them made one hell of a racket but fortunately didn't attract anyone's attention. Then, after locking up, I pocketed the key and mooched off towards the station hall. I chose a spot where I could keep my van under observation. I would be ready to gamble once more, when departure seemed imminent, that I could get aboard in time.

Padua is one of Italy's oldest university cities, and as a result is excellently well provided with bookshops. I thought I could do with something to read on a five-day journey. I spotted a paperbound book entitled, if I remember rightly, *Les Grandes Amours/Piccole Novelle d'Amore*, which in French and Italian respectively means roughly 'Short Tales of Great Loves'. I picked it up and, glancing through its pages, saw it to be a kind of prose anthology of famous love affairs, legendary, classical and modern, rendered into simple French and Italian, in the usual

21 A squad of one N.C.O. and perhaps six men whose job is to prevent any unauthorized leaving of the train.

side-by-side format. I reckoned I'd still got at least a day to spend with Italian influences around me, to be followed by several more travelling through 500 miles of France; it seemed fitting that I should take a 'refresher' course in the French language.

I saw a hurrying and scurrying on the platform. Time to go! I waited for the right moment, made the necessary dash and had just gained entry into my compartment when the train moved off.

There had been no decorated streets, no civic or military ceremonies, no banners waving, no bandsmen to play us off, no pretty girls throwing garlands of flowers, not even one person to wish us '*Buon Viaggio*' or say 'Good bye,' as we, the vanguard of the combined expeditionary forces of the Allied armies, moved slowly away. The war, after all, had ended three months ago; the excitement had died down and departures such as ours were, to the Paduans, no doubt commonplace. It may be that they were as glad to see us go as we were, – but for different reasons.

My new mobile home was a goods van. As soon as we were under way I slid back a door to admit some daylight and examined it at leisure. It was three-quarters filled with large nailed-down packing cases: heavy ammo boxes and other containers of various sizes, all sealed and some roped too. Each had the W.D. stencil, – the Government stamp. I wasn't interested in any of them except for possible use as furniture. What I was interested in were the bales of hay and straw. I could hardly believe my luck.

I suppose a list of the hardships of life on active service would include lack of sleep, lice, dirt, denial of privacy and crude sanitary arrangements near the top. Cold would also be high up, especially if bracketed with wet. All those other afflictions are just bearable if you are only warm and dry; if you are cold and wet they can seem worse than death. I had no blankets for what was going to be a freezing journey, but hay and straw are marvellously insulating – and I had armfuls at my disposal! If anyone was going to suffer from frost-bite in the week ahead it wasn't going to be me.

I'd got just about all I wanted: reserved accommodation, central heating – well, almost! – and seclusion. It had been a long time since I'd enjoyed sufficient of that. Now in my last days as a soldier I could have as much as I wanted, and when it was to my advantage, e.g. when 'grub was up', I could mix with the crowd.

I got to work on making my apartment comfortable. I moved around some of the cases to clear sufficient floor space for sleeping on; then spread a liberal thickness of hay over it for a mattress, with a few sacks (which came to light when I was rearranging the cargo) on top. Some ammo boxes served for a table and chair. By the time I'd finished I had a first class 'sleeper' at my disposal.

I sat on one of the cases and reduced myself to the ranks. By that I mean I removed my greatcoat, cut through the stitches which held my stripes on to the sleeves, and stuffed them into one of its pockets. (I was going to hand the coat in when I got to Blighty anyway.) There was method in this madness. As a Non Commissioned Officer I was a conspicuous individual. As a Gunner, the equivalent of a Private in the infantry, I would be one of a crowd. If for some reason I should <u>want</u> to be a Bombardier I had only to remove my coat.

The scheme worked beautifully. All through that trip I was able to enjoy the best of both worlds, choosing my rank to suit the prevailing circumstances.

In most respects this journey from Italy was a replica of the previous one, but there were two or three unusual incidents which broke the monotony of the trip.

From Padua you have to traverse 300 miles of the plains of Venetia, Lombardy and Piedmont before you find the mountains gradually closing in on each side of the railway, as you head towards the Mont Cenis tunnel on the Franco-Italian frontier. By the time you get to Susa, the last sizeable town on the Italian side, the mountains are real giants, overtopping the 10,000-feet mark. At Susa there is always a delay while an auxiliary locomotive is driven on to the rear of each heavily loaded train to help push it up the steep gradients between the town and the tunnel, nearly twenty miles further on. (The floor of Mont Cenis tunnel is almost a mile above sea level.)

It was late in the afternoon when we neared Susa, which the Tommies naturally renamed 'Susie'. An hour before, while halted at Turin, I had bought a nice little selection of palatable foods to supplement the revolting fare always served in the trackside Army Canteens. I had also acquired some bricks from a building site at our previous stop; this meant I could boil a kettle without going to the forward engine. Cold water could be got fairly easily from the stations en route.

Anticipating that at the altitudes we would soon reach, the temperature might well be sub-zero, I wound on my spare pair of puttees. I liked sitting with my legs dangling out of the train as I watched the scenery. Provided our train's speed was not more than 20 m.p.h. the cold didn't penetrate the double layer of worsted.

I was sitting in this manner, absorbing the grandeur of the mountain panorama as it glided slowly past. The snow, which had fallen intermittently throughout the day, had ceased and I was able to see a glorious spectacle as the sun sank below the Alpine peaks ahead, turning the whole scene into a marvellous symphony of white and gold. Then the first wide-roofed houses with huge icicles dangling from their eaves appeared and we had reached the outskirts of Susa. The train decelerated and came to a halt.

Looking forward I could just see the beginning of the station platform a good 200 yards ahead. I believe I told you that quite a number of the vehicles in front of mine were covered goods trucks, not carrying passengers. The line curved away out of sight, – which is the reason I could only see the end of the platform. On a siding almost level with my position stood a railway engine with 'steam up', as we used to say, but no man was aboard it.

Several minutes of inactivity followed and then I saw the driver, a short, stocky, moustached figure with a grey woollen muffler looped over the top of his peaked cap and knotted under his chin, trudging through the snow from the direction of the station, puffing white clouds of vapour himself as he picked his way between the metals. When he spotted me, I received a friendly wave of the hand and an '*E Freddo?*' (Isn't it cold?) as he crossed over to the stationary loco and climbed onto its footplate. Then with loud shouts his engine backed away, and then crept forward behind the troop train, announcing that it had made contact with the buffers of my wagon with a jolt which nearly threw me off my perch. A minute later we were all on the move once more.

The combined efforts of both puller and pusher engines only achieved a slow cycling pace as we passed through Susa's deserted station platform – deserted that is but for one small figure. The snow had begun falling again, – thickly this time, – as the wagon I was in drew level with the station buildings. Standing on the unroofed section of the platform I saw a small girl, seven or eight years of age perhaps, holding a toy flag in one red-gloved hand and blowing farewell kisses with the other to the soldiers in the forward part of the train. The child was dressed in the colours of her native country's flag: red white and green. On her head the bright red 'tam' she wore was rapidly turning white to match the huge scarf wrapped at least twice around her. Below this was a coat of brilliant green, – the whole as pretty a wintry picture as one could ever hope to see.

Her flag-waving stopped as the 'passenger' coaches curved away out of her sight, but she remained for a while, obviously waiting to see her father (I assumed it was her father) go by in his auxiliary engine. Suddenly, instead of her father she caught sight of me, a lone British soldier sitting on the floor of the truck next to the locomotive. She waved her flag excitedly and blew kisses towards me – a compliment which of course I returned in kind.

You will have read of 'Frontier Incidents' – both in newspapers and 'spy' stories. They're usually dramatic, even melodramatic, affairs. Well, this was a Frontier Incident, of a kind: an unexciting, trivial little event, – but not to me. The memory of it has remained for over fifty years. Why?

For two reasons I believe, – the first being that it was my last memory of Italy, a land I had come to love deeply, – and, because I am a sentimentalist, I found it strangely touching. The second was that I saw something symbolic in it. You see in all my fifteen months in Italy I had not seen one of my own country's flags flying; the Tricolour of France yes, Italy's red white and green, of course, the red and white of the International Red Cross almost everywhere, and even the Star-Spangled Banner of the U.S.A. on occasion, – but the British flag never, – till then. For the toy emblem that the child had waved so vigorously was a little Union Jack. I interpreted the gesture to mean 'Thank you, English soldiers, for coming . . . Love to you all . . . Goodbye.' So it seemed that one person at least, – if only a little girl, – had cared.

My reaction was to think, 'Neither you, nor any of your grown-up countryfolk, need express gratitude to <u>me</u>. What I have done on your country's behalf is negligible compared with what your people have done for me. You owe me nothing, while I owe them everything: health, sanity, life itself. Mine is a debt I can never repay.'

It was completely dark before we entered the ten-mile-long tunnel. After making some tea I bedded down on the straw and was fast asleep in seconds.

It was around 1 a.m. when I awoke. I could tell we were well past the frontier. For one thing the juddering clatter of the pusher engine's buffers on the back end of my 'Wagon-Lit' had ceased, which indicated that it had finished its job and returned to base. The train's speed was such that we were obviously running downhill, presumably into the Isère Valley. I slid open one of the doors. I could see nothing but pitch darkness, though it <u>had</u> stopped snowing. We were in France, – and in just about the coldest part of it too. I slid the door back into place.

I was hungry so I rummaged in my haversack and scraped together some sort of a meal. I lit up my stove (Skirth-type, Mark I, bricks and candle model) to heat up some diluted tinned milk, and when it was ready I made some cocoa. Then I made myself reasonably comfortable on my straw couch and picked up the book I'd bought at Padua station.

As I've told you, it was a collection of love tales, – factual and legendary, un-illustrated and un-erotic, – told in simplified French and Italian. So simplified in fact that I only had to refer to my dictionary about three times per page. I won't bore you with a catalogue of the stories. But I <u>do</u> want to refer to some of the things I learnt from the last tale in that book. It was the only British love story deemed worthy of inclusion. In French, if I remember rightly, its title was '*Les Poètes Aimantes*' ('The Poet-Lovers'), and it was the tale of Elizabeth Barrett and Robert Browning.

Everyone knows of their romance nowadays, but fifty years ago it wasn't so well known; I myself only knew of it from cursory schoolday reading, and of that very little had stuck in my memory. But reading this version I discovered that their story was, in a way, relevant to mine.

After a short stay in Florence, the Brownings went in quest of a quiet spot into which they could retreat to enjoy their newly wedded bliss in seclusion. They found a place such as they had only dared to dream of, in a remote part of northern Italy close to the Austrian border. On the fringe of a picture-book Alpine village they found their '*nid d'amour*', their love-nest, – a beautiful small villa which Elizabeth named the *Casa dei Fiore*, or the House of Flowers. It was there that Elizabeth wrote the Sonnets which expressed her love for Robert – I haven't read any of them, by the way! – and there that her husband wrote some of his most inspired poetry.

There was a link between the Brownings' story and mine. You see, the valley into which the Poet-Lovers had retired to make their *nid d'amour* was the valley I had looked down into from the summit of *Il Montello* mountain on that glorious autumn afternoon three months before. In it, on the outskirts of the small alpine town of Asolo, stood the House of Flowers – and Asolo, with its elegant villas and its silk mill, was a place I and my battery had helped to destroy.

You may wonder why I should harbour feelings of guilt over the destruction of a few unimportant villages, just because sixty years earlier two English poets with whose work I was only barely familiar had made their homes there. But I <u>did</u> have feelings of guilt, – and I <u>did</u> care.

I expect to be told that far too many of my pages have been filled with accounts of insignificant, un-noteworthy happenings. Why should I waste space recording my reactions to a view of a mountain valley where two poets had lived long before I was born, – or to a little girl waving a toy flag on a station platform as my train passed through?

I don't know that I can give a satisfactory answer. Those two things are firmly etched into my memory. Hundreds of others, – doubtless of much greater importance and significance, – have vanished from it. Undramatic, everyday, – even humdrum, – happenings may be meaningless to some, yet of major importance to others. We see life through lenses we have ground for ourselves.

A beautiful valley that the war should have left untouched, but didn't; a pretty little girl waving a flag and blowing kisses. Two trivialities. Of no consequence to anybody perhaps. Except me, – because I happen to be me and nobody else.

Of course my feelings of guilt were unjustified and irrational. I wasn't the barbarian, the vandal. I had done as I'd been told; I was carrying out orders. But what stupid, futile, fruitless orders!

Never mind. It was all over now. Asolo would be built up again. So would Elizabeth's *Casa dei Fiore*. The mill would begin to spin silk once more and the villages with the musical names would welcome back the people who had fled from them, – after the houses we had smashed had been made whole again. All in good time.

And when that good time came and all the Val Musone's war scars had healed, nobody would remember that the devastation of that lovely valley had been the work not of a ruthless enemy but of a supposedly friendly power. That it was the shells from English guns, fired wantonly in the last days of a fifty-one-month-long war, that had disturbed the peace the valley had enjoyed until that very week.

The rhythm of the train wheels was making me sleepy again . . . Strange that the only English love story in that book should have a connection with my doings, and my thoughts and reflections . . . 'Perhaps one day,' I thought, 'one day, I'll write our story down. If I don't, no one else will . . . But if ever I did, would anybody want to read it?'

In any case, I wasn't home yet. 'Don't count your chickens before they're hatched,' was one of my mother's favourite sayings. There was one more river to cross, and we might strike a mine they'd missed sweeping up outside Cherbourg harbour!

I woke up with a start. My watch told me it was after 8 o'clock and must therefore be broad daylight. I had no windows, so could only tell day from night by sliding back the door. I did so. We must be nearing Chambéry now. I wondered whether we'd stop at the trackside canteen there for breakfast.

We didn't. We went through Chambéry and then 'detoured' westward. I consulted my map. We were heading for Lyons to drop a contingent of *Poilus* there.

Our breakfast stop was on the fringe of the mountain country in the Rhône Valley, close to a Red Cross canteen which not only catered for troops in transit but also for an American Army camp close by. They gave us a very welcome hot breakfast.

We had finished our food and were starting to re-board the train when a group of tunic-less Yanks came alongside and began 'throwing their weight about', – in other words, boasting. Unfortunately for them, the fellows they chose to boast to, – about how we would have lost the war but for them, – were a bunch of husky Welsh coal-miners, who looked as though they had been in the fighting zone for years, while the American rookies had only just arrived in France and hadn't even heard a shot fired in anger. Welsh pride was insulted; words led to blows; and a minor war broke out between two technically allied nations. When 'Time!' was called, – by the arrival of two of Uncle Sam's mounted Redcaps, – looking exactly as though they'd just ridden over from a Western film set, – the braggarts had been beaten almost to a pulp and thrown into the nearby river. If it hadn't been frozen over they would probably have drowned. Flattened noses and cut lips produced a patriotic stars and stripes effect as the blood of the vanquished stained the snow which had fallen upon the river's icy surface.

Now my dislike of violence has been often expressed in these pages. But if it is restricted to those who <u>choose</u> to participate, my conscience is not disturbed. This was such an occasion. Those who didn't want to become involved, – like me, – stayed out of it and looked on.

It was a diverting episode, – to both combatants and onlookers, – and was the only occasion I ever heard of in which fighting took place between Britons and Americans on European territory, – a unique, almost historic occasion. But I bet there's no mention of it in any of the official histories of the Great War. If it hadn't been for me writing about it, no one would ever have known there <u>was</u> a Battle of Somewhere-near-Lyons in February 1919.

That final journey took a whole day longer than its predecessors, mainly because of the tortuous route chosen. Had I not been such a travel lover, five nights in a train goods wagon plus one on board ship would have bored me to distraction. But travel has always been one of the three greatest pleasures of my life. (I'll leave you to guess what the other two are.)

I was exceptionally fortunate in preserving my privacy for the entire train journey. Nobody discovered my personal hide-out and I dodged all irksome fatigue duties successfully. As most of the places we passed through were neither ornamental nor historically famous, my memories of them have completely faded, – with one exception.

Somewhere around the fifth day we pulled up in Orleans. Once more I truanted, slipped away unobserved and dashed into the nearby city square, where a statue of Joan of Arc stands. I bought a view-card of it, wrote a message to my sweetheart and dropped it unstamped into the station post box. Ella never received it. I'm inclined to believe that now the war was over the civil authorities had lost patience with foreigners who were too mean to buy a postage stamp.

At Rouen we picked up a contingent of Tommies who took possession of the luxurious horse box vacated by the French-men. Then for more than half a day we crawled at a snail's pace to our destination. I was sure it would be Le Havre following our train's diversion, – but no, it was Cherbourg after all, – for the third time in as many months.

The vessel which had been commandeered to convey us the eighty miles from there to Southampton Water seemed so small that my heart would have sunk into my boots had not the Channel looked as smooth as the proverbial mill pond that evening. It didn't seem possible that the authorities had licensed so small a ship to carry 150 servicemen upon the open seas. By an unusual coincidence the ship's name happened to be *Jeanne d'Arc*. I guessed that in pre-war days she had been a smart little *bateau* running up and down the Seine on pleasure-cruises. Now she was very dingy in her coat of peeling khaki and black cam-ouflage paint.

It was, fortunately, a clear, calm, moonless night when we

steamed out of Cherbourg. Our navigation lights were dimmed, which made me wonder why we couldn't be decently lit up now the war was over. I strolled out on to the deck. It was jolly cold. I remember leaning over the stern railings, – the taffrail?, – and being just able to distinguish the foam of the ship's wake upon the black water running away from her propellers.

Suddenly a shape loomed out of the almost total darkness, drew near and passed by quite closely. It turned on its search-lights, which floodlit us from stem to stern. Messages were exchanged between the two ships' sirens. It was a minesweeper of the Royal Navy greeting us in nautical language – perhaps saying '*Bon voyage*' in its own special way.

An hour or so later the drone of the *Jeanne*'s engines ceased and except for a gentle rolling her movement stopped too. Far ahead I could make out the rhythmic flashings of St. Catherine's Lighthouse on the Isle of Wight. Apart from that there was nothing to see, – except blackness. I sank to the deck, pulled my coat around my knees and fell to thinking.

In another hour, perhaps, I'd set foot on English soil, – this time for good. Home! – and a reunion with the ones I loved, especially my girl. We, aboard the *Jeanne d'Arc*, were the lucky fellows, – some of the first of the two million to be discharged. I couldn't have counted the number of times when, but for the luck of the Devil or the grace of God (– according to one's point of view –), I should have been dead.

How many thousands, no – millions, throughout the world would never go home? Would anyone ever be able to count them? And of those who did, how many would be broken in spirit, body or mind, – or all three? No, it wasn't by luck that I wasn't one of them. It wasn't a thing you could put into words, not ordinary everyday words like 'luck' or 'chance'. I breathed a prayer of gratitude to God for letting me get through nearly two years of savage warfare with only a scratch or two and one ear that didn't work too well to show for it.

A second ship awoke me from my contemplation and I sprang up to watch her pass. She flooded us with light, sounded her siren and then, like her predecessor, vanished into the blackness. I believe she was a destroyer on patrol. Could there still be a lurking U-Boat commander who hadn't heard that hostilities had ceased? It wasn't a very comforting thought!

The *Jeanne*'s engines started up and we were on the move once again. I looked at my watch. The luminous hands were only just distinguishable, but it was enough to inform me that it was 4.10 a.m. Three more hours, perhaps, to daylight.

Those two passing warships brought another thought to my mind, – another memory of my schooldays, which were, after all, only a few years away. I was reminded of an exercise in lettering which I had submitted as part of an end-of-term Art Exam. You had to choose a quotation and then print it as meticulously as you could on a large sheet of cartridge paper.

I had decided on some lines of Longfellow's which seemed just right for Italic script. Our literature teacher ranked the author pretty low in the Poetry League, but as she wasn't going to mark my entry that didn't deter me. I did pretty well and got 19 marks out of 20.

If I write those lines here (not, I am afraid, in exam-standard calligraphy) you will guess why they came into my mind as they did.

Ships that pass in the night and speak each other in passing;
Only a signal shown and a distant voice in the darkness;
So on the ocean of life we pass and speak one another,
Only a look and a voice; then darkness again and a silence.

Second-rate he might have been, but Longfellow had something there, I thought. Something I could understand now, in 1919. In 1915 those lines had had nothing more than a literal significance; four years later I comprehended their subtlety.

I thought of the splendid young fellows who, like those two ships, had come into my life, stayed for so short a time, and then gone. And of some, not splendid and not so young, whom I wished had never come into it at all. I thought again of Bill and Geordie, and of Windy, men I had laughed and cried with and met death with, just a handful of the thousands who would never go home. I hoped that Raymond was on his way already; I knew Alf had returned to Blighty some months before, – perhaps by now he was completely recovered, driving his red bus past the Crystal Palace or testing the latest Thornies down at Basingstoke. I hoped Salisbury was all right; he wouldn't stay in the Army a day longer than he had to. He'd been about the only decent officer I ever met. And of course I thought of the two comrades who had each saved my life, poor Jock, who I'd seen die at Passchendaele, and brave Giulio, who I hoped still lived. My two brothers-in-arms. And Carlo at Thiene, who used to save me some of his smuggled chocolate . . . and a tiny snow-covered figure dressed in red, white and green, blowing kisses at the train I was travelling in . . . and others . . . others whose names have not even been mentioned in my war stories.

All of them, – small and big, old and young, living and dead, high-ranking and lowly, civilians and servicemen, – all like ships that had passed on my small ocean's surface during my little night, then gone, disappearing into the darkness and the silence.

Let me just remind you before I close this section of my book that I was involved in many, many incidents during my twenty months of active service when I was anything but the principal participant, – when I was, like a million others, not even a person, but just

120331 Skirth, J.R., C. of E.

– a mere number and name on an Army's Nominal Roll. I thank God that the above details never had to be inscribed on the Royal Garrison Artillery's Roll of Honour.

CHAPTER TEN

Home at Last

Ron and Ella, boy and girl sweethearts,
get married at last and live happily ever after.

There isn't a great deal more to tell. I arrived in London late
that afternoon. No crowds had gathered to give us a send-
off in Padua, and no crowds accorded us a victors' welcome at

Waterloo. The war was over; we had done our job; we weren't heroes now.

I went to the Union Jack Club to reserve a bed for the night. Then I made my way to the Artillery's Demobilization Centre at Richmond. There I handed in my kit and service clothing (– minus 'souvenirs' –) and in exchange received a passably good 'Demob Suit'. I was given a choice between either keeping my greatcoat or taking two pounds cash; I opted for the money. The stripes were still missing from it but nobody seemed to care. Finally I was handed my discharge certificate, four weeks' advance pay to remind me that technically I was still in the Army, and a travel warrant for my rail journey home.

From Richmond I took an Underground train to Charing Cross. The Strand was splendidly lit up, for the black-out days were now really over. I bought myself a stylish herring-bone tweed overcoat for thirty-seven and sixpence and then spent an hour and a half in a neighbouring cinema, though what the movie was I have no recollection.

Outside the Lyons Corner House stood two pompous Brass Hats (– Lieutenant Generals at least! –), swagger sticks under their armpits, whom I had to pass. I was on the point of halting, clicking heels and saluting before the truth flashed upon me. I didn't <u>have</u> to salute any more, – I wasn't in uniform. I wasn't a <u>soldier</u> any longer – to hell with what they'd told me at Richmond. I was free!

That was the only occasion I can remember when I was deliberately rude to anyone without provocation. I pushed between them and strode into the restaurant. I didn't look back, but I'll bet their faces were redder than the braid on their caps.

I slept and bathed at the club and went down to Bexhill by the morning train from Victoria. And here I have to record an astonishing, extraordinary and most unromantic fact. Neither

Ella nor I can recall any memories of our reunion. What an anti-climax! What an unglamorous, unromantic ending to the longest and most dramatic chapter of our Love Story!

A few pages back I gave you an account of my final journey from Italy which showed how clearly details of that trip were fixed in my memory. Yet now that I come to write the final sentences of the most eventful chapter in the 'drama' of my early life, instead of depicting the curtain falling with the reunited lovers in each others' arms, I have to confess that I can't remember anything of that reunion, – and, even more surprisingly perhaps, neither can Ella!

We are rather puzzled as to the reasons for this but have reached the conclusion that two factors may account for it.

First, my long-awaited leave had brought us together for a tremendously exciting fortnight only ten weeks before. Perhaps this second reunion was in the nature of an anti-climax.

Second, I arrived home at a time when Ella's sister was contracting an illness which was to prove fatal. Evelyn's condition grew steadily worse and a week before her twenty-first birthday (11 June 1919) she died. The loss broke her parents' hearts, and Ella was near heart-broken herself.

So 1919, the year of my return to civil life, also brought great sadness into our lives. It may be that our dulled memories are being kind in not allowing us to recall all that we did and thought.

I entered Training College in London that September. I was living with my parents and used to come home at half-term breaks and between-term holidays. Gradually, Ella's gaiety and vivacity returned, while her parents, though never recovering from the loss they had sustained, bravely accepted the situation.

I returned to teach for a while in the Church school which I had attended as a small boy and where I had served my pupil-teachership, – the school where the playground adjoined the garden of Ella's house. In the spring of 1922 I left Bexhill, having secured a better-paid post in a rural school near Uxbridge. I used to travel through Ealing on my way to Charing Cross, where I caught the train home every second week-end. Ella and I had decided to live in one of London's outer suburbs when we got married and we both liked Ealing very much.

The next year we became engaged. It was her twenty-second birthday and she came up to London to choose the ring: a diamond cluster with a central sapphire. I promised to try for a post in the Ealing area and as soon as I obtained one we would be married.

I had to wait a year more before my ambition was realized and I was appointed to the staff of Little Ealing Senior Boys' School. The appointment took effect from September 1924. There followed a hectic search for suitable living accommodation and it wasn't until early December that I found what I was sure Ella would approve of. (She was all this time still at Bexhill.)

She was immensely surprised to find that a London flat could have an outlook over such green countryside. There was a bowling green below our bedroom window, beyond which was a golf course and a view over Horsenden Hill. The adjoining park had tennis courts and as we both loved tennis this was an additional attraction. We took it on the spot.

We fixed our wedding date as 29 December 1924. I was twenty-seven and Ella nearly twenty-four. It was exactly eight years and five months after our first meeting. Both my parents and hers gave us their blessing.

Of the ceremony itself I can tell you little. I ought to describe the bride's and bridesmaids' dresses of course, for the benefit of any lady readers. But I went through that ordeal in a sort of trance, dimly aware that Ella and I were being married; that the building was the Church of St. Barnabas, Bexhill; that the minister performing the ceremony was the Cannon of Chichester Cathedral, who had made the sixty-three-mile journey specially for us (– he had been our vicar when we were children and must have been informed that we were marrying on that date –); that a host of friends and acquaintances almost filled the church; and that the Bride Wore White. I saw <u>that</u> very clearly indeed and thought she was the loveliest bride I'd ever seen.

I have already told you about our honeymoon at the Regent Palace Hotel. Our last night there (– we only had three! –) was New Year's Eve. A dance was held, of course. We went into the Ballroom and watched for a while and then went up to our room. We had ideas of our own as to how this particular New Year's Eve should be spent!

At one stage of our intimate festivities we made two resolutions; the first was that we would have two babies, – 'a boy for you and a girl for me' as the song goes, – and the second was that we wouldn't have <u>either</u> for some while yet. I said to my three-day wife, 'I know I'm selfish but I've waited a dickens of a long time for this. I want you all to myself; no babies to distract us. This honeymoon's going to last for years.'

Ella whispered, 'I think I shall like that.'

It did too, and it got better as time went on. We had each other to ourselves to make up for those many months of separation. We grew to know and understand each other better, falling more and more deeply in love as time went by.

Our tastes and pleasures were almost identical. Neither of us was extravagant. We couldn't afford to be on six pounds a week of which a quarter went in rent! I was able to supplement my income with private coaching, being determined that Ella shouldn't go out to work while I could keep the two of us.

Living where we did, we were near to both town and country. Twenty minutes by train took us into the heart of the countryside for summer picnics and rambles, and the adjoining park provided courts for playing tennis with our closest friends. They returned the compliment when we visited their home at Hayes. The husband, Steve, was a colleague of mine, with whom I had been in bachelor lodgings before we both got married.

There were 'musical evenings' too. (Our respective parents had given us their family pianos; with their consent we sold both and bought ourselves a quality Chappell Upright.) Steve and his wife loved singing. It was fortunate that our neighbours were understanding and tolerant. Not that we carried on into the early hours: our guests always had to catch a 10 o'clock train home.

When Ella and I were alone we found plenty of amusement at hand. She loved singing as much as I loved listening to her; I accompanied of course and occasionally we 'rendered' our old-time piano duets. If music was the food of love we certainly weren't under-nourished.

After two years we moved to a flat over a baker's shop in West Ealing. This hadn't the unique rural outlook of our first home but it had two great advantages: it was 100-per-cent self-contained and had round-the-clock hot water from the bake-house adjoining. The Christmas of 1927 was one of the coldest ever. All our neighbours' water supplies were frozen up and stand-pipes were fitted in the streets for people to draw water from. Only one building was unaffected and that was Rolfe's Bakery.

Shortly after moving in we adopted an elegant semi-Persian marmalade kitten. The baker didn't care much for cats before we came, but before Toby was half-grown he had taken nocturnal control of Mr. Rolfe's bakehouse and completely rid it of mice. The baker's aversion changed to respect and then affection. From then on our pet could do no wrong. Well, – almost!

One night Toby found his way into the locked-up shop. There was an open crate of eggs up-ended against a wall. (In those days, they came packed in wooden boxes of a hundred or so.) Now Toby looked upon raw egg as an acceptable between-meals delicacy. Once we had caught him red-handed in the act of hooking one out from the bowl in the larder. He knew that if you let an egg drop onto a hard surface the shell broke and the rest was easy.

No one saw what actually happened that night, but when the manageress opened up the next morning she saw the crate still in position against the wall and on the floor below it the ghastly mess that is produced after an enterprising cat has rolled three dozen eggs one at a time on to the tiles below. We assumed he had lapped up the sticky contents of one or two of the smashed shells and hooked out the remainder for the sheer joy of hearing them splosh. When Mr. Rolfe was sent for and informed of Toby's misdemeanour, instead of flying into the temper we anticipated, he was highly amused. 'That darned cat! I'd never have believed it,' he said, refusing to let us recompense him for the damage.

In 1928, four years after we were married, Ella and I spent a memorable Christmas holiday at her parents' home in Bexhill. It is remembered by us, not on account of the special Yuletide festivities, although I am sure there must have been some, but because of the manner in which we celebrated the fourth anniversary of our wedding night. My wife decided that our honeymoon had lasted long enough and said, 'I think I'd like to have our first baby soon.' I said, 'Splendid idea, when?' and she said, 'Now.' (This may not be a strictly verbatim account, but it's true in essence.)

As a result of that 'celebration' a baby daughter was born the following September. We had, in the meantime, moved from the flat in Midhurst Road (over the shop) into a full-sized house in Windermere Road, – still in Ealing.

Actually our planning went slightly awry. We had arranged for our first child to be a boy named John, which is my first name, – but the unborn baby had other ideas and insisted on being a girl. We didn't mind in the least, but we named her Jean, which is as near to John as you can get.

She was as beautiful and well-behaved a baby as any parents could wish for and the older she grew the more we both loved her. (There's only one girl I ever loved <u>more</u>.) Instead of inter-rupting the routine of living we had adopted, she created a new one for us, one which I enjoyed as much as Ella, although my responsibilities were much less. But Jean's arrival on the scene offended the other member of the Skirth ménage, Toby the cat. By this time he had become quite a magnificent animal, – not the sort of pet to take second place to a mere human baby, – so after tolerating the situation for a week or two, he walked out.

He didn't go far, – only across the road to the house almost opposite, where an unmarried lady called Daisy lived. She had been openly in love with him for months and Toby must have known. He, in cat language, asked Daisy if she would like to adopt him; Daisy asked <u>us</u> if we had any objection; <u>we</u> hadn't, so a knotty little problem was solved to the satisfaction of all con-cerned. From then on, though, Toby treated us as complete strangers, despite living only thirty yards away!

'The best laid schemes o' mice an' men . . .' How often I've quoted Robbie Burns! Our honeymoon resolution to have a girl and a boy was never carried out: Jean's little brother was never born. I have no doubt he <u>could</u> have been had we wished it. But we didn't.

Jean was a lovely baby, but oh! the suffering she brought us before she saw the light of day! I was determined that never again should my beloved be subjected to such physical pain. (Had our doctor believed in painless childbirth instead of his 'let-nature-take-its-course' philosophy, things might have been different.) I had suffered mental torments in the war but none comparable with the anguish and torture I had to bear during those interminable waiting hours. I was far too much of a coward to face a repeat performance.

Months later, Ella, who adored her little daughter as I did, said to me, 'I don't think I want any more babies.' Few words of hers have ever made me happier!

So, if ever Jean longed to have a small brother or sister, she will understand now why he or she never came.

As for my feelings, after Jean's birth I never once yearned for a boy. I spent many working hours and frittered away much mental and physical energy assisting in the rearing of other people's sons. Until Jean was twelve I taught only boys. To come home to a girl, tomboy though she could be at times, from the rough, tough atmosphere of a boys' classroom, was to enter another world. I thanked God for it. It was two years before Ella was fully restored to health. When that time came I was convinced I had been blessed with the loveliest wife and the most wonderful daughter in the whole world.

I am nearing the end of my book now. I cannot write its last chapter as it hasn't been reached yet. But before I finish I can look back once again, for the last time, and think of things I have to be grateful for.

Perhaps most of all, we, – for I am now told to include Ella in this, – feel thankful that by the kindness of Providence I came through My War almost unscathed. Ella knew almost nothing of what happened to me then, until she saw the pages these volumes contain. Her one complaint is that I didn't tell her years ago. My answer is that I just could not face talking about things which I had tried to erase from my memory for ever. I wanted desperately to forget.

Now that over fifty years have elapsed, I find I am able to bring them to light and write them down, – still not dispassionately, but at least without the deep emotional effect they would have had earlier. They are now, as the saying has it, 'out of my system', and I think I am the better for having told of them. Ella has forgiven me for my secretiveness and can now share my feelings of gratitude for having survived all the hazards of those war years.

Since our marriage began we have, as all couples must have, experienced bad times as well as good. Some of the bad times were very bad, but the good ones have been very, very good. Together we discovered the truth in the old cliché: 'A trouble shared is a trouble halved,' – to which I think it true to add that most of our greatest troubles never happened at all. We have had our little disagreements, but never a quarrel. Two people with minds of their own cannot agree in every particular over everything, but in major matters we always saw 'eye to eye', – if not immediately then at least eventually.

We have never been rich in material things, – just, what shall I say? Comfortable. Just able to make ends meet and have a little over at the end of the month. But we have been wealthy beyond all calculation in possessions which have no price tags attached, which bring joy into living.

Ella no longer sings because my defective hearing compelled me to give up piano playing (– and my teaching career –) years ago, but we never complain. Together we can both listen to recorded music, and we have memories that no one can take away from us. And, best of all, we are still in love.

It is 26 July 1971. By a happy coincidence it is fifty-five years to the day that chance brought a teenage boy and girl, – the Ronald and Ella of this story, – together.

I say chance brought us together but perhaps it wasn't chance at all. Perhaps the hostess of our little musical soirée had match-making intentions in mind. The truth of the matter will never be discovered because the dear lady went out of our lives for ever, shortly after I went off to the war. If she is still alive and if we were ever to meet her again I'm sure we would say, 'God bless you, Miss Hawkes. Thank you for a lovely evening. It was one we could never forget.'

As you know, I was eighteen when I first thought of Ella as <u>my</u> girl. She was only just sixteen on the day I heard the little ballad which might be the theme music for my Love Story, if I thought it needed any. For so short a time had I known her before we parted that as the days became weeks, the weeks months and the months a year and a half, it seemed in truth 'I had but seen her passing by,' as the burly soldier had sung that spring day of 1917. But it was the last line, the words, 'And yet I love her till I die,' which caused my eyes to cloud with tears then. They still do. That's one of the penalties of being a born romantic.

I <u>thought</u> those words were true in 1917. In 1971 I <u>know</u> they were.

*

As I said, to-day is 26 July. What did I find on my breakfast table this morning? A pretty greeting card.

Far too many pages in this Love Story are filled with what I said, what I did, where I went, and what I thought about this, that and the other. I have devoted very little space to Ella's thoughts. Most of the time, of course, I had no means of telling what they were.

She didn't know that the words she wrote on the card this morning would be seen by any eyes but mine, but I don't think she'll be embarrassed if I copy them below:

> *Happy Anniversary, Darling. All my love as ever, and many thanks for past kindnesses.*
>
>> *Yours,*
>>
>>> *Ella*
>>>
>>>> *Xxx*

A pang came over me.

Of course, you know what anniversary Ella was referring to because you have just been reading about it. I am writing this in the early evening, but at 9 o'clock this morning the significance of the date had not yet dawned upon me.

Hurriedly I seized a pencil and on the opposite fold of the card I wrote what you see below. It wasn't by any means a clever remark, but at least it was sincere. It was the best I could do on the spur of the moment.

> *Thank you, Darling.*
> *All my love too, to the one who deserved them.*
> *Yours,*
>> *Ron.*
> *P.S. I would have remembered before the day was out.   xxx*

I haven't any more to tell you. This really is the end. It's late now and we're rather tired so I think we'll call it a day.

Good Night – and Sweet Dreams, Everybody.

'I had been blessed with the loveliest wife and the most wonderful daughter in the whole world.'

Postscript

Ronald in retirement.

The views I hold on the subjects of Patriotism, Pacifism and War have been virtually unchanged for over fifty years. In 1918, 99 per cent of the population regarded them as treacherously anti-British. During the Second World War I was dubbed variously as crank, visionary, communistic and impractical.

I imagine my war stories must have told you what made me change from ardent patriot to convinced pacifist. The convictions I hold to-day were born on the battlefields of Flanders in 1917. I must remind you that at nineteen I was imaginative, idealistic, sensitive and soft-hearted – no more mature probably than the average nineteen-year-old of to-day, in some respects less so. I should also remind you that the war experiences I have described are only a few of many.

Before 1917 ended, this unbelligerent, sensitive youth had escaped death by inches a dozen times; had seen his comrades die in dreadful agony; had seen and heard men who should have been dead, men broken, torn, limbless, disembowelled, screaming for anyone with a loaded rifle to end their unbearable sufferings; had watched his friends – and others – slowly choke and froth as poison gas suffocated them; could not believe it possible until his own eyes told him it was, that half a man could live for what seemed to him hours; and by the time he was rendered unconscious himself, had come to realize that every friend he had made, every man he'd worked with, had become cannon fodder.

For years afterwards memories of these horrors haunted his dreams and disturbed his sleep; yet awake he could never bring himself to talk of them. And when he thought of those wounded men and the comrades he'd been with when they were killed, he always came to the same conclusion. It must never happen again. Never.

He was sure, certain, positive that NOTHING, NO situation, NO set of circumstances could ever justify human beings being sacrificed in such an agonizing manner, being subjected to such appalling suffering and misery as WAR inevitably brings.

People talk and write of the nobility of war; how it brings out the best in us. I saw many deeds of heroism, so-called, but none of them ennobled me. I can imagine that tales of gallantry thrill the people who write them as much as those who read them. But the man on the spot isn't thrilled in that way. If he risks his life for a comrade, it's not because he's proud to be fighting for his King and Country, not even because he's a soldier. It is because he is what he is and, because of what he is, he feels a compulsion to act. He doesn't have time to consider whether he's being heroic or not; he's far too busy concentrating on his own survival, – for unless he survives his comrade won't. And anyway it usually comes down to this: 'He'd do just the same for me.'

I risked my life for others on a number of occasions; at least in the moment it seemed that I put my life in hazard. Each time it was because I undertook to do something dangerous which had been allotted to a married man. I loved my family and I loved Ella more, but I felt that if a casualty had to be either a single man or the father of a family, the casualty should be the single man – me. There was nothing high-minded or courageous about it. I just acted as my conscience told me to act. I'm not brave. I'm squeamish. I vomit at the sight of blood; all forms of human cruelty sicken me – and I blench at the thought of physical pain. Put those things together and you have the makings of a complete coward. Most of the time I was under fire I was dead scared, shaking with fear, but if my conscience said, 'You ought to do so and so,' I did it.

I risked 'laying down my life' once for a pal of mine called Reggie Starr, – and got taught a salutary lesson. Reggie was my Signaller-Telephonist after Windy was gassed. He was about thirty years of age, a fair-haired, tall, splendid-looking chap from the Midlands. In peace-time he'd been a P.O. linesman. He and I got on very well together and in a few weeks had become firm friends. He had only one aim in life – to get out of the Army and back to the wife and children he loved. I can still see the photo of them that he carried: an attractive young woman and two pretty little golden-haired girls, taken on the sands at Skegness just before he was conscripted.

Reggie was a quiet, unexcitable character. I only saw him nervous once. He was on duty with me at the Command Post when the line connecting us to the Forward O.P. was cut. Snow ordered him out of the dug-out to trace the break and repair it. The mission was suicidal – this was Ypres and an enemy artillery bombardment was at its height.

I handed my work over to a deputy and got Snow's grudging consent to visit the latrines. I found Reggie at the entrance to my bivvy about fifty yards away, trembling from head to foot. I said, 'Give me your box of tricks. I'm going and you're stopping here, and the Old Man can go to hell.' Reg didn't say a word and I set off. Repairing field telephone lines was a job I could do pretty well, having learnt a lot from watching Windy.

The German shelling was terrifying. I traced the line for a couple of hundred yards and then found the break. I crouched in a dry shell hole, praying of course, waiting for a lull. It came. I mended the line and got the 'O.K.' from the Command Post telephone. Shells were falling all around again as I jumped from one shell hole into the next on my way back. My heart thumped with fear as I thought of what might happen at any moment.

Fifty yards from home I had to plunge headlong into a crater that contained something too horrible to describe. I was certain that this was the end; but no, the shell screamed on a few yards over my head and burst some distance in front. I remained in that stinking hole just long enough to regain my breath and then, leaping from one crater to another, I got to within fifty yards of my dug-out when a shell burst so close it helped me into yet another. How I escaped injury baffles me even now when I think of it, but I did.

I got back to the Command Post just in time to see two men with an improvised stretcher picking up what was left of Reggie. The shell which had so nearly got me had pitched a yard outside my bivvy and Reggie had been standing there exactly where it fell.

When I reappeared at the duty table I remember the scowling look Snow gave me. 'Bombardier, you've been a bloody long time. Malingering now, are you? Don't try it on again.'

I didn't answer him. I was choking with sorrow and anger (– I'd been sick in that shell hole, of course –) and couldn't prevent my eyes from filling with tears. I'd hated him before; but I hated him more now. He had helped to kill Reggie. The line repair could have waited until the shelling had stopped, – which it did immediately afterwards. I suppose he didn't know it was partly his fault, – and if he had known he wouldn't have cared two hoots.

But I cared. And do you think I saw myself as a hero? A murderer, perhaps, but not a hero. If I'd minded my own business, poor Reggie wouldn't be dead.

I said this incident taught me a lesson. It did. A lesson in humility. One thing it did not do was ennoble me. Having another man's death, your friend's death, on your hands, if unintentionally, doesn't make you feel noble. I couldn't forget the photograph taken on the Skegness sands the previous summer of the smiling young woman and the two little girls, – somebody had to tell them why Reggie would never come back.

I never volunteered to take on another man's job, – dangerous or otherwise, – after that.

On a number of occasions I nearly 'gave' my life for a comrade on the battlefield; I nearly 'gave' my life for my country. That word, seen on so many war memorials, disguises the real truth. The truth is I didn't offer to give my life, – or anything else. But I very nearly had my life taken from me over and over again. Do you believe the million British who died in France and Belgium in the First World War willingly gave their lives for the cause they were told they were fighting for? Every one of those men was robbed of the life he was entitled to live. In my view not one single soldier, Allied or enemy, gave his life for anything. But millions, – innocent millions, – lost them.

With memories of so many of war's horrors behind me, could I do anything but swear that never, never again would I willingly assist or support any actions which might lead to a repetition of such ghastliness?

'Oh yes,' you'll say, 'we understand and sympathize. But there comes a time when a nation has to fight; when there is no alternative. How much are your principles, sincere as they may be, worth then?'

My answer is a simple one. There is no situation in which you are compelled to go to war. If you enter war you enter of your own free will. Whether you declared war or offered resistance to a potential invader, it is you who made the choice, and therefore accepted the consequences.

When the inevitable Second World War came my pacifist convictions didn't prevent me 'doing my bit'. I could not support something in which I did not believe, but I did everything in my power to assist the victims of it.

Twice in my lifetime Britain has declared war against Germany to protect a weaker ally. In 1914 it was to defend Belgium, in 1939 Poland. What happened? Both countries were over-run in a matter of days. Our 'assistance' was useless. A local war grew into a wider conflict, resulting in eight and a half million deaths the first time and up to twenty million the second.

A war is an evil force. It involves plunging millions of innocent human beings into a blood-bath; condemning the cream of your nation's manhood to horrible deaths; exposing yourself, your wife, your husband, your children to the ghastliness of air attack; causing innumerable other innocent victims to leave shattered homes and become refugees: – anguish and misery beyond calculation. 'Self-defence', your country's 'honour', 'patriotism' are mere words to disguise the reality. Your leaders use them to blind you to the facts, to compel you to shut your eyes, – and your mind.

Perhaps you'll say, 'In certain situations, a nation has no alternative. If we hadn't made a stand Hitler would have taken over. Surely you wouldn't wish Britain to have become one of the occupied territories?'

And there, you see, is the problem that confronts us. We do have a choice, – either to fight or to surrender. Surrender is a dirty word, but war is a dirtier business. I choose the lesser of two evils. But at least I make a choice.

E.M. Forster once said, 'If I had to choose between betraying my country and betraying my friend, I hope I would have the guts to betray my country.' Now I'm not sure how I would react to the situation he imagines, but it started off this train of thought in my mind: if I had to choose between living with my wife and child in an England over-run by an enemy power, or risking my life and theirs (and the lives of another million or so) by declaring war, I hope I'd have the sense to put the safety and survival of those I love most in this world before anything else.

I'll take a broader view. If in 1939 we had offered only passive resistance, we could, in spite of Hitler's declaration that he had no designs upon our country, have possibly become one of the occupied territories. That's an alarming thought. But is it so alarming as the alternative? Can you imagine the survivors of the Holocaust, the mothers and widows of the slain, the soldiers fighting at the front hearing that their loved ones had been killed or maimed in the Blitz, the children parentless, the parents childless, the hosts of permanently disabled, – can you imagine them answering the question 'But it was worth it, wasn't it?'

with 'Oh yes. Anything is better than an enemy occupation!'

My choice is non-resistance to the potential aggressor, a choice which accepts subjugation as a lesser evil than warfare. I am prepared for discomfort and a certain loss of freedom. I am willing to barter this for the assurance that my loved ones will not be harmed physically. I am open-minded enough to give my oppressors the chance of proving to me that being occupied is unpleasant but bearable. Now if, after a fair period of trial, my loved ones and I have become convinced that life under an imposed dictatorship is no better than a living death, we shall mutually decide to end it, in our own way and at a time we shall choose. But it is we who will make the choice between life and death.

On the other hand, if the leaders of our country decide to offer armed resistance, that freedom of choice is taken from us. Once the die is cast we are no more free than we would be under an enemy's domination. They, our leaders, may have condemned us to death. Whatever our fate after they have started a war, we have no say in planning it.

Not so long ago there was a leader who secured the independence of his homeland without firing a shot in anger. He and his followers adopted a policy of passive opposition to the occupying power. They fought with ideas instead of bullets, and ideas won. In the course of time the occupying forces withdrew peacefully and India was free.

It was the founder of the Christian Church who told us to forgive our enemies and turn the other cheek. In 1914, and again in 1939, his earthly representatives, to their shame, swept those words out of sight under the carpet. It seems there was more Christianity in the Hindu Gandhi than in the Archbishop of Canterbury.

Surely if peaceful means succeeded once they could do so again. Dictators are neither omnipotent nor immortal. They fall; they die, – and captives win back their freedom. It's just a matter of time.

To me and to the many who loathe war as greatly as I, the most hopeful sign for the world's future is the attitude of mind of to-day's youth. In countries far and near, daily almost, they show by their demonstrations their awareness of the greatest problems of our time. They parade their motto 'Make love not war' in public, – and often get laughed at for their pains.

Many of these serious-minded, intelligent youngsters have long hair and don strange apparel. I do not think what grows outside the head more important than what the head contains; nor do I consider unconventional clothing an indication of the heart that beats under it. I have only to remind myself of the ways in which the younger generation of to-day renders service to the communities in which they live – and to communities many miles away: the assistance they give to Shelter, Oxfam and War on Want; the elderly and disabled whose homes they visit; the volunteer forces supervising children's playgrounds in underprivileged areas; their help in the conservation of wildlife; and their voluntary aid to hospitals and the Red Cross. Nearly all these activities are unspectacular and un-newsworthy, – much too unsensational to make the headlines.

From the young people of to-day will emerge the leaders of to-morrow. They will make mistakes, as everyone does. But they won't be guilty of the colossal blunders of their predecessors.

In 1914 those predecessors plunged us into war because they hadn't the vision to do anything else. As a result of their stupidity, almost every young man of ability and genius Britain possessed, – writers, thinkers, politicians-to-be, musicians, artists, poets, – was massacred on the green fields of the Somme and in the yellow mud of Flanders. Young men in the prime of youth who would have solved the problems of the post-war world, – had they not been <u>murdered</u> in the name of patriotism. Their ideas and ideals perished with them. And what was the consequence? A mediocrity, a paucity of leadership for a whole generation, such as this country can seldom have seen before or since.

Whatever blunders our young men and women of to-day will make, they will never be capable of a crime as monstrous as <u>that</u>.

I am writing this in the first month of 1972, exactly one year since I began this book of recollections and reflections. Then, I never dreamt it would include a chapter describing my personal brand of pacifism, but it has. I suppose I felt compelled to include it because these opinions are a part of me. Without their inclusion, the self-portrait would be incomplete.

Less than six months' service on the battlefields of Flanders had seen me transformed from a patriotic young soldier into a passionate war hater. My abhorrence of war equated itself with a detestation of the war machine, – the Army of which I was a member. By the end of 1917, it personified everything I despised. I was a cog in that machine, vastly more powerful than myself, so I was compelled to live a hypocrite's existence: to reverse the metaphor, I was a sheep in wolf's clothing. I didn't <u>feel</u> myself to be a hypocrite any more than a stage actor does when he sheds his own personality and assumes that of a character. My justification was that I was powerless to take on any role other than the one I did.

By the time the war ended, my prejudices had become so bitter, so unreasoning and so deeply embedded that I had resolved never to accept any honours, promotions, benefits or even monetary advantages from an authority which I both detested and despised. The consequence of this obstinacy was that I punished myself. Had I listened to the advice given to me, I would have qualified for a disability pension from the date of my discharge.

With the passage of time comes increased tolerance and wisdom. The minor war-time defect worsened steadily as the years passed and eventually compelled an early retirement from my civilian occupation. Ear specialists diagnosed the cause of the deafness and referred my case to the Armed Forces Pension Department; enquiries were made and I was examined by three medical boards. Then followed an investigation into my service record. There can have been few if any blots on the conduct sheet they saw! (I wondered a lot about this, asking myself what had been on the papers that Captain Jordan tore up in Italy.)

So, long after the happenings which had caused me so much physical and mental distress, justice was done. I was awarded a War Disability Pension the year after I retired from teaching, – an unexpectedly generous one on account of my not having applied forty-two years earlier! Thus, out of evil came good, – not only for me but for Ella too.

The Army, which I had detested so bitterly as a youngster, paid its debt, – belatedly perhaps, but nevertheless the account was settled. Their representatives treated me with the utmost courtesy and fairness and gave me every reason to forgive and forget. Well, to forgive if not forget.

extracts reading groups
competitions books new
discounts extracts
competitions
books new
events books
extracts
new titles reading groups
interviews
events extracts
discounts
new books events
events new
discounts extracts discounts
www.panmacmillan.com
extracts events reading groups
competitions books extracts new